Model-based Systems Architecting

Systems of Systems Complexity Set

coordinated by
Jean-Pierre Briffaut

Volume 3

Model-based Systems Architecting

Using CESAM to Architect Complex Systems

Daniel Krob

WILEY

First published 2022 in Great Britain and the United States by ISTE Ltd and John Wiley & Sons, Inc.

ISTE Ltd
27-37 St George's Road
London SW19 4EU
UK

www.iste.co.uk

John Wiley & Sons, Inc.
111 River Street
Hoboken, NJ 07030
USA

www.wiley.com

Any opinions, findings, and conclusions or recommendations expressed in this material are those of the author(s), contributor(s) or editor(s) and do not necessarily reflect the views of ISTE Group.

Library of Congress Control Number: 2021952707

British Library Cataloguing-in-Publication Data
A CIP record for this book is available from the British Library
ISBN 978-1-78630-820-7

Contents

Preface ix

Acknowledgments xv

Introduction xvii

Chapter 1. Introduction to CESAM 1

   1.1. CESAM: a mathematically sound system modeling framework. 1
   1.2. CESAM: a framework focused on complex integrated systems 8
   1.3. CESAM: a collaboration-oriented architecting framework 12
   1.4. CESAM: a business-oriented framework 16

Chapter 2. Why Architecting Systems? 19

   2.1. Product and project systems 19
   2.2. The complexity threshold 22
   2.3. Addressing systems architecting becomes key 25
   2.4. The value of systems architecting 31
   2.5. The key role of systems architects 34
   2.6. How to analyze a systems architect profile? 36

Chapter 3. CESAM Framework 39

   3.1. Elements of systemics 39
      3.1.1. Interface 39
      3.1.2. Environment of a system 41
   3.2. The three architectural visions 42
      3.2.1. Architectural visions definition 42
      3.2.2. Architectural visions overview 46
      3.2.3. Relationships between the three architectural visions 52

3.2.4. Organization of a system model   55
3.3. CESAM systems architecture pyramid   57
    3.3.1. The three key questions to ask   57
    3.3.2. The last question that shall not be forgotten   59
3.4. More systems architecture dimensions.   60
    3.4.1. Descriptions versus expected properties   60
    3.4.2. Descriptions   62
    3.4.3. Expected properties   73
3.5. CESAM systems architecture matrix   78

Chapter 4. Identifying Stakeholders: Environment Architecture   83

4.1. Why identify stakeholders?   83
4.2. The key deliverables of environment architecture   85
    4.2.1. Stakeholder hierarchy diagram   85
    4.2.2. Environment diagram.   87

Chapter 5. Understanding Interactions with Stakeholders: Operational Architecture   91

5.1. Why understand interactions with stakeholders?   91
5.2. The key deliverables of operational architecture   94
    5.2.1. Need architecture diagram   94
    5.2.2. Lifecycle diagram.   95
    5.2.3. Use case diagrams   97
    5.2.4. Operational scenario diagrams.   99
    5.2.5. Operational flow diagram   101

Chapter 6. Defining What the System Shall Do: Functional Architecture .   103

6.1. Why understand what the system does?   103
6.2. The key deliverables of functional architecture   105
    6.2.1. Functional requirement architecture diagram.   106
    6.2.2. Functional mode diagram   108
    6.2.3. Functional breakdown and interaction diagrams   109
    6.2.4. Functional scenario diagrams   111
    6.2.5. Functional flow diagram   112

Chapter 7. Deciding How the System Shall be Formed: Constructional Architecture   115

7.1. Understanding how the system is formed?   115
7.2. The key deliverables of constructional architecture   117
    7.2.1. Constructional requirement architecture diagram   118
    7.2.2. Configuration diagram   120
    7.2.3. Constructional breakdown and interaction diagram   121

7.2.4. Constructional scenario diagram.   123
7.2.5. Constructional flow diagram.   124

Chapter 8. Taking into Account Failures: Dysfunctional Analysis.   127

8.1. Systems do not always behave as they should.   127
8.2. The key deliverables of dysfunctional analysis   134
8.2.1. Dysfunctional analysis from an operational perspective.   135
8.2.2. Dysfunctional analysis from a functional perspective   136
8.2.3. Dysfunctional analysis from a constructional perspective.   138

Chapter 9. Choosing the Best Architecture: Trade-off Techniques.   141

9.1. Systems architecting does not usually lead to a unique solution.   141
9.2. Trade-off techniques.   143
9.2.1. General structure of a trade-off process.   143
9.2.2. Managing trade-offs in practice   145

Conclusion   149

Appendices   157

Appendix 1. System Temporal Logic.   159

Appendix 2. Classical Engineering Issues   163

Appendix 3. Example of System Model Managed with CESAM.   177

Appendix 4. Implementing CESAM through a SysML Modeling Tool   199

Appendix 5. Some Good Practices in Systems Modeling.   209

References.   211

Index.   219

Preface

CESAMES and the CESAM Community

The CESAM Community, which disseminates the CESAM method and is the origin of this book, is managed by CESAMES, a non-profit organization created under the French law of July 1, 1901.

CESAMES emerged in 2009, as a spin-off of the "Engineering of Complex Systems" industrial chair of Ecole Polytechnique, the leading engineering university in France, with the objective of promoting systems architecting in academia and industry. To do so, CESAMES organizes awareness events all year long that allow scientists and industrialists to meet and to share about complex industrial systems. As an example, since 2010 CESAMES has organized on a yearly basis the "Complex Systems Design & Management" (CSD&M) international conference series. This event – that now alternates between France and Asia – gathers each year more than 300 academic and professional participants, coming from all parts of the world. CESAMES also manages working groups and professional workshops, always with the same goal: increasing awareness about systems architecting methods and tools.

Thanks to these events, CESAMES has federated a significant international community of systems architects and engineers who all share the same vision: systems architecting and engineering represent a key factor of competitiveness for companies that has to be developed.

In order to reinforce its visibility and to get more influence at a worldwide level, CESAMES decided in 2017 to manage its activities through the "CESAM Community" banner. However, the mission of the CESAM Community remained of course the same: sharing good practices in enterprise and systems architecture among the community and attesting the competences of the community members in these domains through the CESAM certification.

More precisely, the CESAM Community works to achieve the following:

– **Make architecture a key tool for business competitiveness** by disseminating its use within companies and by communicating the results of its implementation through the visibility and communication actions managed by the CESAM Community.

– **Propose and develop the best practices of systems architecture in industry and services**, through the creation of dedicated publications and the sharing of returns on experience between systems architects and engineers during the events of the community.

– **Propose reference systems architectures**, based on the generic CESAM systems architecting methodology, that are specific to some industrial sectors in order to facilitate the work of systems architects and engineers within these sectors.

– **Facilitate access to the CESAM method** and develop its use in France and worldwide.

CESAMES Systems Architecting Method (CESAM)

The CESAM Community and its members act as the *initial developers and contributors of the CESAMES Systems Architecting Method* (CESAM), which is presented in more detail in this book.

The CESAM is a systems architecting and modeling framework, developed since 2003 in close interaction with many industrial leading companies. It is dedicated to the working systems architects, engineers or modelers in order to help them to better master the *complex integrated systems* they are dealing with in their day-to-day professional life.

The CESAM framework indeed has a number of unique features:

1) First of all, CESAM has sound mathematical fundamentals, which are providing a *rigorous and unambiguous semantics to all introduced architectural concepts*. This first property is clearly key for ensuring an efficient and real

understanding[1] between the stakeholders of a system development project (which is often key for ensuring the success of such projects).

2) These bases ensure that CESAM is a *logically complete lean systems modeling framework*: in other terms, the architectural views proposed by CESAM are just necessary and sufficient to model any integrated system. This second property guarantees both the completeness of a CESAM system model and that no useless modeling work will be done when using CESAM.

3) Finally, CESAM is *practically robust and easy to use* both by systems architects and systems modelers. This was indeed pragmatically observed among the very large number of concrete systems within many industrial areas (aeronautics, automotive, civil engineering, defense and security, energy, railway, space, etc.) that were modeled and architected using CESAM.

Note also that the CESAM framework – due to the right level of abstraction – can be implemented and used with both all existing systems modeling frameworks and systems modeling software tools[2] available on the market.

Last but not least, one shall finally point out, as already stated, that CESAM intends both to propose a generic architecting framework, as introduced in this book, and to progressively offer specific concrete reference systems architectures for a number of industrial application domains in order to facilitate the work of the systems architects and engineers within these areas.

How to read this book?

This book on model-based systems architecting with CESAM is organized in order to be read in many different ways. Typical reading modes are presented below depending on the reader's objectives.

– Discovering what a system is from a pragmatic perspective: the Introduction is an introductory section that introduces systems from a purely practical point of view.

---

1 This feature is in particular fundamental for managing convergence between the stakeholders of a system development project. It explains why collaboration is also at the core of the CESAM framework (see sections 1.3 and 2.4 for more details).

2 CESAM models were, for instance, industrially implemented under CAMEO™ from Dassault Systèmes, Capella™ open-source tool, Enterprise Architect™ from Sparx Systems or Rhapsody™ from IBM (see Appendix 4 for more details).

– Understanding systems architecting fundamentals: Chapter 1 is dedicated to the reader who wants to discover the sound logical basis the CESAM framework relies upon.

– Being aware of systems architecting benefits: you may only read Chapter 2 where the main motivations of systems architecting are described.

– Getting an overview of the CESAM framework: you shall then focus on Chapter 3 where all the core CESAM systems architecture concepts are presented.

– Practicing systems architecting: a systems architect shall know how to model a system, as well as, much more deeply, what are the needs that the system shall satisfy since they will be the compass to be used in order to regularly make the right design decisions. We thus recommend systems architects to read first Chapter 2 to be aware of the main motivations of systems architecting. You may then pass to Chapter 3 up to Chapter 9 in order to get a good overview of the CESAM framework, then learn the main systemic views and their connection with dysfunctional/safety analyses, and how to use them within an architectural decision process (which is discussed in Chapter 9). Conclusion will finally provide you some indications on how to progress in systems architecting.

– Analyzing systems safety: a safety expert shall know how to feed the dysfunctional/safety analyses with relevant systems architecture information. The connections between systems architecture and dysfunctional/safety analyses are explained in Chapter 8.

– Modeling systems: read first Chapter 3 to get an overview of CESAM systems architecture views and follow then from Chapter 4 up to Chapter 7 in order to learn one by one what are the views requested to model completely an integrated system. A last step may be to end by Appendix 3 where you can find a rather complete CESAM model on a realistic case study.

The proposed agenda

This model-based systems architecting which uses CESAM to architect complex systems is organized into 10 chapters, with the addition of some appendices specifically dedicated to more specialized material, as described below.

– Introduction – Systems, which is intended for readers with only a little system background knowledge.

– Chapter 1 – Introduction to CESAM that may be skipped for the first approach.

– Chapter 2 – Why Architecting Systems? Which presents the main motivations of the systems architecting approach and of the CESAM framework.

– *Chapter 3 – CESAM Framework* that provides an overview of all CESAM concepts.

– *Chapters 4 to 7* that present in detail, one after the other, each architectural vision of the CESAM systems modeling framework:

  - *Chapter 4 – Identifying Stakeholders: Environment Architecture.*

  - *Chapter 5 – Understanding Interactions with Stakeholders: Operational Architecture.*

  - *Chapter 6 – Defining What the System Shall Do: Functional Architecture.*

  - *Chapter 7 – Deciding How the System Shall be Formed: Constructional Architecture.*

– *Chapter 8 – Taking into Account Failures: Dysfunctional Analysis* which discusses the nature of the connection existing between systems architecture and dysfunctional/safety analyses.

– *Chapter 9 – Choosing the Best Architecture: Trade-off Techniques* that introduces systems architecture prioritization, a key tool for the systems architect.

– *Conclusion*, which gives some hints to the reader on how to continue the systems architecting journey initiated by this book.

Daniel KROB
January 2022

Acknowledgments

CESAMES and the CESAM Community would like to thank the numerous companies and systems architects and engineers without whom the CESAM framework would have never existed. All concepts and methods presented in this book were indeed prototyped and progressively developed during various missions in close contact with real concrete systems and problems.

The second acknowledgment goes to Ecole Polytechnique, especially to the sponsors of its industrial chair "Engineering of Complex Systems", that is, Dassault Aviation, Naval Group, Direction Générale de l'Armement (DGA) and, last but not least, Thales. This book is indeed, for CESAMES and the CESAM Community, the ultimate outcome of a long and progressive research and maturity process that was initiated around 20 years ago with the creation of the chair.

Introduction

Systems

I.1. Systems from a pragmatic perspective

Let us first point out that we shall only be concerned with *engineered systems* in this book, that is, systems that are designed and constructed by people[1]. As a result, the term "system" will only refer to engineered systems within the scope of this book.

Note that there are of course other objects – for instance, biological or natural systems – that may be considered as systems in an unformal meaning, but we shall not consider them in the perimeter of this book, which intends to focus on a methodological framework for architecting the systems that are developed by engineers. However, notice that engineered systems are not purely technological systems: organizational systems, such as a company or a city, which are a mix of technical systems and organized people, may also be considered to be the result of a voluntary design process and, thus, engineered systems.

From a pragmatic perspective, engineered systems can be classified in the following different types, depending on their level of integration, as described in Table I.1:

– *Product components*, that is, systems that do not make sense independently of the product in which they are integrated: a typical example is an aircraft engine which only works within an aircraft. The classical design strategy for such systems is called the V-cycle: the system is first designed (the left-hand side of the V), then constructed (the bottom part of the V), before being finally verified and validated (the right-hand side of the V).

---

1 See also de Weck *et al.* (2011) where they are called engineering systems.

– *Integrated products*, that is, systems which can be used as such, without being integrated into a larger system. These systems are usually obtained by integrating in a fixed way many product components which are therefore strongly coupled within the resulting integrated product. An aircraft is an example of an integrated product since it results in the integration of aircraft engines, landing systems, wings, fuselage, cabin, avionics components, etc. Note that the design strategy of an integrated product is more complicated than the design strategy of a single product component, since one now has to coordinate the different design cycles of the components forming the final product: in this matter, one speaks sometimes of a W-cycle when one wants to highlight the fact that the overall design cycle of the integrated product is the union of a lot of inter-related V-cycles associated with each product component.

– *Systems of systems*, that is, systems formed of several integrated products, each of them having its own life (see also Luzeaux and Ruault (2010)). These systems typically result from a weak coupling – with interfaces that can be realized or broken, depending on time – of several moving/fixed integrated products. An airport is an example of system of systems since it results in the integration of a fixed, but time evolving, part, made of several integrated products such as local air traffic management system, aircraft maintenance facilities, passenger, luggage and cargo transportation systems, passenger areas, security systems, garages and roads, and a permanently moving part, consisting of the various aircrafts that enter and leave an airport. Such systems are much more difficult to design since the coordination effort to achieve smooth integration is more important due to the huge number of independent systems that one needs to consider. Hence, interface standardization between the various systems forming a system of systems becomes now a key design tool and strategy.

– *Ecosystems*, that is, systems that are formed of several interconnected systems of systems. Here, we are therefore dealing with many inter-dependent components that are interacting from time to time, depending on the needs. The global air traffic management system in its whole – at Earth level – is such an ecosystem that involves all airports, all local and regional traffic management systems and many satellite systems. Such an ecosystem has no owner, and its good design and behavior only results in the agreement of the involved actors.

Table I.1 summarizes these different categories of engineered systems that are illustrated on different aeronautics examples, as presented above.

Type of system	Characteristics	Typical example	Design Strategy
Product component	Does not exist independently of a product	Aircraft engine	V-cycle
Integrated product	Strong coupling of fixed components	Aircraft	W-cycle
Systems of systems	Weak coupling involving moving components	Airport	Interfaces standardization
Ecosystem	Interactions involving moving components	Air Traffic Management	Actors Influence

Table I.1. *Categories of engineered systems. For a color version of this table, see www.iste.co.uk/krob/systems.zip*

As one can see, the notion of system – from a pragmatic perspective – covers various realities. As a matter of fact, engineered systems can indeed be found in all industrial domains where they may, for instance, refer to the following objects:

– *In the automotive sector*: a car, any component of a car (cockpit, chassis, electric/electronic infrastructure, powertrain, etc.) or an advanced driver assistance service (ADAS).

– *On the aeronautical sector*: an aircraft, a helicopter, a drone or any component of these systems (cockpit, fuselage, cabin, engine, landing system, avionics, etc.).

– *In the defense sector*: a military system (vehicle, missile, communication and control system, etc.), a system of systems that involves these systems or any component of these systems.

– *In the energy sector*: an energy production system (nuclear plant, thermal power plant, wind turbine farm, etc.), an energy distribution system or any component of these systems.

– *In the naval sector*: a ship, a sub-marine, a marine drone, a system of systems involving these systems or any component of these systems.

– *In the railway sector*: a train, a metro, a tram, a railway infrastructure, a railway signaling system or any component (e.g. traction, embedded system, station, etc.) of these systems.

– *In the service sector*: an enterprise information system, a service organization or any socio-technical component of these systems.

– *In the space sector*: a satellite, a space launcher, a spaceship, a satellite constellation, a value-added space service or any component of these systems.

Note that most of the systems that we just mentioned here above are either product components or integrated products. This reflects the fact that these two last categories of engineered systems are clearly the ones that one finds the most in the industry, from a pragmatic perspective. On the other hand, it is indeed rather rare in practice that one has to design a system of systems or an ecosystem, which does not however mean that such systems are less important. The point is just that system design always requires a system owner who requests the design of a given system and that unique ownership of systems of systems and of ecosystems is often non-existent.

Note finally that we specially dedicated section I.3 to the presentation and discussion – in more detail – of a number of concrete examples of systems, following the categorization we introduced within this section, in order for the reader to become more familiar with engineered systems.

I.2. The need for a specific approach to deal with systems

Now that we have explained the notion of a system from an empirical point of view, we can see why it is necessary to introduce a particular approach to conceive them, which is indeed the purpose of this book. After all, all the engineered systems that we listed in the previous section, are working perfectly and we could therefore very well conclude that there is no need of a specific approach to their design. The point is that these engineered systems are all characterized by a huge complexity and their design is extremely difficult (see section 2.2 for more details on system complexity). Moreover, traditional engineering disciplines and methods generally fail to take into account a certain number of specificities of complex engineered systems on which we shall now focus. This motivates *systems architecting*, which is the specific system design discipline to which this book is dedicated.

The very first point that we think is important to highlight is the fact that the design and development of an engineered system that is somewhat complex, requires us to deal with a multitude of details in which it is easy to get lost.

Managing all of these details is of course necessary, but the problem is not to see and think of a system as a sum of details, knowing that experience shows that it is easy to lose the overview of a given system and to miss some of its absolutely structuring elements.

To give just one real example of such a situation, during the recent construction of an energy plant, a key industrial equipment arrived on site and it was not possible to install it: the location – a dedicated room in the center of the power plant – where it was to be placed was indeed built, but the designer just "forgot" to think of how to put it there. It was therefore necessary to break the concrete infrastructure to make room in order to move the equipment into place, which generated quality losses, additional costs and delays and new operational safety problems which required some of the dysfunctional studies to be redone. Such examples are unfortunately not isolated at all, and avoiding them is a key challenge for many industries.

In order to avoid such issues, systems architecting proposes analyzing system problems from a high-level perspective, in order to be sure to capture all the most structuring elements of a system, rather than from a low-level perspective, in order not to become lost in the details. To explain this key idea, let us take a mountain metaphor. Look first at the photo of Figure I.1, showing Mont Blanc, the highest summit in Europe, which was taken from Chamonix at 1,200 meters above sea level, a small village in the French Alps, where mountaineering was invented at the end of the 18th century. The point is that Mont Blanc does not look very impressive in that photo and one cannot perceive very well why it has such international fame. However, on the other hand, one can see very well on the photo all the details on the flowers within the streets of Chamonix.

Let us now have a look at the second photo of Mont Blanc provided in Figure I.2. It was taken more or less at the same geographic location as the first photo, the only difference in this case is that we are now 2,000 meters over the sea. We have lost here the details of the flowers of Chamonix village, but gained a wonderful overview of the Mont Blanc massif, which was invisible to us when looking on exactly the same landscape from Chamonix valley. This new perspective provides us with a much better understanding of why these mountains are so famous around the world!

Figure I.1. *Mont Blanc from Chamonix (1,200 meters above sea level).
For a color version of this figure, see www.iste.co.uk/krob/systems.zip*

Figure I.2. *Mont Blanc from the Black Lake
(2,000 meters over the sea). For a color version of
this figure, see www.iste.co.uk/krob/systems.zip*

As we can see from that metaphor, the point of view that one takes when looking on a system can radically change the perception of the considered system and not taking a high enough overview of a system leads to losing the global picture, while risking focusing on details, which are ultimately of no great importance. The first key idea behind systems architecting – the discipline that proposes a specific approach to system design and to which this book is dedicated, as already stated – is therefore to maintain permanently a global vision of the system of interest, meaning both not to forget crucial points for the system design and to guarantee to reach all details, when refining this global vision.

The second key point that we would like to highlight is that any reasonably complex system design always has a socio-technical dimension. An engineered system can indeed always be broken down into a series of technical components, each of them being owned by a given designer. Designing the full system can thus be seen as both, solving a complex technical puzzle where one needs to understand how these various components shall be smoothly integrated within the complete engineered system, as well as aligning all the local designers around a global vision of the system (see Figure I.3).

Figure I.3. *The socio-technical dimension of systems. For a color version of this figure, see www.iste.co.uk/krob/systems.zip*

This explains why the second key characteristics of systems architecting consists of always analyzing systems problems from a global multi-disciplinary perspective rather from a local mono-expertise point of view and ensuring the collaboration between all actors involved in a system design (see also sections 1.3 and 2.5 for more details on the collaborative dimension of systems architecting).

I.3. Examples of systems

The purpose of this new section is to present in more detail some concrete examples of systems. To this aim, we shall use the system classification introduced in section I.1 and present and discuss a significant example of a system for each level of this classification. We shall therefore analyze from a system perspective, first a *computer system* as an example of a complex component, second an *extended vehicle* as an example of an integrated product, then the *railway system* as an example of system of a systems and finally the *world* as an example of a complex ecosystem.

We hope that these examples will allow the reader to become more familiar both with the notion of a system and with the way an engineered system is analyzed from a systems architecting perspective.

I.3.1. *A complex component: a computer system*

The first system that we shall consider is a *computer system* like the ones typically found in a data center as shown in Figure I.4. Let us indeed recall that data centers are dedicated buildings that house operational computer, telecommunications and data storage systems, as well as redundant/backup components and infrastructure for power supply, data communication connections, environmental controls, such as air-conditioning, fire sensing and suppression or intrusion detection and various security devices. Data centers are therefore integrated products – in the meaning of section I.1 – and a computer system is therefore just one of its key complex components.

Figure I.4. *A complex component system: a computer system. For a color version of this figure, see www.iste.co.uk/krob/systems.zip*

To better understand such a system from a systems architecting perspective, let us present its constructional interaction diagram (see section 7.2 for more details on that concept) that focuses on the interactions existing between the different components of a computer system (see Figure I.5) and allows us to both capture all its components and the way they are interconnected.

These interactions involve, in practice, various types of objects such as, for instance, mechanical forces, electricity, data, electromagnetic signals, air, time, etc. It is therefore important to distinguish these different types of interactions when designing a constructional interaction diagram, which can be achieved by using a different color code for each type of interaction (see Figure I.5).

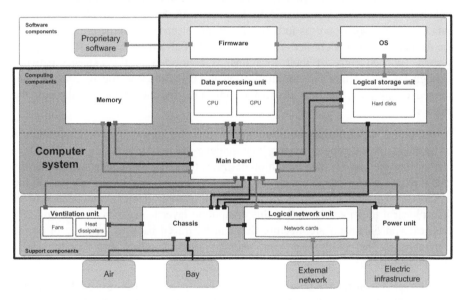

Figure I.5. *Constructional interaction diagram of a computer system.*
For a color version of this figure, see www.iste.co.uk/krob/systems.zip

A key point is also to structure the constructional interaction diagram by organizing the components of a computer system into *logical layers*, each of them formed of components that have the same nature (see Figure I.5 where we used three different colors to distinguish the three logical layers that we introduced for a computer system). Such structuration allows us to more easily understand the architecture of the considered system through the meaning associated with the layers, to simplify the network of interactions between components and to separate the core components from the less important ones. The knowledge of the interactions between the different components of a given system is also key in the context of a modular approach since it highlights the interfaces that shall be standardized – that is, those that exist between the different logical layers – and allows us to better master the standard module configurations that are to be proposed in such an approach.

The generic constructional interaction diagram of a computer system is elicited in Figure I.5. This diagram organizes all computer system components in the following three logical layers:

– **Layer 1 – Support components**: this first layer is formed of all the components of a computer system that support its main functionality, that is, computing. These components are also in direct interaction with key external stakeholders: the *chassis* mechanically interacts with the bay in which it lays in the data center; the *power unit* is interfaced with the electric infrastructure provided by the data center; the *logical network unit*, formed of all network cards of a computer system, independently of their locations, is connected to the external network through the data center telecommunication infrastructure and the *ventilation unit*, formed of all fans and heat dissipaters, manages the air exchanges through the chassis.

– **Layer 2 – Computing components**: this second logical layer contains all core components of a computer system that achieve the core computing functionality, that is, first the *main board*, which orchestrates the other components of this layer, then the *data processing unit* with all CPUs and GPUs[2] (if any), the *memory* and the *logical storage unit* formed of all the possible storage devices, independently of their physical locations. Note that this computing layer is organized according to a classical von Neumann architecture that can be traced back to the very origin of computers in the 1940s (see von Neuman 1945; Godfrey and Hendry 1993; Wikipedia (2021p)).

– **Layer 3 – Software components**: this last layer consists just of the software components of a computer system that can be separated into two groups: the first group is formed of the *operating system* and of the *firmware software* that are both installed by the computer system manufacturer, the second one is formed by the proprietary software installed by the final end-user, which is another key stakeholder of a computer system, during the normal operation of the computer system.

Note finally that the mechanical, electrical, data and air interactions/exchanges between the various computer system components are traced in the constructional interaction diagram with the following different color codes: black for mechanical interactions, red for electrical interactions, green for data exchanges and finally purple for air exchanges.

---

2 GPU means Graphics Processing Unit. It is a specialized CPU (Central Processing Unit) dedicated to graphics processing.

The key point that this first example allows us to see is that the architecture of a modern computer system is fundamentally the same as the one that was imagined by J. von Neuman in 1945, as pointed out above. Good systems architectures are indeed often remarkably stable with time, which explains their importance! Finding a good architecture – which is usually characterized by its simplicity and its apparent obviousness – is however not simple and obvious at all.

I.3.2. *An integrated product system: the extended vehicle*

The second system that we shall consider in this example section is an integrated product system coming from the automotive industry, that is, an *extended vehicle*, in the meaning of ISO 20077 standard (see ISO (2018)). We shall recall in this matter that an extended vehicle is formed of the vehicle plus the off-board facility that allow us to manage the exchanges of technical data between on-board and off-board during the life of a car. The off-board facility, which is usually not perceived by a car driver, but that shall be designed in parallel with any given vehicle, provides access to vehicle data in accordance with clearly defined technical and data protection rules through various interfaces and means of off-board data storage (see Figure I.6). It also manages the regular upgrades of the various software embarked on-board during the maintenance of a car within a garage.

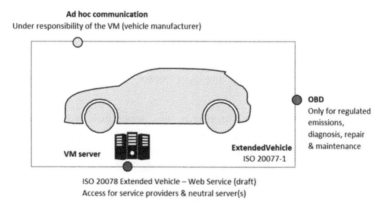

Figure I.6. *An integrated product system: an extended vehicle. For a color version of this figure, see www.iste.co.uk/krob/systems.zip*

To better understand an extended vehicle from a systems architecting perspective, let us present the *functional interaction diagram* of such a system (see section 6.2 for more details on that concept). Such a diagram intends to show the functions that model the technology-independent behaviors of an extended vehicle, together with their internal and external interactions (see Figure I.7).

Again, these interactions may be of various nature: mechanical interactions, electrical interactions, air exchanges and data or information exchanges. In Figure I.7, these various interfaces are presented using different color codes: black for mechanical interfaces, red for electrical interfaces, purple for air interfaces and finally blue for data or information interfaces.

We also used a layered organization, here through *functional layers* since we are dealing with functional architecture, for the functional interaction diagram of an extended vehicle, focusing only on top-level functions. This means that all top-level functions of an extended vehicle were distributed in independent groups of functions, called functional layers, that are exchanging functional flows (data, matter, energy, etc.) through standard functional interfaces. In other words, a function within a given functional layer ideally only discusses with another functional layer through the functional interfaces that this other functional layer provides. Functions overlapping two layers are therefore normally forbidden. This functional layer principle is key to allowing the overall system to easily evolve since a function can be changed in one layer without any impact on the others. Such a layered functional architecture is therefore not only a nice drawing but also has a fundamental impact in terms of ease of evolution of an extended vehicle and mastering the associated costs.

The functional interaction diagram of an extended vehicle is presented in Figure I.7. It is organized into four *functional layers* as described below, which express the functional decouplings that exist between the different functions of an extended vehicle:

– **Layer 1 – Manage user interfaces**: this functional layer groups all the functions that manage the different user interfaces that are offering value-added services to users. It can be broken down into three main functions that cover the management of, respectively, the mechanical user interfaces (e.g. open/close the vehicle), the visual user interfaces (e.g. provide vehicle status) and the comfort user interfaces (e.g. provide heat).

– **Layer 2 – Control extended vehicle:** this functional layer groups all the functions that control the vehicle motion and trajectory. It can be broken down into three main functions which, respectively, manage the sensing of the environment (e.g. measure vehicle speed), make the strategic decision (e.g. decide braking) and act on the environment (e.g. send a braking instruction). Note that these control functions are especially key for autonomous driving and connected vehicle management.

– **Layer 3 – Manage energies:** this functional layer groups all the functions that manage the vehicle energies, that is, fuel, electricity, vacuum, torque and movement. It can be broken down into two main functions which, respectively, manage the production of these energies (e.g. provide torque) and the transformation of these energies into movement (e.g. provide lateral movement).

– **Layer 4 – Protect during crash:** this functional layer is reduced to a single function that protects passengers during crash. It is a safety function that reflects at the functional level the passive safety mechanisms that are implemented inside a vehicle.

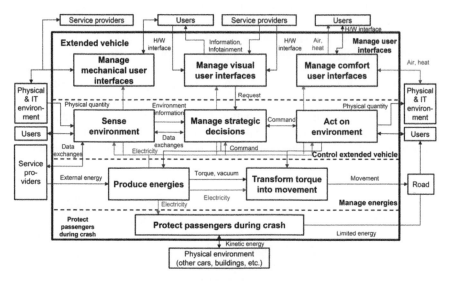

Figure I.7. *Functional interaction diagram of an extended vehicle. For a color version of this figure, see www.iste.co.uk/krob/systems.zip*

The key point that this second example allows us to see is the genericity of the functional architecture, which is introduced through the functional interaction diagram provided in Figure I.7. We were indeed able to capture very different types of technological implementations within the same diagram, that is, usual thermic vehicles, as well as electrical vehicles or hybrid vehicles and even vehicles using other sources of energy, such as hydrogen or gas, which shall all comply to the previous functional interaction diagram. This is a typical example of the strength of functional architecture, which allows us to make architectural decisions – that are usually very structuring – on a given system, independently of its concrete technical implementations.

I.3.3. *A system of systems: the railway system*

The third system that we shall consider within our example section will now be a system of systems, that is, the *railway system* of a given country, to fix ideas. We shall first recall that a railway system at the national scale is formed of various technical and organizational elements such as trains, trackside infrastructures, control and command systems, communication systems, operating centers, depots, railway stations, commercial departments and maintenance organizations. Each of these elements is an integrated product in the meaning introduced in section I.1, and a national railway system appears then as a system of systems in the same meaning, as illustrated in Figure I.8.

To better understand a railway system from a systems architecting perspective, let us again present its *functional interaction diagram* (we refer to section 6.2 for more details on that concept). Such a diagram intends to show the functions that model the technology-independent behaviors of a railway system, together with their internal and external interactions (see Figure I.9). In this last matter, note that the key stakeholders that are interacting with the railway system are typically service operators, customers and end-users, other transportation systems, banks, external operators, energy suppliers, other national railway systems, asset management actors, surrounding environment, malicious people (e.g. hackers, thieves, vandals, terrorists, etc.), legacy systems, atmosphere, mobile network operators (MNO) and satellites.

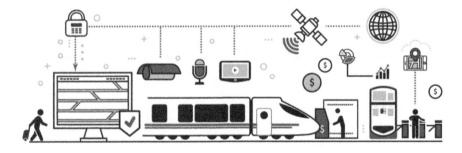

Figure I.8. *A system of systems: the railway system. For a color version of this figure, see www.iste.co.uk/krob/systems.zip*

We can again organize the functional interaction diagram of a railway system according to the functional layer organization that we already used in the previous sub-section, to which we refer for more details among this functional architecture principle. For the sake of completeness, we shall just quickly recall here that this principle consists of clustering functions within independent and decoupled groups, called functional layers (see Figure I.9).

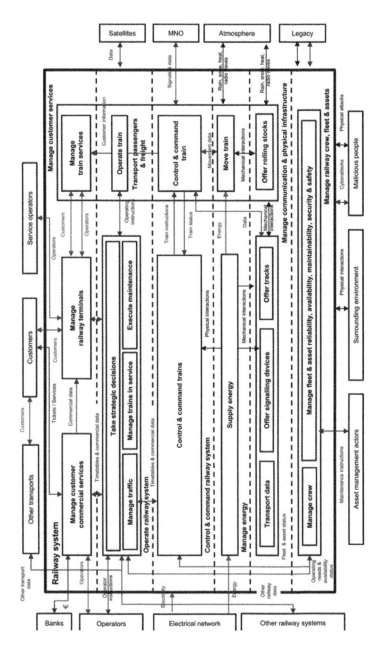

Figure I.9. *Functional interaction diagram of the railway system. For a color version of this figure, see www.iste.co.uk/krob/systems.zip*

Another important point, which we should stress here, is the distinction that one has to make in the context of a railway system, between on-board functions, that is, functions that are managed by trains, also called rolling stocks in the railway industry, and off-board functions, that is, functions that are managed by the fixed railway infrastructure (tracksides, control centers, railway stations, etc.), out of the trains. The "transport passengers & freight" function, which is transversal to all functional layers, being the top-level function naturally allocated to a train, the on-board functions are therefore just the sub-functions of that top-level function of a train, when the off-board functions are the other ones, as it can be easily read in Figure I.9.

The resulting functional interaction diagram of a railway system is organized into the following six *functional layers*, as described more in detail below and illustrated in Figure I.9, which express the natural functional decouplings that exist between the different functions of a railway system:

– **Layer 1 – Manage customer services**: this first functional layer groups the business functions managed by the railway system that are visible from the end-users, that is, either train passengers or freight customers. It breakdowns into two off-board functions and a single on-board function:

   - **manage customer commercial services** in passenger or freight contexts,

   - **manage railway terminals** which may be railway stations or depots,

   - **manage train services** on-board of a train.

– **Layer 2 – Operate railway system:** this key functional layer covers authorization and control of the trains within the railway system and operations of the railway network and its traffic. It breakdowns into four off-board functions and a single on-board function:

   - **make strategic decisions** at the global railway system level,

   - **manage traffic**, again at the railway system level, but from an operational perspective,

   - **manage trains in service,** especially focused on each train within the railway system,

   - **execute maintenance**,

   - **operate train**, which is especially managed by the train driver.

– **Layer 3 – Control & command railway system**: this core functional layer groups the control and command functions of the railway system, including command control of the movements of trains authorized to travel on the railway network and all train control functions required to ensure safety. It breakdowns into a single off-board function and a single on-board function:

- **control & command trains** which groups, for instance, sub-functions such as define route, make safe decisions and control trains,

- **control & command train** which groups train sub-functions such as automatically operate and couple the train, manage driver interface, supervise train speed and movements, make safe decisions, manage juridical recorder, check data consistency, get speed profile/modes and levels, manage communication, manage train interfaces, manage traction/brake commands and provide train speed and position.

– **Layer 4 – Manage energy**: this new layer deals with the basic functions dedicated to energy management, both off- and on-board. It breaks down into a single off-board function and a single on-board function:

- **supply energy**, which provides energy to each train,

- **move train** which includes manage energy, provide traction/brake status, and move and brake functions.

– **Layer 5 – Manage communication & physical infrastructure**: this infrastructure-dedicated functional layer contains the basic functions managed by the end-to-end communication and physical infrastructure. It breaks down into four off-board functions and a single on-board function:

- **transport data** between trains and control & command centers,

- **offer infrastructure**, which reflects the purely mechanical parts of the infrastructure, without any special behavior,

- **offer signaling devices** that corresponds to the parts of the signaling system which do not support any control & command function,

- **offer train rolling stock** that reflects the purely mechanical parts of the train, which do not have any special behavior.

– **Layer 6 – Manage railway crew, fleet & assets**: this last functional layer consolidates all the functions related to human or technical reliability, availability, maintainability, safety and security of the railway system. It breaks down into two main off-board functions:

- **manage crew**,

- **manage fleet & asset reliability, availability, maintainability, security & safety**.

Note finally that we also tried to draft, at a quite high level, in the functional interaction diagram provided in Figure I.9, some key flows that are exchanged either internally between the railway system functions or externally with the railway system stakeholders. In this matter, our diagram tried to highlight the data exchanges, including money, which are represented by blue flows, the people and freight exchanges which are represented by purple flows, the physical exchanges, including matter, mechanical and waves exchanges, which are represented by black flows, and the energy exchanges, which are represented by red flows.

This new example illustrates another important property of the functional architecture of a system, as introduced on the railway system through the functional interaction diagram given in Figure I.9, that is, the fact that the functional architecture easily captures the huge diversity of a system. As a matter of fact, any railway system does not consist of a single railway station, a single operation center, a single control & command system, a single train, a single railway infrastructure and a single maintenance infrastructure. But since all various instances of these different systems share the same functions, it is therefore not necessary to represent all of them from a functional perspective, which is the natural functional point of view that we followed within Figure I.9, which shall be seen as a generic functional interaction diagram, and not of course as an instantiated one, where one should show as many functions as instantiations of them.

I.3.4. *An ecosystem: the world as a system*

The fourth and last system that we shall consider within our example section will be our *world*, that is, Earth, considered as a system. It is indeed clearly an interesting complex ecosystem in which each concrete engineered system is involved. In this matter, the very first world model, based on generalized Volterra equations, was proposed in the seminal work of J.W. Forrester in the 1970s in order to study the impact of the decrease of energetic fossil resources on the human society in terms of population, agricultural and industrial resource and pollution evolution (see Forrester (1971); Meadows *et al.* (1972)).

More recently O. de Weck, D. Krob, L. Lefei, P.C. Lui, A. Rauzy and X.G. Zhang also introduced a new world model in the context of a systemic analysis of the COVID-19 crisis (see de Weck *et al.* (2020)). It is this approach that we shall now quickly present here. In this other framework, the world is divided into the following four main interacting sub-systems (see Figure I.10):

– the *natural environment* that provides natural resources (sun, rain, vegetables, minerals, oil, etc.) to the economy, but from which threats also come such as coronavirus;

– the *economic system* that transforms these natural resources into products and services that are sold to the people, using their work force and respecting regulations;

– the *social system* that consumes the products and services provided by the economical system, provides its work force, respects regulations and is under the stress of coronavirus;

– the *governance system* that regulates the human activities, as managed by the economical and social systems, through suitable regulations.

The resulting constructional interaction diagram synthesizing this way of looking at the world is given in Figure I.10. This first system view exposes the exchanges of matter, people, information and money – plus coronavirus here – that exist between the main systems forming the world. Note that the overall system taken into account here, that is, human society as a whole, including its natural environment, is a closed system on our home planet Earth.

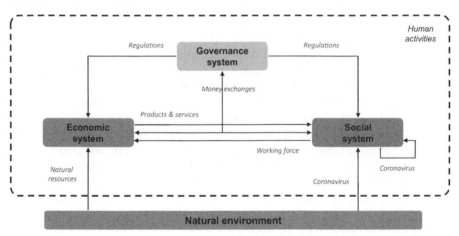

Figure I.10. *An ecosystem: the world as a system. For a color version of this figure, see www.iste.co.uk/krob/systems.zip*

Let us now use this approach to discuss the impact of the COVID-19 crisis on the world as a system. Note first that the impact of the crisis on the economic and social systems depends of course on the health policy chosen by the governance system. Moreover, if a health policy recommends or forces – as often done (cf. World Health Organization (2021)) – a large fraction of the population to stay home, it causes a non-classical *double shock* on the economy, first on the supply side, since economic actors, which are lacking work force, must reduce their production and second on the demand side, since people who do not work anymore are usually paid less and thus are consuming less (cf. Strauss-Kahn (2020)). The unexpected interactions between the various systems forming the world, provoked by the crisis, are therefore huge!

As a result, addressing a systemic crisis such as COVID-19 requires us to solve a complex multi-objective optimization problem that is not obvious at all since one can easily understand that the behavior of our system of interest – the world – will be different depending on whether one wants to minimize the impact of the crisis on the social, health (which shall be considered as a part of the governance system) or economic system or to find the best balance between the impacts on these three systems. The difficulty of this complex optimization problem is moreover increased by the fact that one must also mitigate the long-term consequences of the pandemic on human society and take into account the delays and uncertainties that are specific to such a crisis.

However, the static view provided in Figure I.10 only shows the space in which the COVID-19 crisis takes place. However, we also need to consider time evolution to get a complete picture of such a crisis. This can be achieved by introducing a new systems architecting concept, that is, the *lifecycle* of our system of interest, the world, where we depict its different states over time. In this matter, we now need to understand what the possible future(s) of human society could be after the COVID-19 crisis, which leads us to think in terms of *lifecycle scenarios*, that is, possible temporal evolutions of our system of interest, since our future is by nature uncertain and nobody can predict it. Each such global lifecycle scenario can, for instance, be obtained – using an old technique (cf. Alur and Dill (1994)) that goes back to the origins of distributed computing – through a synchronized product of the domain-specific lifecycle scenarios that model the evolution of each of the main systems forming the world. Using that technique, the point is therefore to construct realistic domain-specific lifecycle scenarios, capturing the possible evolutions of the economic, social and governance systems, that we shall then combine in order to get a global lifecycle scenario for the world.

Let us show an example of the technique that we just introduced, focusing here only on possible evolutions of the economic and social systems as illustrated in Figure I.11. In this example, we considered that the COVID-19 health crisis will result, on the one hand, on the level of the economic system, first on an economic crisis, followed by an economic recovery and, on the other hand, on the level of the social system, taking here a purely health point of view, first on an endemic situation from the perspective of the epidemics, followed finally by a healthy situation. Mixing these two local possible scenarios, we got the global possible lifecycle scenario for the human society which is described on the right-hand side of Figure I.11 where the COVID-19 health crisis will result first in a situation characterized by the conjunction of an economic crisis and a mixed endemic and healthy situation, eventually followed by a global recovery, both from economic and health perspectives.

To obtain more detailed models, we shall of course refine them in terms of space, to capture the geographic dimension of the social system, and time, to make optimal trade-off decisions between short- and long-term impacts of the COVID-19 crisis. Note also that these lifecycle scenarios are of course highly country dependent due to the central role of the governance system in the resolution of such a crisis, as well as the susceptibility of the population with respect to the coronavirus. The main interest of such a scenario approach is that one can compare and evaluate them in order to make the best governance decisions. It is therefore a valuable systemic tool to aid decision-making.

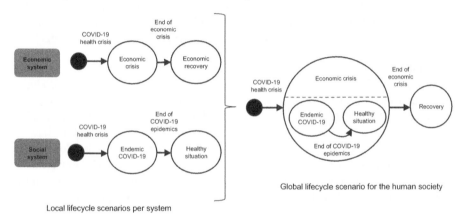

Figure I.11. *Illustration of a standard process for constructing a COVID-19 global lifecycle scenario. For a color version of this figure, see www.iste.co.uk/krob/systems.zip*

This last example allows us to show that the systems architecting approach, promoted within this book, can be used to address systemic issues that are far beyond purely technical problems, even if technical contexts are of course the application domains of such an approach. Finally, readers who want to know more about how to use a system approach in the context of a systemic crisis such as COVID-19 should refer to de Weck *et al.* (2020).

I.4. Systems are everywhere

When one looks at all great challenges that humanity will have to face in the near future, one can find everywhere existing systems that have to be deeply transformed and new systems that have to be developed, leading to various systems architecting and engineering challenges.

First of all, due to the programmed lack of fossil resources, there is obviously an *energetic transition* that the world will have to manage, since energy is at the source of each human activity. This implies reshaping an important part of the economic system that shall be based on new sources of energy, while at the same time developing more sustainable economic policies in terms of recycling, waste management, etc. The industrial consequences of that situation are just tremendous in terms of engineered systems that will have to transform and develop in order to take into account the new energetic paradigm on which the economy has to be reconstructed. Imagine, for instance, hydrogen becoming the dominant source of energy in the future for mobility: it means creating hydrogen production plants, hydrogen distribution infrastructures, hydrogen-based aircrafts, cars, ships, trains, etc. The resulting architecting and engineering challenge would be terribly huge!

Another important trend, to be dealt with, is the *digital transformation* of the economy, leading to increasingly sophisticated services and products. Communication technology, increasing computational power, mobile applications, miniaturization, cloud solutions, Internet of Things, etc., are deeply transforming many engineered systems in various industrial domains. This evolution has, of course, many positive consequences due to the new services that it allows us to propose to the end-users, but it also increases the complexity of the systems it impacts, which are both supporting more functionality while, at the same time, becoming more distributed and therefore less controllable[3]. A typical side effect of

---

3 The introduction of digital technology in most of classical engineered systems created new couplings within these systems, leading typically to new safety issues. Let us take the example of an aircraft to illustrate that point. In old aircrafts, the pilot was directly interacting on aircraft control areas, through mechanical transmission mechanisms, starting from the airplane broomstick on which he/she was exerting forces. The consequence of that architecture was of course that a bad pilot could crash an aircraft through incorrect piloting orders. To avoid this situation, the pilot is no longer connected directly to the aircraft control areas on modern aircrafts: he/she pilots with a joystick that sends the piloting intentions (go quickly up, go smoothly down, etc.) to a central computer that interprets the intentions of the pilot and sends the right instructions to actuators that eventually manage the aircraft control areas. This strategy clearly has a positive impact in terms of piloting since the central computer is obliged to follow the optimal control laws that were embedded at its level. However, it also has a number of side effects. First of all, it just transfers the safety constraints from the pilot to the central computer, which becomes now the weak point in the new architecture, leading to specific engineering standards for trying to ensure safety at that level. Second, it creates new "digital" couplings between the various aircraft systems that are managed by the central computer, leading to new safety issues that were inexistent in classical aircraft architectures.

the digital transformation is the tremendous increase of cyber-security issues, which is its dark side, and nowadays impossible not to consider. Imagine, for instance, the consequences of a cyber-attack on critical systems such as hospitals! Again, the resulting impact of the digital transformation on all existing engineered systems is tremendous.

From a radically different perspective, we shall also point out that the *urbanization* of human society also has a number of architecting and engineering consequences. This other transformation indeed results in an important change of population distributions, leading to larger markets and greater opportunities for citizens, as well as to smarter cities in order to reduce societal stress and to modernize and improve urban infrastructures in terms of transportation, food supply, security, health, entertainment, waste management, etc., which ultimately requires the creation of new engineered systems in these urban contexts.

There are, of course, many other environmental, social, political and technological trends of importance that we did not mention here. However, the common characteristics between all these trends is that they are requiring integrated solutions, based on a lot of different hardware and software technologies and also often involving people, at various local or global scales, that is, systems, in the systems architecting and engineering meaning that we are using here. Systems are thus nowadays everywhere, and better mastering them is crucial. This is the core purpose of this book.

Introduction to CESAM

1.1. CESAM: a mathematically sound system modeling framework

CESAMES Systems Architecting Method (CESAM) is the result of 12 years of research and development (cf. Bliudze and Krob (2005, 2006, 2009), Krob (2006, 2007, 2009, 2012, 2013), Caseau *et al.* (2007), de Weck *et al.* (2009), Aiguier *et al.* (2010, 2012, 2013)) including permanent interactions and operational experimentations with industry. The CESAM framework was indeed used in practice to design and develop thousands of engineered systems within several leading international industries in many independent areas with a success that never wavered (see Chalé Gongora *et al.* (2012), Dauron *et al.* (2011), Berrebi and Krob (2012), Doufène and Krob (2013, 2014, 2015), Giakoumakis *et al.* (2010) or Giakoumakis *et al.* (2012) for some application examples). This huge theoretical and experimental effort resulted in *a both mathematically sound and practical system modeling framework*, which is easy to use by the working systems engineers and architects.

We shall only present in this chapter the more important fundamentals[1] of the CESAM framework that may help to better understand its philosophy. In this matter, the key and core point is the logical consistency of the CESAM framework, naturally provided by its mathematical bases. Due to this strong level of consistency,

---

1 The CESAM framework is based on formal semantics, the mathematical theory – based on mathematical logics (cf. Barwise 1972) – which provides the fundamentals of computer science (see Winskel 1993). The CESAM framework may be understood as an extension of usual formal semantics – which only addresses software systems – to more general types of systems.

anybody who agrees with logical reasoning[2] (which shall normally be the case with all engineers & architects) will indeed be able to use and work with the CESAM framework.

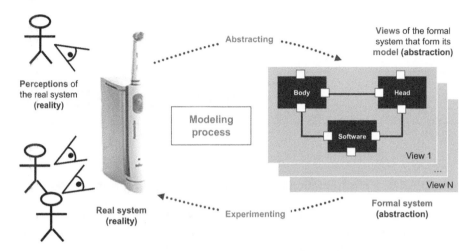

Figure 1.1. *The two abstracting/experimenting sides of a system modeling process. For a color version of this figure, see www.iste.co.uk/krob/systems.zip*

Note now first that systems are considered from a modeling perspective within the CESAM framework. This point of view immediately leads us to distinguish the two core concepts of a "formal system" and "real system". It is indeed important to avoid any confusion[3] between the result of a system modeling process (the formal system) and the concrete object under modeling (the real system). Many design mistakes – often with high costs of non-quality – are indeed made by engineers when they forget that their system specification documentation is just an abstraction

---

2 Logical reasoning is usually mixed with common sense. However, one shall not forget that logics is a body of mathematical knowledge (see Barwise 1972), sadly largely unknown to engineers, that can be traced back to Aristoteles (see Wikipedia 2021g).

3 Unfortunately, this confusion is quite common in systems engineering where such a distinction is usually not made both in practice and in most textbooks, handbooks and standards (such as Blanchard and Fabricky 1998; Meinadier 1998; Sage and Armstrong 2000; Maier and Rechtin 2002; Meinadier 2002; Kossiakoff and Sweet 2003; IEEE 2005; Sillitto 2014; ISO 2018 or Turner et al. 1978). Aslaksen appears to be one of the rare systems engineering authors who proposed a formal definition for a system (see Aslaksen and Belcher (1992) and Aslaksen (1996)). Sound systems modeling formalisms seem to be only found in the control theory and mathematical simulation literature (cf. Cha et al. (2000), Severance (2001) or Zeigler et al. (2000)) or in the few theoretical computer science system literature (cf. Börger and Stärk (2003), Lamport (2003) or Marwedel (2003)).

of reality, but not the "real" reality, and that their job is to ensure permanent alignment – through feedback loops with reality – between their system models and the real system, as it is and not as they think it is.

A *system modeling process* can thus be seen as a permanent back and forth between, on the first side, an *abstraction activity* that constructs a formal model of a real-world object – using the tools of systemic analysis – and on the second side, an *experimentation activity* where the structure or behavior of the real object, as given or predicted by the model, are checked against those really observed in reality, as illustrated in Figure 1.1. The real object under modeling shall thus be considered as a (real) system, in order to distinguish it from the (formal) system that a system modeling process constructs within a systemic modeling framework. By abuse of language, we often identify these two concepts of "system", but it is important never to forget that "the map is not the territory" (Korzybski 1950) in order to know at any time on what we are reasoning! Note also that this approach points out that being a system is absolutely not an intrinsic property of an object[4], but results from a modeling decision of a system designer. This being recalled, we can now provide the definition of a formal system[5] on which relies the CESAM modeling framework (see also Figure 1.2 for the standard representation of a formal system based on that definition).

DEFINITION 1.1.– **Formal system** – A *formal system* S is characterized on the one hand by an input set X, an output set Y and a set of internal variables Q, and on the other hand by the following two kinds of behaviors that link these systemic variables among a given time scale T[6]:

– A *functional behavior* that produces an output $y(t+) \in Y$ at each moment of time $t \in T$, depending on the current input $x(t) \in X$ and internal state $q(t) \in Q$ of the system.

---

4 This last consideration shows that it is merely impossible to give a sound definition of a real system since any object in the real world can be considered as a system, as soon as a system designer decides it.

5 The CESAM definition of a system provided by Definition 1.1 unifies two classical system modeling traditions: it indeed mixes the usual functional definition coming from the control theory & mathematical system simulation literature (cf. Cha *et al.* (2000), Severance (2001) or Zeigler *et al.* (2000)) and the state-machine system definition that emerged in theoretical computer science (cf. Börger and Stärk (2003), Lamport (2003) or Marwedel (2003)).

6 A time scale T is a totally ordered set with a unique minimal element – usually denoted t_0 – and where each element $t \in T$ has a (unique) least upper bound within the time scale, called its successor and denoted t+ within T. Up to rescaling, two types of time scales are key in practice: discrete time scales, where t+ = t + 1, and continuous time scales, where t+ = t + dt, where dt stands for an infinitesimal quantity. Discrete time scales model event-oriented systems (such as software systems, which are regulated by a discrete clock) when continuous time scales are used to model physical continuous phenomena.

– An *internal behavior* that results in the evolution q(t+) ∈ Q of the internal state of the system at each moment of time t ∈ T, under the action[7] of an input x(t) ∈ X on the system.

This definition is deliberately very weak following Occam's razor strategy[8] that prevails throughout the CESAM framework. It simply means that a system is just defined by an input/output and an internal behavior[9]. This is of course not abnormal since we want to capture commonalities between all real systems. These common points are therefore mechanically quite limited due to the tremendous diversity of the real objects that we need to take into account.

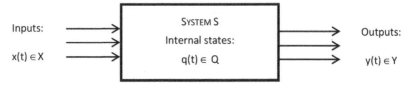

Figure 1.2. *Standard representation of a formal system*

However, we now have a unified systems modeling framework provided by Definition 1.2, in which we can uniformly reason on any type of system, and hence think about systems integration, which was one of our first goals (see section 1.2).

DEFINITION 1.2.– **Real system** – An object of the real world will be called a *real system* as soon as its structure and its behavior can be described by a formal system – in the meaning of Definition 1.1 – that will then be called a *model* of the considered real system.

---

7 When this action is not permanent, one may identify the involved input to a discrete *event*, which occurs only at a certain moment of time t ∈ T, considered as instantaneous within T. Note however that an event is always relative to a given time scale: it may indeed not be instantaneous when analyzed from another, more refined, time scale.

8 Occam's razor (see Wikipedia 2021f) is a key scientific parsimony principle, which expresses that there is no need to introduce a new concept when it can be explained by already existing concepts. The CESAM system modeling framework is constructed in that way: we always only introduced the minimal number of architectural concepts that are necessary for system modeling purposes. The structure of the CESAM framework is also organized in order to cover all the items that we introduced within the definition of a formal system (see end of section 1.1).

9 The internal behavior of a system is modeled by an evolution law of its internal variables, called "*states*".

According to this definition, all human artifacts – independently of their physical, informational or organizational nature – can thus be considered and analyzed as systems. It only changes the nature of the laws – given by physics, logics or sociology – that enable the definition of the functional and internal behaviors, which are making them systems. The two previous definitions also help us to understand that it is neither the nature, nor the size, nor the hierarchical position[10] that makes something a system, since all real objects can be seen as systems. As already pointed out, considering that an object is a system remains first of all a modeling (human) choice: it just means that this object will be abstracted through a systemic point of view, that is, in the framework provided by Definition 1.2.

Note finally that the definitions we proposed above imply that a system S is completely specified (for a given time scale) if and only if one is able to provide (see Figure 1.3):

1) *The states of S*, that is, a description of the evolution law of its internal variables, which can be typically achieved through a state-machine (see, for instance, Börger and Stärk (2003) or Booch *et al.* (2004)).

2) A description of its functional dynamics, which can be naturally obtained by defining:

– *the static elements* of S, in other terms the signatures of the functions required to express its functional behavior, as given, for example, by a static block diagram (see Severance (2001) or Friedenthal *et al.* (2012));

– *the dynamic behavior of S,* that is, the temporal dynamics[11] of these functions, which can be, for instance, defined by a sequence diagram (see Booch *et al.* (2004) or Friedenthal *et al.* (2012)).

These last considerations are at the core of the CESAM systems architecting matrix (see section 3.5) and explain the generic nature of the key columns – states, static elements and dynamic behaviors as described in Figure 1.3 – involved in that modeling matrix.

---

10 A common mistake is, for instance, to consider that a "sub-system" of a system (see section 1.2 for more details) is not a system, which is, of course, absolutely not the case according to our definitions. This last remark allows, in particular, to recursively apply the principles of systems modeling within a given system hierarchy.

11 We here mean the underlying "algorithm" that expresses how the functional behavior of S is obtained as a result of the interactions of a certain number of elementary functions.

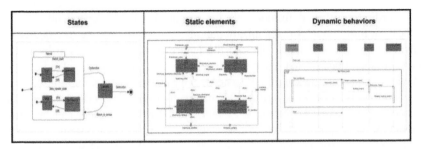

Figure 1.3. *Structure of a standard complete system specification. For a color version of this figure, see www.iste.co.uk/krob/systems.zip*

Note that it may be useful to consolidate in a specific view all the exchanged input/output flows that appear when describing the functional dynamics of a system. Such a view – which, strictly speaking, is already contained in the two other functional views introduced here above – is indeed important for constructing the glossary of all flows exchanged within a given system context. This will lead us to the last column – objects – of the CESAM systems architecting matrix (see again section 3.5).

Up to now, we only dealt with an *extensional formalism* for systems. When using Definition 1.1, we are indeed obliged by construction to explicitly describe extensionally the behavioral and structural dimensions of a system (definition in extension). But there is another different, but totally equivalent from a mathematical perspective, system specification formalism, which is of *intentional nature*. This means that here we do not need to describe the behavior or structure of a system as before, but rather to express its expected/intended properties (definition in intension).

That new formalism is based on a formal logic, called *system temporal logic*, which is presented in full detail in Appendix 1. The only point to stress here is that we will now need to work with systems whose input, output and internal states sets X, Y, Q and timescale T are fixed. The associated system temporal logic allows us then to syntactically define well-formed logical formulae[12], called *temporal formulae*, which specify the sequences O of inputs, outputs and internal states values of such a system that can be observed among all moments of time t within the timescale T, as stated below:

$$O = (O(t)) \text{ for all } t \in T, \text{ where we set } O(t) = (x(t), y(t), q(t))^{[13]}.$$

We are now in position to introduce the notion of formal system requirement, which refers to logical predicates within system temporal logic (see Appendix 1 for several examples).

---

12 Also called predicates in formal logic.

13 We use here the formalism of Definition 1.1.

DEFINITION 1.3.– **Formal requirement** – Let S be a formal system with X, Y and Q as input, output and internal states sets and T as timescale. A *formal requirement* on S is a temporal formula expressed in system temporal logic, based on X, Y, Q and T, as described in Appendix 1.

Most of engineers would, however, be afraid to work with system temporal logic. Hence, one quite rarely[14] uses formal requirements to specify real systems. The only utility of the previous definition will then just be to remember that one works with logical formalisms when managing systems requirements, which is usually not known. This explains why we now propose the following unformal definition that intends to reflect what should be a good requirements engineering practice[15].

DEFINITION 1.4.– **Requirement** – A *requirement* on a real system S refers to any sentence that intends to express a formal requirement on a formal system that models S.

Note that each formal requirement R specifies a set of systems, which is the set of all formal systems that satisfy R. A set SR of formal requirements specifies then also a set of formal systems, that is, the set of formal systems that satisfy all elementary requirements of SR. This simple property establishes a connection between sets of (formal) requirements and sets of (formal) systems. One can then prove that this connection is bijective, which means in other terms that it is mathematically strictly equivalent to specify sets of systems using either Definition 1.1 or sets of requirements. We thus have introduced two different equivalent ways of specifying systems.

A wrong conclusion would now be to use either one, or the other, formalism, for defining systems. The two formalisms that we introduced are indeed absolutely not equivalent in terms of engineering effort: some properties are indeed much easier to state using the formalism of Definition 1.1 when some others are much simpler to state using requirements[16]. The working systems engineer will thus always have to

---

14 Temporal logic is only classically used for the verification of real-time critical software systems.

15 A good system requirement shall indeed always be unambiguous, which is quite difficult to achieve when trying to express a formal requirement in natural language.

16 The fact that a system behaves according to a given state machine is, for instance, easier to state by explicitly describing the concerned state machine, which gives rise to a single systemic view. Using requirements would contrarily require us to define one logical formula per transition – stating typically that when the system is in state q and event e occurs, it shall pass in state q' – which would give rise to N requirements, where N is the number of involved transitions, which is clearly much more complicated than the first formalism. Conversely, a safety property can usually be stated using just one unique safety requirement, but would give rise to many behavioral descriptions if one would like to express it in that other way.

mix extensional and intentional formalisms, according to their relative "human" costs. A good system specification is therefore a specification that shall mix, on the one hand, behavioral or structural descriptions in the line of Definition 1.1 and Definition 1.2 and, on the other hand, requirements in the line of Definition 1.3 and Definition 1.4.

Note finally that requirements will also provide us with the first column – expected features – of the CESAM systems architecting matrix (see section 3.5)[17].

1.2. CESAM: a framework focused on complex integrated systems

The second key point to stress is that CESAMES Systems Architecting Method (CESAM) is fundamentally a *complex integrated systems-oriented framework*. This means that CESAM is especially dedicated and adapted to the architecting and modeling of complex systems, that is – in equivalent terms – of non-homogeneous systems which result from an integration process.

To be more specific, let us first recall that *systems integration* is the fundamental mechanism[18] that allows us in practice to build a new system from other smaller systems (typically of hardware, software or "humanware" nature), by organizing them so that the integrated system can accomplish – within a given environment – its missions (see, for instance, Figure 1.5 for an example of systems integration). For the sake of completeness, a more formal definition of this key mechanism is provided below (see Figure 1.4 for an illustration of that definition).

---

17 As a matter of fact, the systems architecture paradigm can also be expressed using the formalism of requirements. Any systems architecture problem can indeed be stated as the research of a system S that satisfies a set of requirements associated with the environment of S. As an immediate consequence of this genericity, the generic structure of a system provided by the CESAM framework naturally reflects in the generic structure of the systems architecture process, which is the core property on which the CESAM systems architecting method relies.

18 Integration is thus an operator between systems that maps a series of systems into another new system. It is interesting to point out that most of the existing system "definitions", which can be found in the systems engineering literature (see, for instance, Meinadier (1998, 2002), Sage and Armstrong (2000), Maier and Rechtin (2002), IEEE (2005), de Weck *et al.* (2011), ISO (2018) or Sillitto (2014)), are defining systems as the result of an application of the integration operator. From a mathematical perspective, this gives unfortunately rise to inconsistent definitions since the set on which this operator acts is never defined. However, all these "definitions" are clearly expressing a real pragmatic dimension of all systems, which is rigorously captured in our framework by the notion of integration as provided in Definition 1.5.

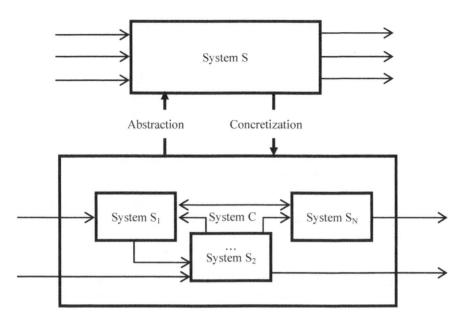

Figure 1.4. *Formal integration of formal systems*

DEFINITION 1.5.– **Integration** – Let S_1, ... , S_N be a set of N (formal) systems. One says then that a (formal) system S is the result of the *integration* of these systems if there exists, on one side, a (formal) system C obtained by the composition of S_1, ..., S_N and, on the other side, dual abstraction and concretization operators[19] that allow us to express:

– the system S as an abstraction of the system C;

– the system C as a concretization of the system S.

The fundamental purpose of this somewhat technical definition is to position integration as a different mechanism from a simple composition of models in order to try to capture structural emergence in our approach. Definition 1.5 indeed clearly shows that the description of an integrated system, obtained through the interconnection of other systems, requires:

---

19 In order to avoid mathematical technicity, we will not define here the notions of abstraction and concretization that shall be considered in the meaning of the theory of abstract interpretation (see, for instance, Cousot and Cousot (1996) for more details on this topic).

– models of each system contributing to the integrated system;

– a new integration model, specific to that integrated system.

In other words, we are claiming through the last definition that *the mere knowledge of the models of the components of a system is never sufficient to model this system!* This strong modeling postulate can be seen as the direct translation of the universal phenomenon of *emergence*, which is always a mechanical consequence of integration: an integrated system will indeed always have emerging properties, that is, specific properties that cannot be found in its components, nor be deduced from the properties of its components.

This emergence postulate can be observed on all simple integrated systems of day-to-day life. Let us consider, for instance, a wall formed solely of bricks (without mortar to bind them) for the sake of simplicity. A simple systemic model of a brick can then be characterized by:

– a functional behavior consisting, on the one hand, of providing reaction forces when mechanical action forces are acting on the brick and, on the other hand, of absorbing the light rays;

– an internal behavior provided by three invariant states "length", "width" and "height".

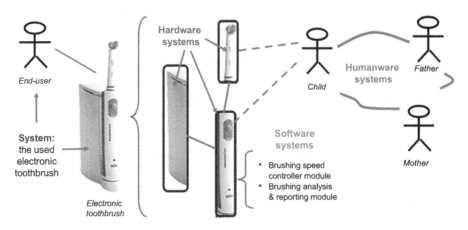

Figure 1.5. *Example of an integrated system: the used electronic toothbrush. For a color version of this figure, see www.iste.co.uk/krob/systems.zip*

By composing such brick models, a (formal) wall will just be seen as a network of bricks connected by mechanical action/reaction forces. However, it will be difficult to get anything else from such a (formal) wall than a resulting functional behavior consisting of absorbing the rays of light, since it is the behavior of all its elementary components. This is however clearly not the usual behavior of a (real) wall, since we want to take into account the holes in (real) walls for windows, that should just let the light pass! Note also that it is difficult – and probably vain – to try to express the form of a (real) wall – which is one of its typical internal states – depending on the lengths, widths and heights of the bricks that compose it. All these facts call for the obvious need to create a dedicated systemic model, more abstract, to specifically model a (real) wall.

These considerations may appear to be common sense, if not naive, but we unfortunately noticed that their consequences are usually not understood, which directly causes a lot of non-quality issues as observed on many modern complex engineered systems. Most engineers and managers indeed still continue thinking that mastering the components of an integrated system is sufficient to master the system as a whole. However, the very nature of the integration mechanism requires not only having people responsible for the components when one has to design a given integrated system: it is key to also have somebody specifically in charge of the integrative dimension of the considered system – formally of the integration model of the integrated system – that is, a systems architect, who unfortunately often does not exist[20] in most industrial organizations, as strange it may sounds when one is aware of the underlying systemic fundamentals!

Note also that emergence obliges one to utilize a top-down design strategy – rather than a bottom-up approach[21] – when dealing with integrated systems. As a matter of fact, it is indeed not possible to predict the emergent properties that result from integration: any bottom-up design strategy will thus statistically create numerous undesirable emergent properties that will be difficult to master. In such a context, the only possible efficient design strategy is to start by imposing the expected properties of the integrated system and then deriving from them the properties required for its components, which naturally lead to a top-down design strategy.

Finally, note that the integration mechanism naturally hierarchizes systems, while giving a recursive dimension to systemic analysis. Engineered systems are indeed obtained in practice by a number of successive systems integrations: each integrated system thus generates in this way an integration hierarchy, which is also an abstraction hierarchy due to the nature of integration, called the *systemic*

---

20 As a consequence, integration models of integrated systems are also often non-existent in practice....

21 This is unfortunately still the most common design strategy in the industry for integrated systems....

hierarchy of the initial system. This allows us, in particular, to speak about the system, sub-system, sub-sub-system and other levels (that are also called sometimes "layers" or "tiers") of any integrated system.

1.3. CESAM: a collaboration-oriented architecting framework

CESAM is however not only a mathematically sound system modeling framework, specifically focused on complex integrated systems. It is also an *architecting framework*, which means that it is intended to efficiently support all the design decisions that a systems architect needs to regularly make during a complex system prototyping or development project. We must recall in this matter that modeling is not an end in itself[22], but just a tool for architecting, which is the key design process addressed by the CESAM framework. Architecting here means finding a solution that fulfills a series of external needs and constraints. It can be seen as an optimization process, which has to construct and to select the "best" system among a series of possibilities. Choice is thus intrinsic to that activity. Being able to make "good" choices in a rational way is thus always key in any system design project. This is exactly the purpose of the CESAM framework, which provides to the working systems architect a number of systemic views as a support to *collaborative architectural decisions*.

It is indeed important to remember that a technical system never exists alone and that it cannot be designed independently of the people who are engineering it. "Good" systems architecture is in particular always an architecture that all stakeholders share. The first job of any systems architect (by applying the core principles of systems architecting to the engineering organizational system to whom he/she belongs) shall thus always be able to understand and identify the organizational architecture in which a given system development takes place: the technical architecture of the technical system under design is indeed highly correlated to that organizational architecture (we refer to section 2.1 for more details on this important topic). This explains why a systems architect must always manage the two following types of activities, which are of very different nature:

– on the one hand, *technical activities* fundamentally centered on the definition of global system integration models, making explicit interfaces between all components of a system;

– on the other hand, *facilitation activities* centered on the construction of convergence on these models, creating a common vision between all stakeholders of the system.

Figure 1.6 illustrates these two kinds of systems architecting activities, which all rely on systems models (the images were blurred for privacy reasons). The initial

---

22 Which most systems modelers unfortunately forget!

version – denoted initial version 0 – of the system architecture presented in that figure is the result of a technical activity, when the second version – denoted shared version 1 – is the result of a facilitation activity involving all key stakeholders of the considered system. It is quite interesting to see the differences between these two system views: this illustrates the value brought by facilitation, which is crucial for collaboratively constructing robust systems.

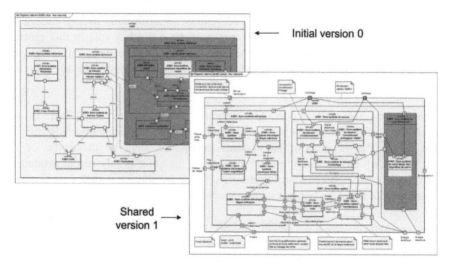

Figure 1.6. *Using models to converge on the same vision of a system. For a color version of this figure, see www.iste.co.uk/krob/systems.zip*

System models are thus key for ensuring a collaboration of quality, which is mandatory in the context of complex integrated systems development (as we will see more in detail in section 2.5). In these matters, the basic tool for managing collaboration and creating architectural convergence is *the collaborative systems architecture workshop*. We will now quickly sketch its mode of operation in order to better understand the "human" dimension of systems architecting.

The principle of such a workshop is quite simple since it consists "merely" of putting in one place all the stakeholders[23] that must converge on a given

23 This means that these stakeholders were comprehensively and correctly identified, which is in itself a difficult exercise with multiple traps. Moreover, it can also easily be understood that it is difficult to carry out convergence with 150 people! The effective implementation of a collaborative workshop also presupposes that one previously achieved an organizational architecture analysis, which sufficiently abstracted the "field" of a given system architecture, in order to identify a limited number (typically no more than 15) of top-level players, truly representative of the entire organizational scope of the target system, with whom we shall manage the required convergence work.

architectural solution and then submitting to them the first version of the intended system architecture. This is indeed key to obtain stable systems architectures. The groundwork for a collaborative systems architecture workshop is then to discuss and collaboratively modify the proposed system architecture, so that the final architecture, which is resulting from such a process[24], becomes a collective asset (see Figure 1.7 for an example).

This method naturally leads to shared visions, which usually deeply engage all the involved actors. Note that the systems architect has a key role in this process since he/she must always ensure that the system architecture, on which all stakeholders converge, remains a satisfactory response with respect to all the needs that one shall take into account.

However, this modus operandi assumes a key prerequisite, that is, all stakeholders of the workshop have a common systemic representation language. In other terms, the meaning of all system descriptions shall be the same for all participants, which is usually not the case. It is therefore highly recommended to start a collaborative systems architecture workshop by sharing with the participants the semantics of each systemic representation that will be used[25].

Once these core bases are established, the work of convergence towards a shared architecture can be attacked, starting with a collective analysis of the proposed initial architecture. We then often see in practice that the first problems that occur are again syntactical problems, due to the fact that the vocabulary that is used to describe the elements of an architecture is not necessarily shared among its stakeholders! To solve this other recurrent issue, it can, for instance, be helpful to also share with all participants a glossary of key technical terms, in order to be sure that these terms have exactly the same meaning for everybody.

---

24 To carry out such a work in practice, a simple way to proceed is typically to make the system model visible to share by printing the various associated architectural views on large A0 posters. One can then easily collectively discuss and change an initial system architecture by directly annotating these architectural diagrams (cf. Figure 1.7 for an illustration of this method). Note that the systems architect must manage that "live" modification process in order to permanently guarantee that the proposed changes have the consent of all participants and do not lead to sub-optimality at the system level.

25 This is again one of the important uses and purposes of the CESAM framework.

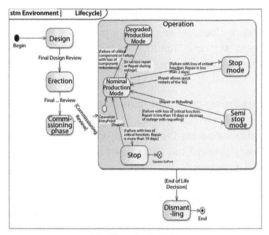

Initial life cycle of a system

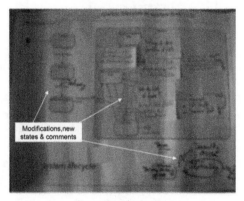

Shared life cycle of a system

Figure 1.7. *Initial and final models as managed during a collaborative systems architecture workshop. For a color version of this figure, see www.iste.co.uk/krob/systems.zip*

Once these barriers are removed, we can consider that we have a solid base to attack the technical activities, strictly speaking. The work consists then of discussing the proposed system architecture and modifying it collectively, if necessary (see Figure 1.7 for an illustration of such a process), so that the final architecture, resulting from the exchanges, is shared by all at the workshop's end. Note that it is also mandatory to have an arbitration mechanism for decision-making, which will handle all the disagreement points, if any (in which case, a new loop with stakeholders may be needed to explain them the definitive choices).

As one can see here, the systems architecting technical process shall always be deeply integrated into a "human" engineering process without which no shared and no "humanely" robust systems architectures would emerge (which by the way is often a *sine qua non* condition for them to also be technically robust).

1.4. CESAM: a business-oriented framework

Let us finally also stress on the fact that CESAM is also a business-oriented framework. As already pointed out and shown in the example section of our initial chapter, the CESAM framework was indeed used in many applications. In order to contribute to the increase in quality of system projects, which is a key issue for our modern societies, we thus want to share with the system community a part of that quite important practical experience.

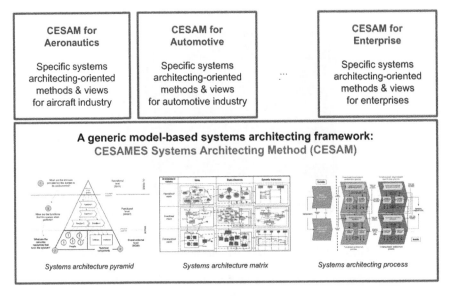

Figure 1.8. *Tentative structure of the CESAM frameworks. For a color version of this figure, see www.iste.co.uk/krob/systems.zip*

The CESAM framework is therefore intended to be organized into two layers:

– **a generic layer**, consisting of a *generic model-based systems architecting framework* whose fundamentals are presented in the current book;

– **a specific layer**, consisting of a *number of specific systems architecting methods and systems architecture views* per main application area (aeronautics, automotive, enterprise, etc.).

We plan to progressively publish in the following decade these different parts of the CESAMES systems architecting body of knowledge. Note that we already provided some insights on the specific layer of the CESAM framework – which is still under construction – in the example section of the initial Introduction of this book where we presented some reference systems architectures for computer, car and railway systems and for world modeling.

This strategy plans to offer to all systems architects and engineers both a sound, complete and robust method for architecting complex integrated systems as well as to provide them with a series of domain-specific systems architecting methods and systems architecture views. These elements, which will be already expressed and/or formalized within the CESAM framework, will be starting points to ease their systems architecting activities (see Figure 1.9 for an illustration of what could be such a starting point in the aircraft industry[26]). It is indeed much easier to deform an existing system architecture in order to adapt it to a series of new needs, rather than constructing it from scratch.

---

26 The architecture of Figure 1.9 is a constructional integration architecture (boxes are modeling components) of an aircraft – an Airbus A320 here – aligned with the underlying functional architecture (gray zones are modeling functional domains). It was constructed on the basis of operational pilot documentation, freely available on the Internet.

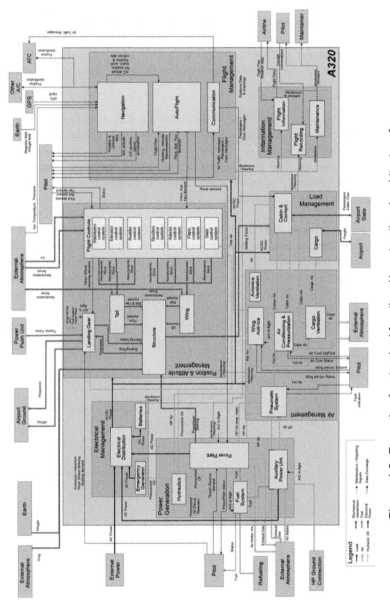

Figure 1.9. *Example of a standard functional/constructional architecture for an aircraft. For a color version of this figure, see www.iste.co.uk/krob/systems.zip*

2

Why Architecting Systems?

2.1. Product and project systems

Before going further, we need first to introduce a distinction that will be fundamental to a better understanding of both what systems architecting is and how to read many classical engineering issues. It indeed appears that all engineered systems are always involving two kinds of systems (see Figure 2.1):

– The first is clearly the *product system*, that is, the integrated hardware and software[1] object which is under engineering in order to be finally constructed and put in service.

– The second is the *project system*, that is, the engineering organization (or in other terms the engineers) who is designing and developing the product system.

These two types of systems are of quite different nature: the product system is usually a technical-dominant system, while the project system is clearly a human-dominant system. However, as shown in Figure 2.1, these two systems are highly and permanently coupled during all design and development phases of the product system: the project system typically monitors the implementation status of the product system through adapted implementation actions that change this implementation status.

The product/project distinction seems very simple. However, it appears in practice that most of engineers are thinking in terms of project activities realization and not of product characteristics achievement. Many engineering issues are therefore arising from the fact that system development projects are often too

---

1 One may also possibly include a "humanware" dimension into a product, if one must put a person, a group of persons or even an organization within the scope of the system under engineering.

project-system-oriented and not sufficiently product-system-focused. One must indeed understand that there are two totally different ways of managing a system development:

– *Mode 1 – Project system management*: this first management mode – also the most common in practice – groups all classical project management activities where a system development project is followed by means of a project agenda and a task achievement monitoring.

– *Mode 2 – Product system management*: this other management mode intends to monitor the progressive maturity increase and achievement of the desired product system, which shall be followed by means of systems architectural views.

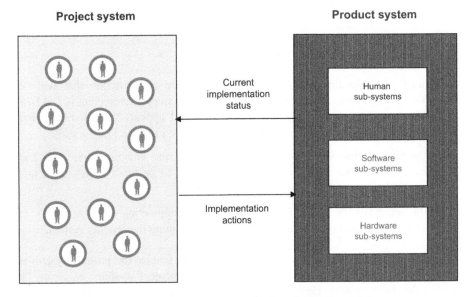

Figure 2.1. *Product versus project systems. For a color version of this figure, see www.iste.co.uk/krob/systems.zip*

These two management modes shall of course not be opposed, since they are fully complementary. A key good practice, on which systems architecting relies, claims in particular that these two modes of management – respectively, based on project agendas and on systems architectural views – are both mandatory in the context of *complex systems development* (see sections 2.2 and 2.3).

The project system management mode is indeed not sufficient for ensuring the good achievement of the product system quality and performance when such a product became complex. One unfortunately observes in practice (see next section) too many situations where system complexity is so high that project teams are no longer able to master their product. These teams are thus discovering too late that they will not deliver the expected product within its cost, delay, quality and/or performance objectives. The key motivation of systems architecting is just to provide these engineering teams with new product system-oriented tools to better master a complex integrated system development[2].

Note finally that most of the engineering issues occurring with complex systems can be classified into two categories, according to the product/project distinction, that is, on the one hand, *product problems*, referring to purely architectural flaws leading to a bad design of the product, and, on the other hand, *project problems*, referring to organizational issues leading to a bad functioning of the project. Table 2.1 provides an overview of typical such problems. More details on examples and analyses illustrating these different complex systems issues can be found in Appendix 2.

Product system problems
Product problem 1 – The product system model does not capture reality *Typical issue:* the system design is based on a model which does not match with reality
Product problem 2 – The product system has undesirable emergent properties *Typical issue:* a complex integrated system has unexpected and/or undesired emerging properties, coming from a local problem that has global consequences
Project system problems
Project problem 1 – The project system has integration issues *Typical issue:* the engineering of a system is not done in a collaborative way
Project problem 2 – The project system diverts the product mission *Typical issue:* the project forgets the mission of the product

Table 2.1. *Typical examples of product and project issues*

---

2 As a good practice, each systems architect shall always try to quickly understand whether a given system development project is only project-oriented and not project/product-balanced. This can be done by analyzing the words used within the project meetings. If the project team speaks only of agenda, milestones, activities, contractual relationships, deliverables, etc., without any reference to the underlying product, one can easily deduce a project orientation for the project. This is statistically an important risk for the project since it does not fully master the product it is developing.

2.2. The complexity threshold

At this stage, it is now time to explain more precisely what "systems complexity" is and how it is connected with systems architecting. An element of the answer is provided by the Constructive Systems Engineering Cost Model (COSYSMO; see, for instance, Valerdi (2008) or Wikipedia (2020)). This *cost model* – which extends to general industrial systems a classical model well known for information systems since the 1980s[3] – is based on an integration complexity measure of a product system[4] that recursively measures[5] the number of external and internal product interfaces within a given industrial system.

The COSYSMO cost model connects then the effort of engineering, expressed in men-months, that is required to develop a given product system (denoted Effort in the below equation) to this intrinsic measure of complexity (denoted Complexity in the below equation), by the following relationship[6]:

$$\text{Effort} = A \times \text{Complexity}^{1+B}, \tag{2.1}$$

where, on the one hand, A is a constant, depending on the size and performance[7] of the project system, and, on the other hand, B is a statistic scale factor, only related to

---

3 That is, the Construction Cost Model (COCOMO) developed by Barry Boehm in 1981 (see Boehm (1981), Abts *et al.* (2000) or Wikipedia (2021b)). This other model expresses the effort for constructing an information system (in men-months) in terms of function points, which was aimed to be an intrinsic complexity measure of an information system, independent of its programming language.

4 In this matter, note also that the notion of "complex system" cannot be formally defined. One can however define the notion of "complexity" associated with a system, as introduced in this section. This complexity definition will then allow discussing whether a given system is of low, medium or high complexity – but not whether it is complex or not, which is a typical false debate for us, even if many people like to discuss on the difference between complicated and complex, which is irrelevant from a purely scientific perspective, which can only deal with measured complexity – or eliciting the connection between engineering effort and complexity, as provided by the COSYSMO model that we present here.

5 The exact complexity measure provided by COSYSMO is more complicated than that. However, the approximation that we are making here, for the sake of simplicity, is totally valid.

6 Such a relationship is a statistical model, constructed on the basis of the analysis of several real engineering projects.

7 A is 1.0 by default, but multiplicatively grows depending on product or project parameters such as number of critical algorithms to develop, number of needs and operational scenarios, level of knowledge on requirements and architecture, expected level of service, migration and technological risks, project team experience, stakeholder cohesion, etc.

the product system, that can evolve in a range of 0.05 for simple systems up to 0.5 for large systems.

The key issue to point out here is the *nonlinear nature* of equation [2.1], which results in a largely non-intuitive relation between integration complexity and engineering effort, and thus system delivery delay, which is directly connected to such an effort[8]. It is indeed important to see that integration complexity is proportional to the square (N^2) of the number N of components of a given system[9]. As a direct result, the engineering effort is then proportional to N^3, where N stands again for the number of components of the underlying system, when a large system is involved, due to the 1.5 exponent in equation [2.1] in this situation. In more familiar terms, this means that the engineering effort is multiplied by 8 (respectively, 1,000) when the number of components of a system is multiplied by 2 (respectively, 10), with a project team who would be able to easily absorb the increase of complexity[10].

As a result of the complexity laws, the engineering effort in a system development project will be quickly too important, when complexity increases, for being anymore handled by a single person. In other terms, there will be always a *cognitive rupture moment* where complexity is too high to be any longer efficiently individually mastered by a systems architect or engineer. This rupture point is of course difficult to formally define, and it depends on the system maturity of a given industry[11], but as far as we could regularly see in practice, it can always pragmatically be observed when systems designers began to express strong cognitive difficulties[12].

---

8 Typical relation is delay = 2.5 x effort$^{1/3}$, where delay and effort are, respectively, expressed in months and men-months. We refer to the appendix of Printz (2001) for a rational explanation of that empirical law discovered by Boehm (1981).

9 When a system has N components, the number of its internal interfaces is indeed $N^2/2$ on average.

10 Which probably never occurs: the increase of engineering effort will thus probably be much more than the simple impact of the single B parameter, due to the A factor in equation [2.1] that will also heavily evolve in such situations.

11 The system maturity of an industry may moreover evolve among time due to its industrial cycles (see Case study 2.1).

12 Typical verbatims in such complexity situations are: "it is impossible to make a reasoned decision", "we have the feeling of not mastering anymore anything", "we are spending all our time trying to understand our problems and then there is no more time to solve them", "we are fighting against the more and more increasing pressure of our environment", "cost and delays are exploding and we cannot do anything to avoid it", …

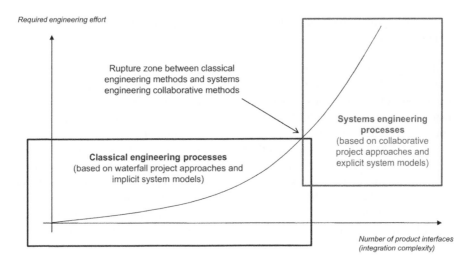

Figure 2.2. *Project effort and integration complexity relationship. For*
a color version of this figure, see www.iste.co.uk/krob/systems.zip

The consequence of this situation is that we can now distinguish two types of engineering, depending whether the complexity of a given system lies before or after the complexity rupture zone that we pointed out (see Figure 2.2). The first type of engineering, working perfectly well for low-complexity systems, is just what we shall here call "*classical engineering*": it is usually based, on the one hand, on waterfall development project approaches, induced by a separation of engineering organizations by domain specialties, and, on the other hand, on implicit system models where structuring technical knowledge only lies in the brains of a limited number of technical experts.

Such an engineering paradigm unfortunately does not work anymore when the system complexity threshold that we pointed out is crossed. One indeed arrives then in a domain where transversal collaboration becomes key in order to complete individual expertise (which is of course still mandatory) and where explicit system models are now mandatory due the fact that it will be basically impossible to implicitly handle the complexity one is facing. In other words, one enters into "*systems engineering*", which is the engineering approach, especially dedicated to the mastering of integration complexity that we will discuss more in detail in the next two sections.

As a matter of fact, one shall finally also notice that integration complexity is increasing in most areas due to the impact of many new technological paradigms. The replacement of analogical control by numerical control, the new electrical architectures, the future new sources of energy such as hydrogen and the better integration of sustainability constraints are, for instance, deep trends, which are regularly creating new software, electronic or electrical interfaces between components within numerous industrial systems, hence in the same way, increasing the integration complexity of the corresponding systems. Most industries will thus cross the complexity threshold along the lifecycle of their products and be obliged to deal with systems engineering and architecting, as soon as they want to be able to efficiently face the complexity challenge.

System maturity cycles: the European space industry case

The European space industry is a sector where systems complexity is well mastered, due to the very early introduction of systems engineering that goes back to the 1960s, when Europe decided to construct its own spatial capability. Systems engineering was then chosen as a key tool to reach this objective. It took afterwards two to three decades to totally master this practice which is today well integrated within all engineering processes.

In the 1990s, the failure of the very first Ariane 5 launch (cf. Appendix 2 for more details on that case) led however to a deep evolution of the systems engineering processes. The issue was to better integrate and monitor the emergent side effects of critical real-time embedded software with its difficult associated safety issues. A new industrial cycle began when these difficulties were mastered, which, quite interestingly, arrived nowadays at its end due to the growing pressure of the new agile low-cost competitors like SpaceX or Blue Origin.

The European space industry indeed totally reshaped with the creation – announced in June 2016 – of a new company – Airbus Safran Launchers – that integrates vertically two key players. In that context, systems engineering evolved in order to better integrate agility, leading to an agile systems engineering way of working, where system maturity is managed collaboratively through regular suitable agile rituals: this transformed practice continues therefore to play a key role in the success of the new challenges that the European space industry will have to face in the near future.

Case study 2.1. *System maturity cycles: the European space industry case*

2.3. Addressing systems architecting becomes key

Due to the complexity threshold, as presented in section 2.2, which is – in our understanding – the root cause of most engineering issues observed in complex systems development (we here refer to Appendix 2 for some examples of such issues), addressing systems architecting becomes therefore key for engineering organizations that are dealing with complex systems. These organizations are indeed all facing the need to work more efficiently in transversal mode, due to the integrative core nature of the systems that they are designing and developing.

This is exactly the context where systems architecting will bring its full value. This discipline allows reasoning about hardware and software components (technical dimension) and human factors (human dimension) related to a given system, both in a unified framework and in subsidiary with all existing disciplines and engineering fields (see Figure 2.3). To achieve this goal, the fundamental principle on which systems architecting relies is a *logical vision of engineering* brought by systemics. As one can easily understand, it is indeed merely impossible to strongly consolidate all formalisms that are used to model and work with the different components of a heterogeneous system[13]. Systems architecting thus proposes a purely logical approach to federate all these "local" formalisms, rather than trying to consolidate them in a unique global formalism.

The main idea here is to simply use logic[14] as a pivot language in order to be able to work in the same way with all hardware-, software- and "humanware"-oriented disciplines, involved in a given complex system design and development context. Each discipline can indeed easily formulate its requirements, constraints, findings or models using the universal language provided by *logical predicates*, which are formally Boolean functions telling us whether a given property is satisfied or not depending on the values of its entries (see Wikipedia (2021i)). In a system context, a logical predicate is thus nothing more than a statement that may be true or false for a given system. A typical reasoning in systems architecting will thus be based on logical predicates associated, on the one hand, with the whole considered system and, on the other hand, with the different involved components and disciplines[15].

---

13 Electromagnetism or fluid mechanics are, for instance, based on partial differential equation formalisms such as Maxwell or Navier–Stokes equations, when signal processing relies on a distinction between time and frequency domains, leading to Fourier or Z transform formalisms, which have nothing to do with the logical and discrete formalisms used in information technology. Human factors are moreover of a totally different nature, without any strong mathematical background, but they shall also be included in the global picture. We thus do not believe the existence of a "universal theory of systems" that could federate all these different formalisms since they are analyzing the world in a lot of mutually incompatible ways. To the best of our knowledge, systems architecting remains thus the only tool to consolidate all these points of view.

14 In the mathematical meaning of that term (see, for instance, Barwise (1972)).

15 Imagine, for instance, that thermic experts tell us that the predicate P1 = "the engine works well only when the refrigerating fluid temperature is less than 30°C" is true, when we know through another discussion with fluid mechanics division that the predicate P2 = "the refrigerating fluid temperature can be over 30°C when the pressure is low". Somebody who has the global vision on those two domains can then easily deduce that P3 = "the engine may not work correctly when the pressure is low" is true, since it is a logical consequence from P1 and P2, formally $P1 \wedge P2 \rightarrow P3$ (where the $\wedge$ symbol means AND). This is typically a – here quite simple – systems architecting type of (logical) reasoning.

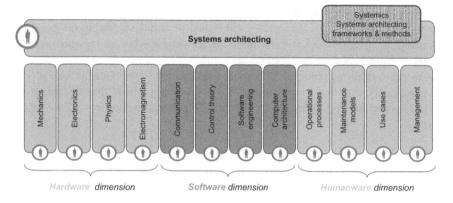

Figure 2.3. *The integrative and collaborative dimension of systems architecting. For a color version of this figure, see www.iste.co.uk/krob/systems.zip*

As one can see, there is therefore absolutely nothing magic in the promise of systems architecting proposing a unified framework for working with all dimensions of systems: it is just a rather simple consequence of the universality of logic[16]! One may also notice that systems architecting can thus be fundamentally seen as an *observational* modeling approach[17]: the construction of a system model – in the meaning of systems architecting – is indeed the result of the observation of all components and engineering domains involved in the considered system of interest and of the federation of all these observations into a unique logical model of system level.

---

16 This probably also explains why systems architecting is so difficult to penetrate in practice in engineering organizations. Most of engineers are indeed well trained in analysis and control theory, but not at all in logic, which happens to be the core mathematical discipline on which relies systems architecting. It is really a pity if one remembers that logic is one of the oldest scientific disciplines in the world, which can be traced back to Aristoteles in the 4th century before Christ (see Wikipedia 2021g).

17 A typical example of observational model is Ptolemy epicyclic system: it was a purely geometric model, used from the 3rd century before Christ up to Copernic in the 16th century, that explained the movements and variations in speed and direction of the apparent motion of the Moon, Sun and all visible-to-the eye planets (cf. Murschel (1995) or Wikipedia (2021c)). This model fitted perfectly with the observations since it was constructed on that basis. It was also predictive, in particular, with respect to phenomena such as Moon and Sun eclipses. However, it is nowadays considered as completely false from a physical perspective. This example shows that an observational model can be specific and predictive, thus usable for practical needs, but not necessarily truth...

Last but not least, it is important to also point out that systems architecting always integrates a strong collaborative dimension: it is indeed simply not possible to construct a system model without implying all people who are representing the different involved system components and engineering domains, as soon as one wants to get a realistic model[18]. Moreover, sharing a system model is also a key good practice for ensuring its robustness. Collaboration is thus at the very center of any systems architecting approach (cf. Figure 2.3, as well as section 2.5 for more details).

All these elements allow us to easily understand that systems architecting is the superior discipline which is required to efficiently address systems integration issues. At this point, it may thus be useful to precisely position systems architecting within systems engineering (see Figure 2.4).

For this purpose, let us first recall that systems engineering is nothing other than systemics applied to engineering. Systemics[19] here refers to the discipline that deals with – formal and real – systems. It provides holistic vision and holistic analysis methods (cf. section 3.1 and Wikipedia (2021n)), integrating crosswise all dimensions of a given topic. Systemics applies to many application domains such as archaeology[20], biology[21], city planning[22], enterprise[23] or psychology[24] to provide a

---

18 The best way to construct an unrealistic system model is indeed probably to construct it alone in its corner...

19 Systemics can be traced back to the 1950s with the seminal work of H. Simon published in 1962 (cf. Simon (1962)). One usually also cites von Bertalanffy, who tried, but without being terribly convincing, to construct a "general systems theory" (cf. von Bertalanffy (1976)).

20 We refer in this matter to Case study 2.2.

21 Systems biology defines itself as the computational and mathematical modeling of complex biological systems and as an emerging engineering approach applied to biological scientific research (cf. Wikipedia (2021k)). Systems biology is a biology-based inter-disciplinary field of study that focuses on complex interactions within biological systems, using especially a holistic approach applied to biological research, instead of the more traditional reductionism approaches.

22 Systemics applied in city planning means considering all the many different dimensions of a city (economy, energy supply, entertainment, people welfare, traffic, water distribution, waste management, etc.) when making an urbanistic decision. Due to the numerous interactions between the sub-systems of an urban system, it is indeed quite easy to make an optimal local decision, which is globally under-optimal (e.g. developing public transportation in an area to resorb local traffic congestion, but that, as a side-effect, is increasing the value of the considered area, thus bringing middle-class people in that area and moving population, and at the very end, creating new traffic jams since the new inhabitants had two cars in average, one for each person in a husband–wife couple). One thus understands that systemic models are of interest for urban design.

few non-exhaustive examples. From a systemics perspective, systems engineering is thus just another application domain.

This fact must of course not make us forget that *systems engineering* (cf. Wikipedia (2021l) for more details) also has its own tradition that goes back to the 1950s, with first textbooks in the 1960s (see Wikipedia (2021n)) and its first industrial processes formalization with the seminal NASA systems engineering handbook in the 1970s (see NASA (2016) for current edition). Many other textbooks (such as Turner *et al.* (1978), Aslaksen and Belcher (1992), Aslaksen (1996), Blanchard and Fabricky (1998), Meinadier (1998, 2002), Sage and Armstrong (2000), Maier and Rechtin (2002), Kossiakoff and Sweet (2003), de Weck *et al.* (2011) and Sillitto (2014)) and industrial standards (such as ANSI/GEIA (2003), IEEE (2005) and ISO (2018)) were constructed then in the line of these initial works. More recently, the International Council on Systems Engineering (INCOSE) emerged in the 1990s. It is currently federating and developing the domain at the international level (see, for instance, INCOSE (2011) for the INCOSE systems engineering handbook).

Following INCOSE (see again INCOSE (2011)), systems engineering is defined in particular as "an interdisciplinary approach and means to enable the realization of successful systems. It focuses on defining customer needs and required functionality early in the development cycle, documenting requirements, then proceeding with design synthesis and system validation while considering the complete problem (operations, performance, test, manufacturing, cost and schedule, training and support, disposal)". When one more precisely analyzes the systems engineering processes, one can however break them down naturally according to a product/project distinction as discussed in section 2.1, that is, in the following two types of activities of quite different nature:

---

23 Systems approach applied to enterprise typically gives rise to enterprise architecture frameworks (see Wikipedia 2021d), such as, for instance, TOGAF® (cf. The Open Group (2011)) or our own CESAM for enterprise framework (see section 1.4).

24 Systems psychology is a branch of both theoretical psychology and applied psychology that studies human behavior and experience as complex systems. Individuals are considered within groups as systems (cf. for instance, Wikipedia (2021m)). A consequence of such an approach is that one cannot cure an individual who has psychological or sociological problems without trying to understand the groups to whom he/she belongs. Root causes of his/her problems may indeed be found at the group level and shall then be addressed at that level and not at the individual level. For instance, if an alcoholic father beats his child, one must typically understand the cause of his alcoholism and tackle it, rather than taking the child out of his/her family.

– Project-oriented activities, such as systems projects planning, follow-up and monitoring, engineering referential and configuration management, reporting and quality, which may be seen as systems project management.

– Product-oriented activities, such as requirements engineering, operational, functional and constructional architecting, safety and trade-off analyses, verification and validation, which cover exactly the scope of systems architecting.

Systemics applied to archaeology: the Cretan case

A puzzling example of systemics applied to archaeology is the recent understanding of how the Cretan civilization disappeared suddenly in the 15th century BC (cf. Antonopoulos (1992) or Novikova *et al.* (2011)).

The story started when the study of the Thera site in Crete revealed enigmatic geological strata: they were indeed identified by an expert in hydrology like a riverbed, but no river could be located there for both geological (due to the geology of the site) and archaeological reasons (due to the presence of a human habitat at exactly the same place). Moreover, the biological analysis of these strata highlighted then several marine fossils of high sea origin, although the sea was quite far away from the site where the strata were.

By putting together their archaeological, geological, hydrological and biological data and by crossing them with those from other Cretan sites, archaeologists gradually understood that they discovered the last traces of a tsunami, which destroyed the city they were studying.

This hypothesis was subsequently validated, by checking with Carbon 14 dating techniques that the similar observations made on other archaeological sites took place in the same time period! Last but not least, volcanologists were involved in order to identify the possible origin of such a tsunami, which was localized in Santorini. Oceanographers constructed then an oceanographic model to successfully demonstrate the possible propagation of a tsunami between Santorini and Crete, which are separated by a distance of about 200 kilometers.

As one can see, the combination of many disciplines – a nice example of systems approach – was necessary to globally understand an apparently local phenomenon.

Case study 2.2. *Systemics applied to archaeology: the Cretan case*

In that perspective, systems engineering can be seen as the union of systems project management and systems architecting, which can thus also be analyzed as the core part of systems engineering, dedicated to the design and construction of robust systems models. System architecting shall thus be seen as the discipline synthesizing the methods and the tools that allow an exhaustive and coherent modeling of a system (in its triple operational, functional and constructional dimensions) in order to manage it efficiently during its lifecycle (design, test, deployment, maintenance, etc.)[25].

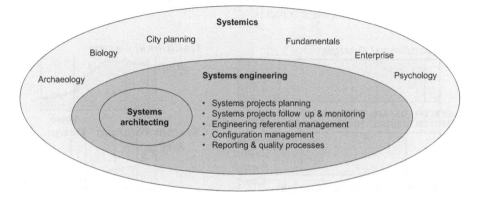

Figure 2.4. *Relative position of systems engineering and systems architecting within systemics. For a color version of this figure, see www.iste.co.uk/krob/systems.zip*

2.4. The value of systems architecting

To complete our discussion on systems architecting, let us now focus on the value brought by this discipline, which was in particular well analyzed by E. Honour in 2014. The key point to understand is that the systems engineering approach in which systems architecting takes place mainly consists of redistributing the engineering effort towards upstream phases of the project, in a "definition" phase, in order to anticipate design risks as early as possible within a system development project.

Figure 1.3, extracted from Honour (2014), illustrates this paradigm, consisting of initially spending more time in order to better understand the system to develop and thus reduce the project risks in the future, compared to a traditional design. Such an approach strongly relies on systems architecting since the initial "definition"

---

25 Other alternative definitions are also proposed by 1) ANSI/IEEE (2000): systems architecting is the process of describing the structure of a system, given by its components and its internal interfaces, and the relationships of the components of the system with its environment among time (i.e. starting from the design and including all possible evolutions of the system); 2) Wikipedia (2021j): systems architecting is the process of defining a set of representations of an existing (or to be created) system, i.e. of its components (hardware, software, "humanware", functions, roles, procedures, etc.), of the relationships that exist between these components and of the rules governing these relationships.

phase will typically contain a strong part dedicated to the construction of a systems architecture file that will allow us to analyze the system under design in all its dimensions[26], the other part being devoted to project planning. In that perspective, systems architecting can thus be seen as a good risk management practice in complex systems development contexts.

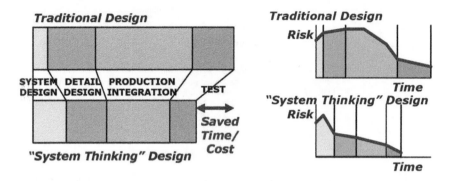

Figure 2.5. *Systems architecting as a risk management practice[27]. For a color version of this figure, see www.iste.co.uk/krob/systems.zip*

Much evidence supports this point of view (see, for instance, again Honour (2014) for many concrete examples). Among them, we will consider a quite interesting one which comes from NASA. In 1992, the financial controlling office of NASA indeed analyzed 32 major spatial programs conducted between 1970 and 1990, comparing the final budget overrun with the budget ratio, which was allocated to the initial "definition" phase, from the preliminary design review (PDR), which especially included the initial systems architecting analyses, as discussed above. The finding of that financial analysis was quite clear: budget overrun was indeed statistically inversely proportional to the budget dedicated to the definition phase. More precisely, it could be seen that budgets were more or less always at least doubling when the definition phase was weak and that the optimal ratio to dedicate to the definition phase seemed to be about 15% of the global budget (see Figure 2.6). Consequently, this means probably that, to cover optimally product and project risks, a complex systems manager should allocate around 5% of its global budget to systems architecting, strictly speaking, with another 10% being reserved for project-oriented initiation and preparation activities.

---

26 Typically, such as environment, lifecycle, use cases, operational scenarios, needs, functional modes, functions, functional dynamics, functional requirements, configurations, components, constructional requirements, constructional dynamics, critical events, dysfunctional modes and behaviors, verification and validation.

27 This figure was reproduced from Honour (2014).

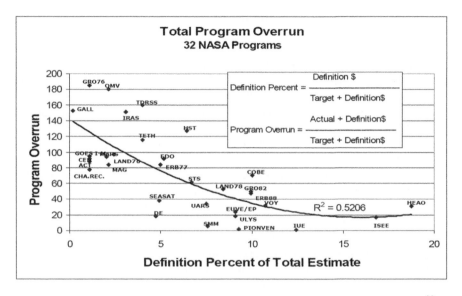

Figure 2.6. *NASA statistics supporting the importance of the definition phase*[28]

One can thus understand that systems architecting is a key tool for mastering systems design and development projects with respect to their quality, cost, delay and performance constraints (QCDP), as soon as one deals with complex systems produced by the integration of many technical systems (hardware and software) and human systems (people and organizations). We shall finally recall some key principles[29] provided by systems architecting that allow us to achieve this objective:

– **Provide simple, global, integrated and shared visions of a system:** "being simple" and capturing completely all dimensions of a given problem in complex environments, which does not mean "being simplistic", is always very difficult....

– **First, think about needs and not about solutions:** this last point being unfortunately the common rule in most systems development projects. One shall thus remember that the "customers" of a system project shall fundamentally feed the systems architecting process.

– **Sort out all "spaghettis" in a system design:** in order to avoid mixing everything (objectives, functions, technical constraints, etc.) and confusing ourselves while confusing others, which are also again very common bad practices in too many complex systems contexts.

---

28 This figure was reproduced from Honour (2014), where it was traced back to Gruhl (1992).

29 That one shall always have in mind during a systems design and development project.

2.5. The key role of systems architects

Systems architecting would of course not exist without the right key people, that is, systems architects, to support the architectural process! The systems architect shall indeed fundamentally be the core responsible for the systems integration issues. He/she shall thus ensure that the interfaces of the subsystems of the target system under design are reasonably robust for the purpose of the system development project[30], or, in other terms, that they will not be questioned (or as little as possible) by the technical managers in charge of the different subsystems.

To achieve such objectives, it is necessary to play on a different dimension than the purely technical one. A key problem within system design is indeed that it is usually not sufficient to have the "best" possible system architecture that is automatically picked up and used by everybody. The global optimum, typically with respect to quality, cost, delay and performance criteria, for an integrated system is indeed never[31] the union of the local optima of each of the subsystems that comprise it: the consequence is that each subsystem shall necessarily individually be suboptimal with respect to these criteria, if one wants to reach global optimality at the system level.

This fact is unfortunately not easy to accept for a subsystem responsible who is not designing its sub-system with a global vision, like the architect of the whole system[32]. To solve this "human" problem, which is intrinsic to the design of integrated systems, one must put stakeholder alignment mechanisms at the heart of any systems architecting process. These alignment activities shall in particular ensure that the structuring systems architectural choices will always be shared by their stakeholders. Systemically speaking, such mechanisms will indeed guarantee that the technical interfaces of the product system will always be discussed and

---

30 And possibly beyond, but this is another issue, namely that of the reusability of reference systems architectures and of product lines/family design. We will not discuss it here.

31 This is true as soon as the system does not show a linear behavior with respect to its entries, which is never the case for complex systems. This result can be traced back to R. Bellman in the 1950s (see Bellman (1957)).

32 The difficulty of understanding the importance of system architecting comes from this situation. Engineers usually deal with technically homogeneous subsystems of a given system (i.e. the "boxes" of Figure 2.7) which are clearly visible to all. On the other hand, the systems architect takes care of the system interfaces (i.e. "arrows" in Figure 2.7) that nobody sees because they are, strictly speaking, not material. The architecture work is therefore done somewhere in the invisible, and it is thus difficult to detect for the uninitiated, while fundamental since it fixes the framework in which to do engineering (a bad architectural framework can typically only lead to a "bad" system).

accepted at the "human" interfaces to which they are allocated within the project system (see Figure 2.7).

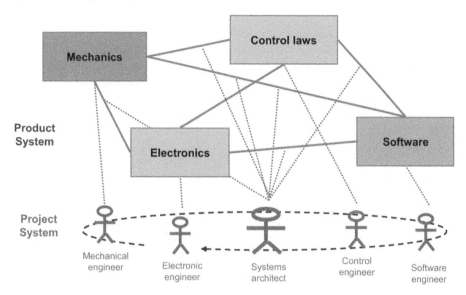

Figure 2.7. *The key role of the systems architect. For a color version of this figure, see www.iste.co.uk/krob/systems.zip*

This quick analysis therefore shows that a systems architect must always be fundamentally capable of making the project actors converge on the architectural choices for which he/she is responsible. This convergence work – which is a substantial and essential part of the systems architect job[33] – is however not simple at all. It indeed requires mastering, among purely technical competency, a set of completely different soft skills that could be qualified as "human" architecting and engineering since they strongly involve the "human" dimension of the project system. At that level, the systems architect shall, for instance, typically have the following key capabilities[34]:

– *Identifying all stakeholders of a given system architecture*: it looks like an apparently simple activity, but it is often terribly difficult to achieve in practice since it requires confronting the complex and changing reality of engineering organizations. Ensuring the completeness and validity of a particular organizational analysis is indeed never easy. It is notably more than classical to forget key players

---

33 And that makes a good "systems" architect a kind of six-legged sheep ....

34 Which are typically prerequisites to achieve the success of any actors' convergence within a systems architecting context.

within a given engineering scope and to identify erroneously others[35]. Moreover, organizations are also often changing rapidly. A stakeholders mapping should thus be constantly updated, if one wants to keep pace with reality.

– Aligning these stakeholders on the same architectural solution: this is a real "facilitation" skill, in the best sense of the term, since it requires real difficult technical and human know-how. A systems architect will only succeed in achieving stakeholders' convergence on given architectural choices if he plays consistently on both the technical side, that he/she should of course perfectly control to be credible, and the human level, in order to secure strong consensuses that will stand the test of time.

2.6. How to analyze a systems architect profile?

To conclude this chapter, we will briefly present the key characteristics of an (ideal) systems architect profile. As a matter of fact, such profiles are indeed quite rare and always difficult to find. Having some clues on that still poorly explored topic may thus be helpful for any engineering organization that would like to increase its systems architecting capability.

With the CESAM framework, systems architecting skills are indeed analyzed from the following three completely different perspectives, as described in Figure 2.8:

– Dimension 1 – business and technical skills, referring here first to standard capability such as scientific education, analysis capability and business orientation, as well as to a multi-area knowledge, both from product and engineering domain points of view.

– Dimension 2 – soft skills, that is, leadership, communication and facilitation ability (key for being able to create consensus within stakeholders), curiosity and open-mindedness, together with a strong customer orientation (key for analyzing correctly a systemic environment).

– Dimension 3 – architectural skills, with, first of all, abstraction and synthesis ability, modeling and needs capture capability, systems architecting main processes mastering and integration, verification, validation and qualification knowledge.

A good systems architect must indeed have a *well-balanced profile* with respect to all these three dimensions. This gives the key clue on how to identify systems architects. One shall indeed measure the maturity of a future systems architect on the

---

35 This can be, for instance, achieved by badly analyzing the role of somebody in a given organization.

previous three axes and check that this maturity is high in all of these axes, typically by analyzing concrete realizations done by the candidate, in order to ensure good systems architecting capability within somebody.

One may also pay attention to the following three unfortunately quite common anti-profiles that should not be confused with systems architect profiles. The first anti-profile is the *technical expert profile*, which refer to somebody who is excellent with respect to dimension 1, but much poorer on the other ones. A good systems architect was probably very good in several technical domains, but is clearly not a technical expert anymore, in the usual meaning of that term. The second anti-profile is the *manager* one who mainly developed in dimension 2. Good technical managers are usually very bad systems architects due to the fact that they have a project-oriented, and not a product-oriented, mindset. Thus, never take a managerial profile for a systems architecting mission, it will not work! The last anti-profile is a bit vicious since it corresponds to somebody who would have a good level in dimension 3, but not in the others, that is, typically with poor soft skills. We are here referring to a *methodologist profile*, in other terms to somebody who knows very well all systems architecting and engineering methods, but without having the ability of creating consensus among the actors of his/her ecosystem[36]. A good systems architect shall clearly have strong methodological capability, but he/she shall never be confused with a methodologist[37] (and vice versa).

Last but not least, do not confuse systems architecting with systems modeling. Modeling is a key tool for the systems architect, but never an end in itself. A systems architect shall master systems modeling, but more importantly, he/she shall know why and how, and thus when, to model something. We refer to Appendix 5 for some good practices in that matter.

---

36 Systems architecting is never a "behind the door" activity, which does not mean that solitary design work is not necessary .... An architectural work must always *identify the needs of the stakeholders and the constraints of the involved engineering domains*. This requires a huge presence on the field! A good architecture is indeed always an architecture shared by all stakeholders, both external and internal: thus, a permanent alignment of all concerned contributors shall be ensured.

37 Systems architecting is indeed not a quality process, taken here in a purely normative meaning. This does not mean that quality is not fundamental in systems architecture, on the contrary.... Its effectiveness *is thus not measured by the syntactic realization of deliverables*, but by the intrinsic quality of the proposed architectural choices (which can often only be validated through peer reviews). *The production of documentation is also not its main objective*: an architectural work must remain smart and produce the "minimal effective" quantity of technical documentation which is required.

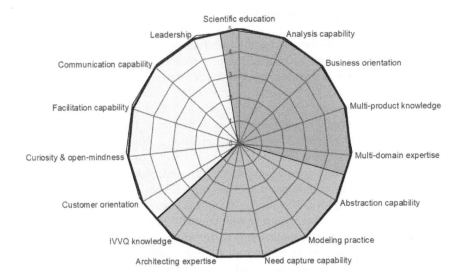

Figure 2.8. *Ideal profile of an ideal systems architect. For a color version of this figure, see www.iste.co.uk/krob/systems.zip*

CESAM Framework

3.1. Elements of systemics

Before going further, we first need to introduce the notions of interface and of system environment. These elements of systemics will indeed be useful for presenting further the CESAM framework. We refer to Definition 1.1, Definition 1.2 and section 1.1 for the fundamentals of systemics, that is, the core definitions of a system, on which the CESAM framework is constructed.

3.1.1. *Interface*

The concept of interface is the first key systemic concept[1] that we need to present. In this matter, let us thus now recall that an *interface* models an interaction, an exchange, an influence or a mutual dependence between at least two systems (some interfaces may indeed be complex and involve several systems[2]). Beware that an interface may not necessarily have a concrete implementation: it is just a way of expressing the relative impacts that different systems have each on the others[3].

---

1 Remember indeed that a systems architect deals fundamentally only with interfaces... (cf. section 2.5).

2 The toothbrush has, for instance, a complex interface with the user during the brushing phase since toothpaste, water and user mouth, teeth and hand are then involved at the same time.

3 Most people, for instance, confuse networks and interfaces. A network is indeed strictly speaking not an interface, but another system with which the system of interest has also a specific interface. In the first stages of a design, one may of course abstract it and only consider the logical interface between the systems it connects, but the abstract interface involved in such a mechanism shall not be mixed with the network system in itself.

With respect to a given system S, interfaces may then be either *external*, when they are involving the considered system and some other external systems, or *internal*, when they are only relative to sub-systems of S. Figure 3.1 illustrates this notion on the electronic toothbrush example by showing two external interfaces between the toothbrush and the end-user (here one with his/her mouth, the other with his/her hand) and several internal toothbrush interfaces (i.e. two mechanical interfaces and one inductive interface between the base and the body of the toothbrush).

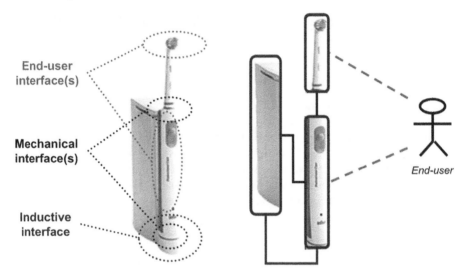

Figure 3.1. *Examples of interfaces for an electronic toothbrush. For a color version of this figure, see www.iste.co.uk/krob/systems.zip*

Note also that the technical interfaces, corresponding to a concrete interaction or exchange between several systems, are usually easier to identify since they refer to a visible relationship between the involved systems. However, the invisible interfaces, relative to an influence or interdependence between different systems that may typically be of strategic, political, societal or regulatory nature[4], are also crucial. They are unfortunately much more difficult to find. They can thus be easily forgotten and discovered too late, only at the moment where the designer will "see" their impact...[5]

---

4 Think also on the possible impacts of competitors, new technology, industrialization or maintenance on your system.

5 Such an issue typically occurs when existing stakeholders, who were forgotten during the initial analysis, remember to the project team that they exist! We refer to the first section of Appendix 2 for an illustrative case study of this situation.

3.1.2. *Environment of a system*

The recursive nature of systemic analysis naturally leads us to introduce the notion of (systemic) environment of a system. We here mean a closed[6] super-system of a given system S, which will thus be a natural basis to begin a recursive analysis of S. To be more specific, we will say that a system Env(S) is an *environment* for S if it is a closed system that results from the integration of S and of another system Out(S) that will be called the outside of S within its systemic environment Env(S).

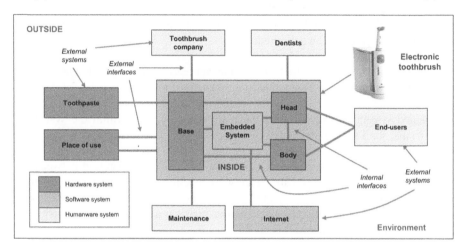

Figure 3.2. *Environment of an electronic toothbrush. For a color version of this figure, see www.iste.co.uk/krob/systems.zip*

A real system has of course many real systemic "environments" in the meaning of our definition, the physical universe in its whole being typically a common environment for any real system ... However, the pragmatic constraints of any system design and development project lead us to define *a reference environment* for any concrete system S, which will be called the environment of S by a slight abuse of language. This reference environment is the smallest "useful" systemic environment of the system of interest S. It is just the system that results from integration of S and all other real systems, external to S, that have an influence on its design. We will thus neglect in this way all other real external systems when one considers that they have no strong interdependence or no strong interaction with S[7].

---

6 A closed system is a system which is considered to have no external interfaces.

7 One can, for instance, typically consider that the Proxima Centauri star has simply no influence on most of the engineered systems on Earth, even if it is probably sending them a number of neutrinos each day...

Defining the environment of a system means defining its border, that is, defining what is inside the system and what is outside the system. Figure 3.2 typically illustrates this key distinction on the electronic toothbrush example. We described there the main external and internal systems relatively to the considered case study, also specifying their hardware, software or "humanware" nature.

Note also that defining this border is typically the first key systems architecting decision that one must make in practice, since it allows us to precisely specifying the system of interest which is under design. This decision is usually quite difficult[8] to manage in real life, especially when a system is a small part of another system in which it should precisely be delimited.

One shall also beware of the fact that one can reason on many different systems, all of them being naturally connected to the system of interest, such as, for instance, the used system (where one put the user within the system of interest) or the maintained system (where one puts the maintenance system within the system of interest) that shall never be mixed.

The inside/outside distinction is also at the heart of the separation between the different visions that are used in systems architecting (see next section for more details). One can typically not speak of needs and requirements with respect to a system without having defined a clear border between a system and its outside, as we will see in the remainder of this book.

3.2. The three architectural visions

We are now in position to introduce the three systems architectural visions which will be our first key systems architecting tool for analyzing any system.

3.2.1. *Architectural visions definition*

The heterogeneity of the environment of a system requires us to address it by means of different axes of architectural analysis in order to be able to integrate the whole set of various perceptions of the different system stakeholders[9]. Such a

---

8 In the worse cases, it may typically take several months to precisely identify the scope of the system of interest.

9 For an electronic toothbrush, these perceptions can be typically the one of mothers who want good dental hygiene for their children, of stressed business people who want to clean their teeth as quickly as possible, of dentists who understand whether the toothbrush is efficient or not with respect to teeth cleaning and of engineers who know how the electronic toothbrush works and how to construct it.

consideration naturally leads us to organize these points of view according to different architectural visions that are both necessary due to the variety of any systemic environment and useful since they allow decoupling the representations of a given system in different "properly" interrelated separated views[10], which always leads to better clearness and flexibility in terms of system design and development management[11].

As a matter of fact, each integrated system S can always be fully analyzed from three different and complementary perspectives that give rise to three complementary generic *architectural visions*, that is, the operational, functional and constructional visions, each of them grouping different types of systemic models, as defined below:

– **Architectural vision 1 – operational vision:** strictly speaking, the operational vision of S groups only the models of the environment of S – and not of S itself – which are involving S. Such operational models are thus describing the interactions of S with its environment.

– **Architectural vision 2 – functional vision:** the functional vision of S groups all system-level models describing the input/output dynamics of S, without making reference to its concrete components[12]. Such functional models are thus abstractly modeling the behaviors of S.

– **Architectural vision 3 – constructional vision[13]:** the constructional vision of S groups the system-level models of S constructed by the composition of the lower-level models associated with its components. Such constructional models are thus describing the structure of S.

---

10 This way of managing different views on the same system is in fact quite common in usual life. Think, for instance, of a tourist visiting a city. He/she will probably use many different views of the city, typically provided by a touristic guide, a metro map and a city map. To find his/her way, he/she may, for instance, first choose the monument to visit in the touristic guide, then move there using the metro map and finally manage the local approach using a city map. In architectural terms, the tourist is thus finding information in different coupled views and integrating them in order to make the "good" decision!

11 A classical difficulty is that such views can correspond with totally – and even sometimes opposite – different perceptions on a system, depending on the involved stakeholder.

12 That is, without referring to any technological choice or to any chosen solution.

13 Other names classically exist for that vision. One may, for instance, also speak of *structural vision*. Some frameworks are also speaking of *logical vision* to denote the constructional vision in the CESAM meaning. The term "*physical vision*" also refers to the refinement of the constructional vision for implementation purposes (see the last section of Appendix 3).

An illustration of these three different architectural visions is provided by Figure 3.3 on the electronic toothbrush example. We sketched there our three different types of models, with their connections (see the last section of the current section for more details), each of them illustrating a different architectural vision. One sees that the operational vision is not interested by the toothbrush behavior or structure, but just by describing its interactions with (in this example, only some) external systems, which are here power supply, end-users and the Internet. On the other hand, the functional vision gives the main toothbrush behaviors – that is, provide electrical power, generate brushing power and provide brushing capability – that produce these external interactions as captured by the operational vision, when the constructional vision shows how to concretely implement these internal behaviors through suitable components, here a base, a body, a head and embedded software.

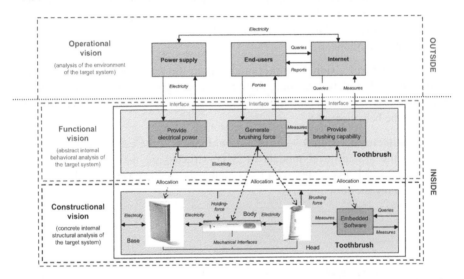

Figure 3.3. *Illustration of the three architectural visions on an electronic toothbrush. For a color version of this figure, see www.iste.co.uk/krob/systems.zip*

It is also important to point out that the previous architectural visions definitions are consistent. In this matter, the key point is here only to be sure of the existence of functional models as defined above. This is however directly connected to the emergence postulate (see section 1.2) that claims that the mere knowledge of the models of the components of a system and of their interaction laws is never sufficient to model the system that results from their integration. This fact explains why any system has always purely functional models, whose core fundamental role is to express the emerging behaviors[14] that one will never be able to capture and read within constructional models[15].

Various perceptions on a system: the Concorde case

The Concorde supersonic aircraft is a typical example of how various – often contradictory – perceptions on the same system can impact it.

From an engineering perspective, Concorde was indeed an outstanding success. Most British and French engineers are usually very proud of this great technological achievement.

But from a business and societal perspective, it was a total disaster. The supersonic aircraft was typically not able to offer a real service to the end-customer. Concorde was indeed the fastest, as well as the most expensive aircraft, with very few destinations offered (only Paris-New York and Paris-Rio de Janeiro) and at the end, a quality/price ratio which was strongly non-optimal. Due to chemical and noise pollution, it was also not an environmentally friendly aircraft, which blocked it for a long time to get the landing authorization in New York City as a result of the opposition of many neighbors' protection organizations.

When possible, which is not always the case, as taught by the final collapse of the Concorde story, the role of the systems architect is to find the best architectural balance between all these different competing points of view.

Case study 3.1. *Various perceptions on a system: the Concorde case*

---

14 Unfortunately, this is not the common understanding of the functional vision. When doing "functional analysis", most people are indeed just modeling the functions of the components of a given system, which is only a part of functional analysis in our meaning since this activity shall focus on describing transverse functions at the system level, and not at the component level.

15 To understand this phenomenon, consider the example of a car whose constituent high-level systemic components are the car body, the powertrain, the cockpit, the chassis and the embedded electronics. The interaction of these components typically allows for features like "obstacle detection", which requires the cooperation of a radar (placed in the car body), embedded software (within embedded electronics), a LED or a buzzer (positioned in the passenger cockpit), and possibly chassis or powertrain, if one wants to act on brakes and/or to reduce engine torque, when an obstacle is too close to a car. Such a "transverse" feature is clearly difficult to catch in a purely constructional car model, where one will see the flows exchanged between the various involved components of the vehicle, without being able to account for their overall logic. Only a functional model at the car level will capture the semantics of such a transverse function.

We can thus now understand why it is necessary to have three different types of models in order to model in practice a real system: the operational vision indeed captures the external viewpoint while functional and constructional views capture the internal perspective, by modeling, respectively, first the emergent behaviors and second the concrete constitution of the considered system.

As we will see more in detail in the sequel, architectural visions are of course key for a systems architecting perspective: the first job of any systems architect will indeed always be to classify the modeling information according to our three architectural visions[16], so as to obtain homogeneous system models, each of them associated with a well-defined architectural vision.

3.2.2. *Architectural visions overview*

Let us thus now present more in detail the three different – operational, functional and constructional – architectural visions that we introduced in the last section.

3.2.2.1. *Operational vision*

The *operational vision* provides "black box" models of a given system, where one does not describe the system of interest, but rather its interactions and its interfaces with its environment. Its core motivation is to understand the motivation – that is, the "why" – of the system.

In this matter, the key point to understand is that an operational analysis manipulates concepts at the environment level, which are mixing – by definition – both the system of interest and its external systems. The operational concept of "mission" of a system is a typical example of such a situation. Formally speaking, a *mission* of a given system S can indeed just be defined as a function of the environment of reference Env(S) of that system[17]. When one analyzes, for instance, the "guarantee dental hygiene" function[18], whose functional behavior consists of transforming dirty teeth into healthy teeth and/or maintaining teeth in a healthy state, one can see that a toothbrush can clearly not achieve this feature alone, which also requires at least an end-user, toothpaste and water, plus perhaps a dentist. Such a function can thus only be allocated to the environment of the toothbrush, in the meaning of section 3.1, and not to the toothbrush alone. In other words, "guarantee

---

16 That will be segregated more precisely according to a systemic analysis grid and organized in different abstraction levels, as we will see further in this book.

17 In other terms, $Mission(S) \equiv Function(Env(S))$, for every system S.

18 Due to the functional nature of a mission, we recommend naming it as a verb in infinitive form (cf. next section).

dental hygiene" cannot be considered as a function of the electronic toothbrush, but rather as a function of its environment, which means that it shall be interpreted as a mission – and not as a function[19] – of the toothbrush, according to our above definition.

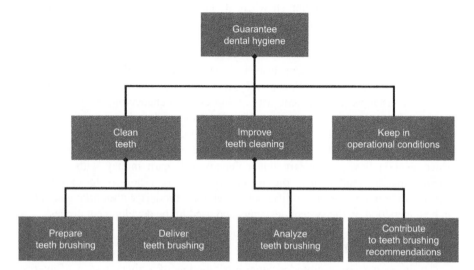

Figure 3.4. *Operational vision – mission breakdown structure (MBS) of an electronic toothbrush. For a color version of this figure, see www.iste.co.uk/krob/systems.zip*

---

19 The role of functional analysis is in particular to extract the functions of a system of interest that are hidden within its missions, that is, the internal behaviors of the considered system that are only involving the system and nothing else around it (and thus also partially contributing to the missions). For an electronic toothbrush, we may, for instance, analyze that the toothbrush is only achieving the "brush teeth" function, which basically only provide brushing forces, as a partial contribution to the "guarantee dental hygiene" mission of the electronic toothbrush. To illustrate this subtle distinction, we may take the other classical example of the cigarette system. Most of people will probably say that the core function of a cigarette is to "smoke", but again it is easy to see that one cannot smoke without at least a smoker, a source of fire and air, plus probably also an ashtray. The "smoke" behavior can hence be only allocated to the environment of a cigarette and it shall be interpreted as a mission – and not a function – of a cigarette. One may indeed understand that "smoke" refers to a complex protocol requiring first a smoker, a cigarette and a source of fire that provides first its own "deliver fire" function, passing then through a loop where smoker "inspires pure air", cigarette "propagates fire" and "delivers tar" and smoker "expires dirty air", up to arriving to the cigarette consumption, with a final request by the smoker of the "keep ashes" ashtray function applied to the burned cigarette. This analysis shows that the underlying cigarette functions – or in other terms the intrinsic behaviors of a cigarette – are here "propagate fire" and "deliver tar".

The operational vision relies on other operational concepts such as lifecycle, operational contexts, operational scenarios or operational objects (cf. section 3.4 for more details). All these concepts may also be managed at different levels of abstraction/grain. Figure 3.4 shows, for instance, the *mission breakdown structure* (MBS) of an electronic toothbrush where its core missions are put in a hierarchy according to the fact that a high-level mission needs the lower-level missions to be achieved.

The operational vision can also be seen as a natural interface between engineering and non-technical people. Typical examples of operational models are indeed, for instance, development, assembling or maintenance models (that specify how a product system will be managed by the associated design, manufacturing or support systems), as well as marketing or usage models (that describe how a product system will be seen by the market or used by the end-users) and business models (which explain how the constructing company will earn money with a product system). In this matter, the role of the operational vision is to express the information contained in these different stakeholder models within a language that can be understood by the system designers and used in the development process.

3.2.2.2. Functional vision

The *functional vision* provides "gray box" models of a given system of interest where one begins to apprehend the inside of the system, but only in terms of input/output abstract[20] behaviors, and not concrete implementation choices, in order to begin a deeper understanding of what the system does, without however knowing at this point how it is concretely structured. Its core motivation is to elicit in that way the behavior – that is, the "what" – of the system.

The core notion of the functional vision is of course the notion of "function" of a system, which refers to an input/output behavior of the considered system. In other terms, a *function* associated with a given system models a transformation process – which can be achieved by physical, software or even "humanware" resources – that transforms a given series of inputs into a given series of outputs. This explains why a common pattern to name a function is a verb followed by a complement, the generic patterns being typically to "do something" or "transform inputs into outputs". In any case, one must always check when defining a function whether it expresses such a transformational behavior.

Contrarily to the operational vision, all functional concepts – such as functional modes, functional scenarios or functional objects (see section 3.4 for more details) – are now uniquely referring to the system of interest, without involving any external system. All these concepts can again be managed at different levels of abstraction/grain.

---

20 That is, independent of any technological implementation.

Figure 3.5 shows, for instance, the *functional breakdown structure* (FBS) of an electronic toothbrush, where its main functions are put in a hierarchy according to the fact that a high-level function needs the lower-level functions to be achieved (i.e. the "algorithm" of the high-level function involves the lower-level functions as sub-routines).

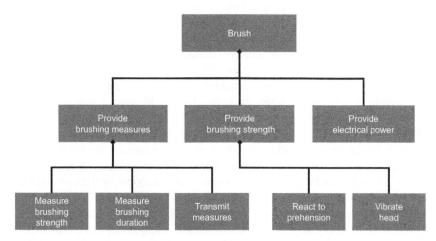

Figure 3.5. *Functional vision – functional breakdown structure (FBS) of an electronic toothbrush*

We may now point out that a key difficulty of functional analysis is the identification of *transverse functions*, that is, of functions that cannot be directly allocated to a single component of a given system. Such functions are indeed capturing the emergent behaviors resulting from the cooperation between the different components of a system, which by definition cannot be easily observed at the constructional level. It is therefore always important to identify these functions in order to master the integration process since these functions are also telling us where different teams in charge of different components shall work collaboratively[21]. Within a functional breakdown structure, one may thus normally

21 We already provided an illustration on that situation in footnote 15 to which the reader may first refer. Another similar example is the thrust reversing function on an aircraft: this function, which reverts the air flow passing in an aircraft engine to decrease the speed of the aircraft when on ground, is provided by the cooperation of a cylinder that pushes a trap located in the nacelle, the engine itself and a critical embedded software that coordinates the involved nacelle and engine components when thrust reversing operates. Such a function is typically transverse, since distributed on several hardware and software components, which are moreover provided by different suppliers (typically one for the nacelle, one for the engine, one for the embedded system): identifying the function and putting it under control in the aircraft development project is thus totally key to ensure the success of its integration.

always find both component functions and transverse functions. Unfortunately, most engineers often forget the transverse functions in their analyses, which leads them to lose the most important value of a complete functional analysis from a systems architecting perspective.

Another key point is that the functional vision is fundamental in systems architecting since it provides the deep invariants of any system. Any communication network will achieve, for instance, always the same basic functions such as "receive messages", "route messages" or "deliver messages", totally independently of its implementation technology, that may be either purely manual (think to your snail mail operator) or based on many different techniques (Hertzian waves, twisted cables, copper wires, optical fiber, etc.). In a totally different direction, consider a state as an organizational system: one may observe that it always relies on the core function "collect taxes", consisting of taking money from the citizen pockets and bringing it into the state's pocket, which is basically invariant among time, even if the tax collecting mechanisms evolved a lot from Roman antiquity up to our modern societies. In other words, *technology changes, but functional architecture remains*. As a natural result, functional architecture always provides a robust basis for architecting a system. It indeed allows the systems architect to reason on a system independently of technology and thus to define, analyze and evaluate different implementation options for a given functional architecture. Such an approach is key to choose the best solution, which cannot be done if one directly works at the constructional level, where one will be glued into a given technical choice, without the possibility of easily making another.

Good systems architectures are also based on *functional segregation principles*. This simply means that some key functional interfaces must be strictly respected at the constructional level[22]. This gives rise to layered architectures where components are clustered in different independent layers connected by functional interfaces, as one can see in the three first examples provided in the Introduction. Another classical example of such a layered functional architecture is a communication network architecture, which is organized in different independent layers, starting from the physical layer up to arriving to service layers (see, for instance, Wikipedia (2021h) for more details). One must therefore, for instance, be able, on the one hand, to change a signal processing protocol within the physical layer without any impact on the service layer and, on the other hand, to implement a new service or a service evolution in the service layer without any impact on the physical layer. Such a result is typically achieved by means of robust functional interfaces that shall be stable

---

22 In this matter, the role of the systems architect is to guarantee that such interfaces will never be violated in the design.

over time, in order to absorb the technological evolutions that will naturally always arrive in the life of any system[23].

It is finally interesting to observe that the standard vocabulary used to discuss the functional vision is traditionally different, depending on whether the considered system is a technical or an organizational system. The term "function" is, for instance, usually reserved for technical systems (that may be of either hardware or software nature), when one rather uses the terms "process", "activity" or "task" to express the same behavioral concept, when dealing with organizational systems. It shall however be clearly understood that processes, activities or tasks are in fact nothing other than functions of a given organizational system, considered at different levels of abstraction.

3.2.2.3. Constructional vision

The *constructional vision* provides white box models of the system where one describes all concrete hardware, software and "humanware"[24] components of a system with their interactions. Its core motivation is to elicit in that way the concrete structure – that is, the "how" – of the system. It is thus probably the most intuitive part of a systems architecture.

The core notion of the constructional vision is of course the notion of "component" of a system that refers to a concrete part of the considered system. In other terms, a *component* associated with a given system models a physical, software or even "humanware" resource that belongs to the system. Each atom of a system shall therefore belong to one and only one of its components. A common pattern to denote a component is thus just to use its usual technical or business name.

Exactly as in the functional vision, all constructional concepts – such as configuration, constructional scenarios or constructional objects (see section 3.4 for more details) – are again uniquely referring to the system of interest, without

---

23 Another motivation for such functional segregation is abstraction. It would indeed be basically impossible to develop a service if one would access directly to the physical layer of a computer system since the physical world is here usually highly non-deterministic with many probabilistic phenomena that must be hidden to a service developer.

24 Remember that men can be part of systems with either strong organizational dimensions such as information systems, for instance, or when a human stakeholder plays such a key role (e.g. pilot, driver, operator, etc.) that it may be important to include him/her in the design, considering then an operated system, rather than the underlying technical system alone.

involving any external system. All these concepts can be managed at different levels of abstraction/grain. Figure 3.5 shows, for instance, the *product breakdown structure* (PBS) of an electronic toothbrush, where its components are put in a hierarchy according to the fact that a high-level component results from the integration of its lower-level components.

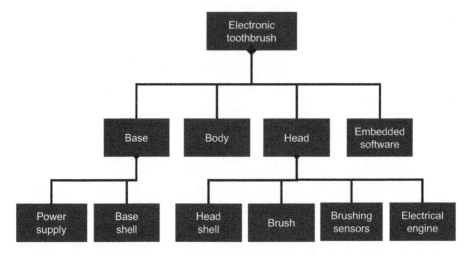

Figure 3.6. *Constructional vision – product breakdown structure (PBS) of an electronic toothbrush. For a color version of this figure, see www.iste.co.uk/krob/systems.zip*

Note finally that the term "architecture" usually only refers to the constructional architecture of a system. One shall thus be aware of the fact that we will use this term in a much broader acceptation through our entire book, especially when speaking of systems architecture, which refers to the union of all architectural visions for a given system as introduced above.

3.2.3. *Relationships between the three architectural visions*

Last but not least, it is also important to point out the network of relationships existing between the three architectural visions, since they are at the heart of the systems architecting process. It is in particular especially important to maintain these relationships during the different design phases, which is difficult due to the "highly iterative and recursive nature" of systems architecting (NASA 2016).

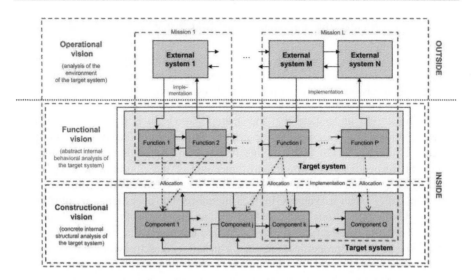

Figure 3.7. *Relationships between the three architectural visions. For a color version of this figure, see www.iste.co.uk/krob/systems.zip*

Figure 3.7 illustrates the generic relationships between the architectural visions as explained below:

– The operational vision connects first with the two other visions due to the fact that missions are naturally implemented by functions, as well as components. Another way to make this connection is to observe that all external flows between the different external systems and the system of interest, as provided by the operational vision, must be internally captured or produced (depending the external flows are input or output flows, from the internal point of view of the considered system) by functions of the system of interest[25].

– The functional vision connects back in the same way with the operational vision and forth with the constructional vision due to the fact that each abstract function must be concretely allocated to/implemented by some set of constructional components.

– The constructional vision connects then back to the two other visions according to the implementation and allocation relationships that we just pointed out.

25 In other terms, it is sufficient to prolong each external flow, as identified in the operational vision, within the system, to get the first functions of the system of interest. Functional analysis will then internally continue the same kind of analysis up to exhaustively identifying all functions, which shall be ultimately checked by a functional synthesis in order to prove that all identified functions are forming a coherent functional network.

Note, in particular, that **one should not think**[26] that operational artifacts only allocate to functional artifacts, which on their side only allocate to constructional artifacts. Such a vision would indeed be dramatically false. Operational, functional and constructional visions shall indeed be analyzed as a circle of three interdependent visions. Figure 3.8 illustrates this situation.

One must first understand that the operational vision is nothing other than a mixed functional and constructional description of the part of the environment of the system of interest, which involves this last system. As an immediate result, the functional (respectively constructional) dimension of the environment Env(S) of a given system S naturally maps with the functional (respectively, constructional) dimension of S. Such a property implies therefore that operational architecture is connected both to functional and constructional architectures of a given system. As a matter of fact, the geometry of a given system's environment – which is one of its typical constructional properties – maps, for instance, directly with the geometry of the considered system, without any connection with functions[27]. The same situation also holds for most of the physical properties of the environment.

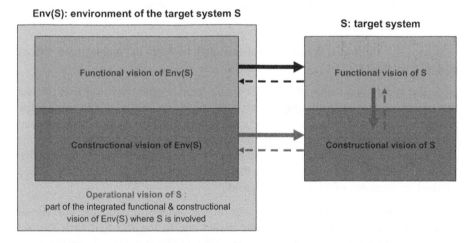

Figure 3.8. *Relationships existing between the three architectural visions. For a color version of this figure, see www.iste.co.uk/krob/systems.zip*

On the other hand, one must also notice that there may be feedbacks from the constructional vision onto the functional vision and/or the operational vision and/or from the functional vision onto the operational vision. The choice of a specific

---

26 Which is unfortunately a common mistake.
27 The shape of my body typically implies the shape of a chair, without requiring any functional analysis.

technology at the constructional level may indeed typically induce functions that were not directly requested. Deciding to implement a given service through an automated device creates, for instance, immediately the "distribute electricity" function. In the same way, the choice of a specific function at functional level may allow new services that were initially not designed. As another example, just remember that nobody could imagine the creation of an entire new world of new services thanks to the apparently simple Internet functionality[28]!

3.2.4. *Organization of a system model*

We are now in position to derive the first consequences of the CESAM framework, that we begin to introduce, on the structure of a system model. We are indeed now aware of two dimensions of any system, the first one being provided by the three architectural visions used to model a system, and the second one being given by the abstraction/grain level on which a given system may be analyzed. On this last point, we shall just recall that any integrated system can be analyzed on the different levels of its integration hierarchy, that is, at system, sub-system, sub-sub-system and other levels.

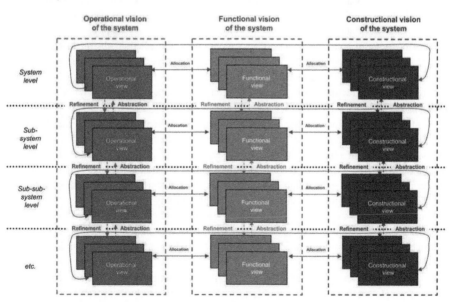

Figure 3.9. *Organization of a system model. For a color version of this figure, see www.iste.co.uk/krob/systems.zip*

---

28 Which, functionally speaking, is nothing other than to allow exchanges between different computers.

Hence, any system model can be naturally organized in a matrix way where the different system views are classified according to their architectural vision and the level of analysis within the system integration hierarchy, as depicted in Figure 3.9. Note that the horizontal relation between these views is allocation or implementation, as explained in the previous section, when the vertical relation is refinement, when going from a high-level view to a higher-level view, and abstraction, when doing the converse. Refinement means here providing more details with respect to a given architectural view, when abstraction stands for a not too destructive idealization[29] of a series of views, where one will reason on high-level clusters, from a lower-level perspective, thus losing the details for getting the big picture on a given architectural topic[30]. On the one hand, refinement is clearly the right tool when one wants to precisely analyze a problem. On the other hand, abstraction[31] is crucial for being able to define an architectural strategy without becoming lost in an ocean of details (see Cousot and Cousot (1996)).

---

29 An abstraction/refinement mechanism is formally provided (see Cousot and Cousot (1996)) by a pair (α,ρ) of applications between sets of so-called concrete objects and sets of so-called abstract objects, where the *abstraction application* α maps each set of concrete objects into a set of abstract objects and the *refinement application* ρ maps each set of abstract objects into a set of concrete objects. These applications are called an abstraction/refinement pair if and only if $\alpha(\rho(A)) \subseteq A$ for each abstract set A (refining an abstract set and then re-abstracting the result cannot enlarge the initial abstraction) and $C \subseteq \rho(\alpha(C))$ for each concrete set C (abstracting a concrete set and then refining the result cannot reduce the initial concrete scope).

30 Abstraction and refinement are core mechanisms for systems architects, especially when creating architectural hierarchies. A quite frequent problem in architecture is indeed the excessive number of objects generated by a step of an architectural analysis. In order to handle them effectively and to achieve their real global understanding, we typically have to cluster and to synthesize them into abstract objects. This abstraction activity can be achieved by partitioning the objects in clusters of "similar" weakly inter-dependent objects, then systematically clarifying the key characteristics (goal, function, feature, etc.) of each group and consequently naming each group. Such a process will naturally lead to architectural hierarchies such as mission, functional or product breakdown structures, as introduced in the previous sections.

31 As a matter of fact, one observes in practice that abstraction is not at all an easy activity. Most of people are in particular not able to manipulate efficiently this mechanism. The key difficulty is indeed to find the "good" abstractions of a given problem, that is, the good balance between too abstract and too detailed views. The key point is here to be able to manipulate coarse grain views, with which one can reason more easily and thus make the good strategic decisions, but that can also be refined in fine grain views. This requires the abstract views to be holistic in order to capture all dimensions of a given problem. What happens unfortunately often in real life is that one creates too simple abstractions to be useful!

3.3. CESAM systems architecture pyramid

3.3.1. *The three key questions to ask*

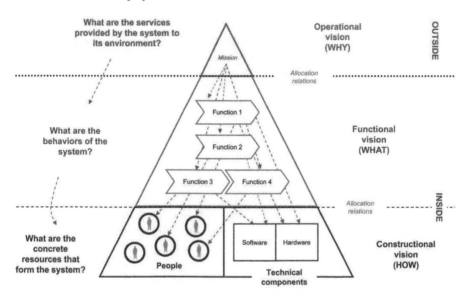

Figure 3.10. *The CESAM systems architecture pyramid. For a color version of this figure, see www.iste.co.uk/krob/systems.zip*

As discussed in the previous section, any system can be analyzed from an operational, functional and constructional perspective. In order to achieve such analyses in practice, one must simply remember to ask three simple questions[32] to cover these different architectural visions:

– *Key operational question*: WHY does the system exist?[33]

– *Key functional question*: WHAT is the system doing?[34]

– *Key constructional question*: HOW is the system formed?[35]

One usually summarizes these different questions in the *CESAM systems architecture pyramid*, which is a simple graphical way to represent a system,

---

32 These questions shall just be seen as a mnemonic trick to remember the scope of each architectural view. Modeling of each view is indeed much more complicated than that.

33 Or more precisely what are the services provided by the system to its environment?

34 Or equivalently what are the behaviors/functions of the system?

35 Or in other terms, what are the concrete resources that form the system?

presented in Figure 3.10. Such a pyramidal representation intends just to recall that details – and thus clarification of the model of any given system – will permanently increase when moving from the operational to the functional vision and from the functional to the constructional vision.

Note that the key point is of course the order in which these three core questions are asked during a system design process. The systems architecting process consists indeed of following the previous order, that is, passing from the first question ("why?") to the second one ("what?") up to the third one ("how?"), in that exact order. Be however careful not to manage successively, that is, one after the other, these three types of analyses that should largely overlap in practice. At some point, it is indeed just impossible to reason operationally without any vision of the concrete solution that will answer to the operational architecture[36]. This typically leads to manage coarse grain functional and constructional analyses during the operational analysis. In the same way, it is often not possible to reason functionally without any idea of the concrete components that may implement the functional architecture. This obliges to manage middle grain constructional analyses during the functional analysis. As a result, good systems architecting practice is clearly to manage in parallel the three architectural analyses at the same time, but not at the same grain of analysis.

Organizing the systems architecting process in that way will allow passing from technical-oriented to value-oriented system design strategies. In most of classical system design strategies, the technical components are indeed usually the starting point and it is only at the end of the development phase that one begins to look how the developed system fits to its stakeholders needs. Such an approach is a *product-push* strategy from a marketing perspective, and it may work well as soon as one is only making incremental improvements on existing products in stable markets.

Unfortunately, industry must nowadays increasingly manage many technological ruptures within unstable environments. In that case, just pushing new products will have a high probability of failure. To increase success, one must thus invert the design logic in order to put stakeholders and their needs as a starting point to the product development. Systems architecting shall thus just be seen as the key methodological tool to implement such *a need-pull* strategy.

---

36 An operational architecture that cannot be implemented in a concrete solution has a name: a science fiction movie. Such movies are indeed typically showing us use cases of technology that are just not concretely feasible. Think, for instance, of Star Trek's hyper-propulsion or teleporter: the movie can be seen as an operational proof of concept of such technology, from which one could derive a coarse grain functional analysis. Unfortunately, we will never be able to achieve a detailed functional analysis due to the fact that no constructional architecture exists in response to the operational architecture.

3.3.2. *The last question that shall not be forgotten*

The three previous questions are however not the only ones that one should ask in the context of complex systems design and development. The last fourth key question, unfortunately often forgotten in real systems contexts, refers to the product/project duality as introduced in section 2.1. It simply consists of asking which person – in other terms, "who?" – is the project counterpart of the different product elements described in the three architectural visions of the product, that is:

– WHO owns each architectural element of the system?

This question can then be divided according to the three architectural visions as follows:

– *Operational perspective:* who are the stakeholders of the system?

– *Functional perspective:* who is in charge of the functions of the system?

– *Constructional perspective:* who is responsible for the components of the system?

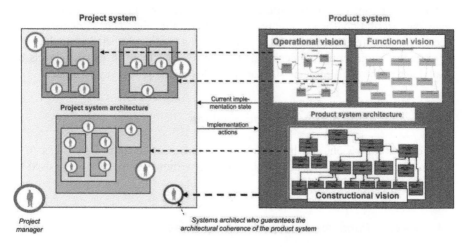

Figure 3.11. *Alignment of the project system architecture with the product system architecture. For a color version of this figure, see www.iste.co.uk/krob/systems.zip*

Asking these different questions is clearly fundamental from a systems architecting perspective. First, it is just impossible to capture the right needs without deeply interacting with the stakeholders of the system of interest, which requires identifying them as early as possible, leading to the first above question. Second, we may recall that the robustness of a system design is directly correlated to the fact that all transverse functions are managed, that is, under the responsibility of somebody within the project, which motivates the second above question. Third, one cannot influence the design of a system without involving all functional and constructional responsibles, which again obliges knowing them well, which requires answering the second and third above questions. In this matter, we shall also recall that the role of a systems architect is usually to manage complex socio-dynamics implying all these various actors, which cannot be done without understanding their personal motivations, their synergies and their antagonisms with respect to a given system design and development project. We are here again in the "who" sphere and not in a technical domain.

Note finally that the "WHO" question is also crucial in the construction of the project organization. A good project architecture indeed results from the mapping of all architectural elements of a given product system into the project system, that is, onto people, where they shall be put under a single responsibility. This project/product alignment principle is indeed crucial to be sure that all operational, functional and constructional elements of a product system are taken in charge by somebody in the project system, which is obviously a *sine qua non* condition for the completeness of any engineering analysis, as well as to guarantee that no product architectural perimeter has two project leaders, which would mechanically lead to many engineering conflicts[37]. Figure 3.11 illustrates this alignment principle on the electronic toothbrush example: the boxes appearing on the project system side are, for instance, engineering project teams that correspond there to the first levels of breakdown of the different views that are provided on the product system side.

3.4. More systems architecture dimensions

Architectural visions are however not the only architectural dimensions of a system. We shall now introduce a number of new dimensions that can be used to refine each architectural vision.

3.4.1. *Descriptions versus expected properties*

As already discussed in section 1.1, one must now recall that there exist two complementary ways of specifying a system. The first one refers to *descriptions*: in this specification mode, one explicitly[38] describes the behavior and structure, either of the system of interest (if one is reasoning functionally or constructionally) or of its environment (if one reasons operationally).

---

37 Such situations unfortunately often exist in practice, with sometimes up to 10 people responsible for the same product system architectural perimeter!

38 Hence, descriptions are considered as specifications *in extension*.

The second way deals with *expected properties*: one is now not explicitly describing a system, but rather stating the (operational, functional and constructional) properties, expected/intended[39] to be satisfied by the system. Note these expected properties are usually called *requirements* in systems engineering (see section 1.1 for more details). This gives rise to the six different – but altogether exhaustive[40] – specification modes that are presented in Figure 3.12, that is:

– descriptions: operational descriptions, functional descriptions, constructional descriptions;

– expected properties: needs[41], functional requirements, constructional requirements.

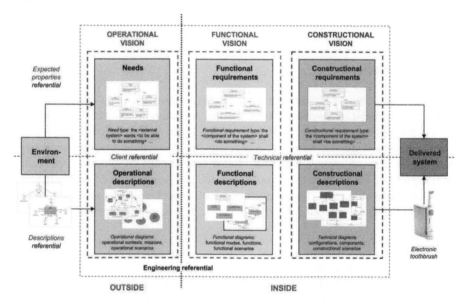

Figure 3.12. *Descriptions versus expected properties. For a color version of this figure, see www.iste.co.uk/krob/systems.zip*

---

39 Hence, expected properties are considered as specifications *in intention*.

40 This key property is ensured by the mathematical foundations of the CESAM framework (see section 1.1).

41 We will use here the term "need" instead of "operational requirement", even if they are equivalent. We indeed prefer to reserve the term "requirement" for functional and constructional uses in order to strictly separate the domain of the question (expressed with needs) and the domain of the solution (stated with requirements).

As explained in section 1.1, one can equivalently (from a theoretical point of view) completely specify any system by using either descriptions or expected properties. However, these two specification modes are absolutely not equivalent from an engineering effort perspective (see again section 1.1). On the one hand, descriptions are indeed well adapted to define and to synthesize the behavioral and structural dimensions of a system. On the other hand, performances of a system are typical expected properties. But the converse is totally false. As a good practice, an efficient and optimal – in terms of time spent in engineering – system specification shall mix descriptions (to be reserved for defining behavioral and structural elements and their dynamics) and expected properties (to be reserved for performances). This trick allows drastically reducing the requirements volume in a specification file, thus improving its readability, since descriptions are usually encoded by many requirements.

3.4.2. *Descriptions*

Descriptions can be separated in four different views, each of them modeling a different dimension of a system. States are first modeling time. Static elements are then depicting the core objects of each architectural vision, when dynamics are describing their temporal behavior. Flows are finally consolidating the exchanges involved in these dynamics. One should also note that all these system views are both exhaustive (they allow the complete modeling of a system) and non-redundant (each view provides a specific perspective, which is not covered by the other views) due to the foundations of our system architecting framework (see section 1.1).

3.4.2.1. *States*

A *state T* associated with a given system S is modeling a period of time, that is, a set consisting of one or more intervals of time, where the system S can be analyzed in a homogeneous way from the perspective of a given architectural vision. A state can usually be specified by its initiation and termination events[42], which are both modeling phenomenon occurring instantaneously, that is, at a specific moment – not interval – of time. As one may imagine, the initiation (respectively, termination) events correspond to moments of time – the same type of event can indeed occur at different moments of time – where the period of time modeled by T begins (respectively, ends).

---

42 $T = \cup [t1, t2]$ for all moments of time $t1$ and $t2$ where an initiation (respectively, a termination) event occurs at time $t1$ (respectively, $t2$).

States are used to model time. In each architectural vision, a key temporal analysis consists indeed of break downing in different states the timeline of a system from birth to death. In such analyses, one can then model the usual temporal behavior of a system as a succession of states in which lies the system, one after the other. Think, for instance, of a normal day of a human person which begins in the "sleeping" state, passing then to the "morning dress" and "breakfast" states, before arriving to the "transportation" and "working" states, passing a new time in the "transportation" state, then in the "relaxing", "dining" and "TV listening" states, before going back again to the "sleeping" state. We will discuss more precisely in Chapter 5 that kind of analysis for systems, based on states.

There are therefore logically three different types of states for any given system S, depending on the considered architectural vision, which are defined as follows:

– Operational states are called *operational contexts*: an operational context for S is a period of time OC(S) characterized by the fact that external interactions of S during OC(S) only involve a certain fixed set of stakeholders or external systems of its environment.

– Functional states are called *functional modes*: a functional mode for S is a period of time FM(S), which is characterized by the fact that the behavior of S during FM(S) can be modeled by only using a certain fixed set of system functions.

– Constructional states are called (technical) *configurations*: a configuration for S is a period of time TC(S) – usually identified with the involved components – characterized by the fact that the structure of S during TC(S) only consists of a certain fixed set of system components.

In other terms, one changes operational context, functional mode or configuration if and only if a new stakeholder, function or component appears within the life of a given system. Passing from the "rainy" to the "sunny" operational context typically means that the rain stakeholder disappeared and was replaced by the sun stakeholder. Replacing stakeholder by function or component would then lead to similar examples for the two other types of states that we introduced.

Table 3.1 illustrates the notion of states with some examples for an electronic toothbrush, where we provided the set of architectural (static) elements characterizing each state.

One can see in these examples that there is no one-to-one correspondence between these different states. The toothbrush can indeed typically be in the "bathroom" operational context and in either an "active" or a "passive" functional mode (in that last case, it would mean that the toothbrush is broken, but that the user did not notice it) and in either a "children" or an "adult" configuration.

States types	Toothbrush states	Initiation event	Termination event	Characteristic set of architectural elements
Operational contexts	Bathroom	Entering in bathroom	Going out of bathroom	Bathroom, power supply, end-user
	Teeth brushing	Start brushing	End brushing	Bathroom, end-user, toothpaste, water
	Reparation	Failure detection	Back in bathroom	Communication device, end-user, repairer
Functional modes	Idle	End working	Start working	Provide (only) mechanical reaction
	Active	Start working	End working	Provide electrical power, brushing forces & measures
	Passive	Failure	Failure fixed	None (all functions are broken)
Configurations	Children	Child-head on	Child-head off	Children-dedicated brushing head
	Adult	Adult-head on	Adult-head off	Adult-dedicated brushing head
	Broken	Component crash	Component replacement	Some non-core components disappeared

Table 3.1. *Examples of states for an electronic toothbrush*

In the same way, the toothbrush can be in the "active" functional mode, but in either a "bathroom" or a "reparation" operational context (this last case corresponds to the situation where the toothbrush was repaired in the reparation workshop) and in a lot of different configurations. The toothbrush may finally also be in a given configuration, but in various operational contexts or functional modes as one can easily check in Table 3.1. These examples thus show that each type of state may be allocated with many other types of states without any simple relationship in this matter.

Let us end by providing the standard representation of states – in most modeling languages – which are usually modeled by means of oval shapes, as one can see in Figure 3.13.

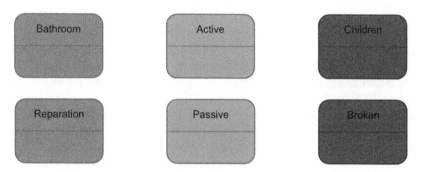

Figure 3.13. *Standard representations of states. For a color version of this figure, see www.iste.co.uk/krob/systems.zip*

3.4.2.2. *Static elements*

A *static element* with respect to a given system S refers to an input/output mechanism associated with S from the perspective of a certain architectural vision. We are using the term "static element" to emphasize that this new system description does not focus on the temporal dynamic (see the next section for that other point) of the involved input/output mechanism, but provides just a non-temporized definition of such a mechanism without providing its "algorithm".

There are therefore logically three different types of static elements for a given system S, depending on the considered architectural vision, which are defined as follows:

– Operational static elements are called *missions*: a mission of S is an input/output behavior of the environment Env(S) of S, involving both S and other external systems.

– Functional static elements are called *functions*: a function of S is an abstract implementation-independent intrinsic input/output behavior of S, that is, that only involves S.

– Constructional static elements are called *components*: a component of S formally refers to a concrete implementation-dependent intrinsic input/output behavior of S. A component of S is therefore naturally identified to a concrete part of S.

Missions shall never be mixed with functions or components, since they do not refer to the system of interest, but to its environment. Functions and components both refer to the system of interest, but in two different ways. Functions are indeed independent of any concrete implementation of the system of interest, when components always refer to its specific concrete implementation. There are thus two types of functions: on the one hand, transverse functions that can only be implemented by using several components; on the other hand, unitary functions that can be implemented by using a single component (such functions are thus "simply" modeling the behaviors of the components). Transverse functions are very important since they model transverse system behaviors that, by definition, cannot be easily analyzed at the constructional level. One may finally observe that the existence of such transversal (or equivalently emergent) behaviors is intrinsic to any system since it is directly the consequence of the emergence postulate (see section 1.2).

Note also that the standard way for stating a mission or a function of a given system is to use the "do something" pattern in both cases. The only difference lies in the subject associated with the verb that describes the mission or function. This subject shall consist of external systems or stakeholders in the case of a mission ("external systems cooperating with the system shall do something") when it shall only be the system alone for a function ("the system shall do something"). On the other hand, components are usually stated using only names referring to concrete objects forming the system.

Table 3.2 illustrates the notion of static element with some examples for an electronic toothbrush. We provided some inputs and outputs for each proposed static element.

As already mentioned, static elements are related by *allocation relations*. Each function contributes, for instance, to one or more missions, which corresponds to the fact that a mission can be obtained by composing a function with some other input/output behaviors (cf. the examples given in footnote 19): such a situation is then expressed by saying that this mission is allocated to the considered function. In the same way, a component can contribute to a mission and/or a function, which will be expressed by saying that such a mission or function is allocated to the considered component.

We may also provide the standard representations of the three different types of static elements – in most modeling languages – which are usually modeled by circles for missions, ovals for functions and boxes for components, as one can see in Figure 3.14. We also expressed in this figure the different allocation relationships – represented by dashed arrows – that may exist between these different operational, functional and constructional static elements.

Static elements types	Toothbrush static elements	Inputs	Outputs
Missions	To clean teeth	Dirty teeth	Cleaned teeth
	To improve teeth cleaning	Clean teeth	Cleaner teeth
	To keep in operational conditions	Working toothbrush	Working toothbrush
Functions	To provide brushing strength	Grip forces, Low voltage (LV)	Brushing forces
	To provide brushing measures	Raw measures, Low voltage (LV)	Measurement data
	To provide electrical power	Medium voltage (MV)	Low voltage (LV)
Components	Body	Grip forces, Structural forces	Low voltage (LV)
	Head	Low voltage (LV)	Brushing forces, Structural forces
	Base	Medium voltage (MV), Support forces	Low voltage (LV), Support forces

Table 3.2. *Examples of static elements for an electronic toothbrush*

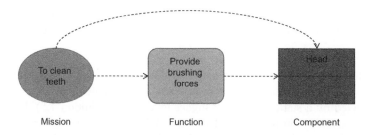

Figure 3.14. *Standard representations of static elements. For a color version of this figure, see www.iste.co.uk/krob/systems.zip*

Note finally that static elements can occur at different abstraction levels that also correspond to different integration levels, resulting in both associated abstraction and integration hierarchies. Hence it is always crucial to be able to specify how different types of static elements are connected by such relationships. The standard representations of these abstraction/integration relationships are provided by

Figure 3.15, where we also put the associated allocation relations (beware that full arrows – which express abstraction relationships – are squared when dealing with components).

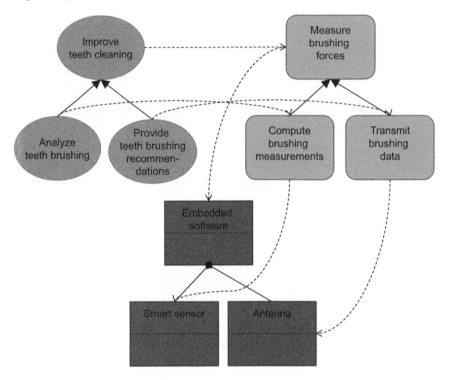

Figure 3.15. *Standard representations of integration relations between static elements. For a color version of this figure, see www.iste.co.uk/krob/systems.zip*

For the sake of completeness, one also needs to explicitly represent the full *integration mechanism* that relates the different static elements of lower level that are abstracted by a static element of higher level (see Definition 1.5). Figure 3.16 shows an example – in the line of Definition 1.5 – where oriented arrows labeled with an exchanged flow represent interfaces[43] – between different constructional components of the same level of abstraction (here the head, body and embedded system that are forming the "brush" part of an electronic toothbrush). Similar representations also exist with functions or missions.

---

43 We recall that an interface between two static elements E and F is formally nothing other than the couple (E, F). With such an interface, one may associate both flows exchanged between E and F and flows exchanged between F and E (we refer to the section dedicated to flows that follows for more detailed information on flows).

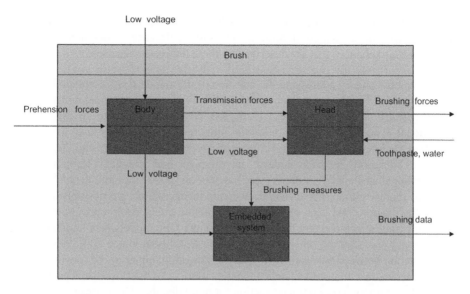

Figure 3.16. *Interfaces standard representation. For a color version of this figure, see www.iste.co.uk/krob/systems.zip*

3.4.2.3. *Dynamics*

The *dynamics* of a static element of a system S refers to its temporal behavior or equivalently to an algorithmic description of such a temporal behavior. Dynamics are completely crucial if one wants to precisely specify the behavior of any system or any system mission, function or component.

There are therefore logically three different types of dynamics for a given system S, depending on the considered architectural vision, which are defined as follows:

– Operational dynamics are called *operational scenarios*: an operational scenario of S is an algorithmic description of the interactions existing between the system (considered as a black box) and its environment.

– Functional dynamics are called *functional scenarios*: a functional scenario of S is an algorithmic description of the interactions existing, on the one hand, internally between the functions of S and, on the other hand, externally with the environment of the system.

– Constructional dynamics are called *constructional scenarios*: a constructional scenario of S is an algorithmic description of the interactions existing, on the one hand, internally between the components of S and, on the other hand, externally with the environment of the system.

Note that these three types of scenarios have exactly the same nature since they are all describing exchange algorithms. The only difference comes here from the nature of the exchanges that are described by these different scenarios.

Let us now end by addressing the question of the standard representations of the different types of dynamics, which are typically given – in most modeling languages – by *sequence diagrams*. Figure 3.17 depicts this formalism with an example of operational dynamic description, here the initiation of a toothbrush use, where one specified the interactions existing between all involved stakeholders and the system. Sequence diagrams provide indeed an efficient and classical formalism for representing distributed algorithms (see Booch *et al.* (2004) for more details). In this mode of representation, the different elements in interaction are positioned on the top of the diagram and each of them has a timeline going from top to bottom that represents time (each element having its own time). One models then an interaction by putting – one after the other – arrows, going from the initiator to the receiver of an interaction between two elements, with an indication, either of the function, used by the interaction initiator to manage the interaction, or of the flow that is exchanged during the interaction (see our next section for more details). These arrows shall then follow the sequential order of a given global interaction, as depicted in Figure 3.17. Note finally that one indicates the interacting sequences that are highly coupled by a large rectangle at the level of a given involved system.

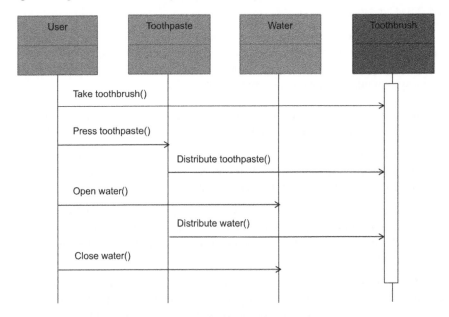

Figure 3.17. *Standard representations of an operational dynamic. For a color version of this figure, see www.iste.co.uk/krob/systems.zip*

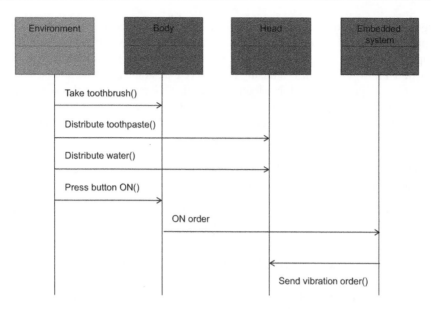

Figure 3.18. *Standard representations of a constructional dynamic. For a color version of this figure, see www.iste.co.uk/krob/systems.zip*

For the sake of completeness, we shall also provide an example of constructional scenario that can be found in Figure 3.18, which represents the exact constructional counterpart of the previous operational scenario. Functional scenarios are represented exactly in the same way, components being just replaced by functions. Note that the difference between a functional or constructional scenario and an operational scenario is only that the environment is a black box in the first situation, when it is the case of the system in the second situation[44].

3.4.2.4. *Flows*

A *flow* associated with a system S models an object – matter, energy, data, information, etc. – which is exchanged, either externally between the system and its environment or internally between two functional or constructional elements of the system.

Flows may be quite different depending on the vision. To illustrate that last point, let us take the example of a traffic light system. When the traffic light is red, it operationally sends a stop request to the drivers that are looking at it. The operational flow exchanged between the traffic light and the drivers can then be

---

44 There are of course also mixed scenarios where one may provide details on both the environment and the system.

modeled by a "stop order" flow. On the functional level, one would however typically say that the traffic light is just sending red light (which is interpreted as a stop signal by the drivers) to its environment, which may be modeled by a "red" functional flow. Finally, it is amusing to observe that, at the constructional level, the red color is just produced by lighting the first (starting from the top) traffic light – which may typically be white – in connection with the use of a red filter. The associated constructional flow can thus be modeled by "white 3" to express that situation.

There are therefore logically three different types of flows for a given system S, depending on the considered architectural vision, which are defined as follows:

– Operational flows or objects: an *operational flow or object* of S is an object that is exchanged between S and its environment, that is, between S and an external system of its environment.

– Functional flows or objects: a *functional flow or object* of S is an object that is an input or an output of one of the functions of S, that is, which is exchanged, either between the functions of S, or between a function of S, and an external system of its environment.

– Constructional flows or objects: a *constructional flow or object* of S models a concrete object that is exchanged either between the components of S, or between a component of S, and an external system of its environment.

Flows are usually simply stated using only names that are referring to concrete objects that are exchanged between different systems. Table 3.3 illustrates these various notions of flows, with some examples for an electronic toothbrush.

Flow types	Flow	Nature
Operational Flows	Toothpaste	Matter
	Brushing data	Data
Functional Flows	Low voltage	Energy
	Brushing measure	Data
Constructional Flows	Electricity	Energy
	Brushing pressure signal	Data

Table 3.3. *Examples of flows for an electronic toothbrush*

Note that flows are naturally related by allocation relations. As illustrated by the traffic light system example provided above, an operational flow OF may be allocated to either a functional flow or a constructional flow, which may be operationally interpreted as OF. In the same way, a functional flow FF may also be allowed to a constructional flow that may be functionally interpreted as FF. Flow hierarchies are therefore naturally induced by these allocation relations.

Let us end by providing in Figure 3.19 the standard representations of the three different types of flows – in most modeling languages – which are all modeled by "objects" or "blocks" in the usual meaning given to this concept in object-oriented modeling (see Booch *et al*. (2004) or Friedenthal *et al*. (2012)).

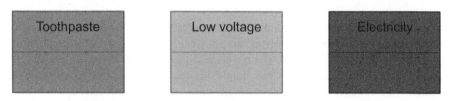

Figure 3.19. *Standard representations of flows. For a color version of this figure, see www.iste.co.uk/krob/systems.zip*

3.4.3. *Expected properties*

As already stated in section 1.3, expected properties are formally speaking *logical predicates* related with the system of interest (see Chapter 1 or Appendix 1 for more technical details on that core logical concept that goes back to Aristoteles). An expected property is thus nothing other than a Boolean function[45], that is, a function P that maps a system on TRUE or FALSE, depending on whether the property that P models is satisfied or not by the considered system:

$$P: S \longrightarrow P(S) \in \{ \text{ TRUE, FALSE } \}.$$

This consideration allows avoiding confusing expected properties with their constitutive elements. An expected property indeed typically expresses that a given system shall behave or be structured with a certain external or internal performance[46]. The involved behavioral or structural elements and performances shall thus not be mixed with the property, since they are just not logical predicates.

It is also important to remember that one can analyze in practice a given system S, either from an external perspective or from an internal perspective. This consideration leads to the key distinction between needs and requirements, which are the two first main types of expected properties on S:

---

45 This is thus also true for needs and requirements according to the definitions that follow.

46 In other terms, expected properties express the performances that shall be satisfied by the system of interest or by its environment, depending on whether one deals with the functional/constructional or operational visions.

– External perspective[47] – need: a *need* with respect to S is a property that is expected or imposed by the environment Env(S) of S, expressed in the language of the environment[48] (i.e. only referring to operational descriptions and performances).

– Internal perspective – requirement: a *requirement* on S is a functional or constructional property that shall be satisfied by S, expressed in the language of the system (i.e. only referring to functional or constructional descriptions and performances).

One shall of course understand that these definitions are fundamentally relative to a given system. A need with respect to a system S is indeed a requirement on the environment Env(S) of S. In the same way, a requirement on S is also a need with respect to a subsystem of S. One should hence always remember to point-out explicitly the system of interest to which any need or requirement refers.

Note also that we used here a voluntarily different terminology depending on the external or internal perspective we may take with respect to expected properties. A good system architecting practice indeed consists of strictly separating the domain of the *question* – expressed using needs – from the domain of the *solution* – expressed by means of requirements[49]. In other terms, needs shall be only reserved to model questions, when requirements shall model the corresponding answers. This point is crucial since many engineering problems are due to the fact that stakeholders are often expressing their "needs" in an intrusive way, that is, in terms of requirements in our meaning. This bad practice both limits the ability of the designers to propose better alternative solutions and prevents them from knowing the real needs hidden behind requirements[50], which may ultimately lead to bad

47 External perspective is here a synonym of operational vision.

48 One cannot thus use the language of the system to express a need.

49 This point is illustrated by Case study 3.2.

50 In a recent customer specification file for military vehicles, one could, for instance, find the demand C ≡ "the vehicle shall be painted in green", which was just copied/pasted from previous files. This expected property is typically not a need but a constructional requirement. A good systems architect shall then try to understand the functional and operational expected properties from which C derives. In this case, C can be traced back to a functional requirement F ≡ "the vehicle shall not be seen", itself coming from a quite simple need N ≡ "soldiers shall not die when in operations". At this point, one now has the rationale of the green color, which was motivated by the fact that it allows to be invisible in European battlefields where green is dominant. However, conflicts are no longer taking place in Europe, but rather in the Middle East where ocher and sand colors are dominant. The analysis of the root need allows us to understand that C is a very bad constructional choice to implement the functional requirement F, which is still valid. One shall of course rather request C' ≡ "the vehicle shall be painted in ocher/sand colors", which could not be suspected if only staying at the constructional level.

solutions from an end-user perspective, even if fitting perfectly to their requirements.

Note finally that requirements on a system S can be of course refined into two sub-types depending on whether one is dealing with functional or constructional visions:

– **Functional requirement:** a *functional requirement* on S is a property that shall be satisfied by the behavior of S, expressed in the functional language of the system (i.e. only referring to functional descriptions and performances).

– **Constructional requirement:** a *constructional requirement* on S is a property that shall be satisfied by the structure of S, expressed in the constructional language of the system (i.e. only referring to constructional descriptions and performances).

To write down properly these different types of expected properties, one shall use the standard statement patterns – referring to the notions introduced above – that are provided in Table 3.4.

Need	The "external system[51]" shall "do something/be formed of something" with a certain "operational performance" in a given "operational context".
Functional requirement	The "system" shall "do something[52]" with a certain "functional performance" in a given "functional mode".
Constructional requirement	The "system" shall "be formed of something[53]" with a certain "constructional performance" in a given "configuration".

Table 3.4. *Standard statement patterns for needs and functional and constructional requirements*

Table 3.5 illustrates the three previous different types of expected properties – written in accordance with the above standard statement patterns – on

---

51 Or equivalently a stakeholder of the system (see section 4.2).

52 "To do something" shall always refer here to an existing function of the considered system.

53 "To be formed of something" shall always refer here to an existing component of the considered system.

an electronic toothbrush, with a picture of the toothbrush part which is (partially) specified by them. In this example, the proposed need was derived first into a functional requirement that was derived then into a constructional requirement. One can thus immediately trace back the last constructional choice to the associated service provided to the end-users, which is useful – especially to analyze the stakeholder value brought by a given technical decision – since this service cannot be seen at the constructional level.

Note finally that the previous types of expected properties are *complete* by construction with respect to the CESAM framework. In other words, one can always specify any system in intension by *using only* needs, functional requirements and constructional requirements, without anything else.

Need	End users shall get a positive[54] feeling when efficiently cleaning their teeth.
Functional requirement	The electronic toothbrush shall display an encouraging message within 1 second when cleaning performance has been met.
Constructional requirement	The electronic toothbrush shall have a user interface of 2.5 cm x 1 cm in each configuration.

Table 3.5. *Examples of expected properties per architectural vision*

Needs or requirements? The tanker case

In the 1970s, important leaks occurred when pumping out liquid natural gas from tankers. The issue was that dangerous cracks appeared in the shell of the tankers due to the very cold temperature – close to 0 K – of the liquid gas.

To solve that problem, engineers began to think in terms of technical solutions, which led them to imagine a metal for tankers shells that should not crack at liquid gas temperature. This was however a very bad idea since the resulting solution would probably request many years of R&T and cost hundreds of millions of euros.

---

54 Positive refers here to the performance.

Another way of reasoning is to express the problem in terms of the question to solve, which is "how to avoid the liquid gas entering into contact with the shell metal?" Such a question expresses a simple constraint on the gas (which is a need – within CESAM formalism – with respect to the shell metal of the tanker) that has to be fulfilled.

Such a question has then a simple and quite cheap solution, consisting of putting pieces of folded cardboard under the leaking points. The gas is then retained by the cardboard before quickly evaporating at environmental temperature, which avoids all troubles.

As one sees on that illustrative simple example, there may be a huge gap between thinking in terms of solutions (requirements) and in terms of questions (needs).

Case study 3.2. *Needs or requirements? The tanker case*

There is in particular no need to introduce the concept of "non-functional requirement" that exists in many other architectural frameworks (cf. IEEE (2005), INCOSE (2011) or ISO (2018)) and often refers to "ity" properties of a system such as availability, maintainability, operability, safety, reliability and security. All these properties can indeed easily be expressed in terms of needs. To be more specific, let us take the example of a maintainability property for a given system, which would probably be expressed by most engineers by stating that M ≡ "the system shall be maintainable". However, to "be maintainable" can clearly not be considered as an internal function of a system since it does not refer to any of its input/output behaviors, but rather to a permanent status of the system. Property M is therefore neither a functional or constructional requirement[55] nor a need[56] within our framework. It has thus absolutely no status at all, which shows that it is probably a bad specification! The good way of expressing the property M is then just to identify the hidden stakeholders behind – which are here just maintenance teams – and to understand what these stakeholders are expecting. In our example, this would lead us to reformulate M by stating instead M' ≡ "the maintenance teams shall maintain the system with a certain performance"[57], which is now obviously stated as a need since it expresses an expectation of the environment of the system. The reader can do the same kind of exercise for the other classical "non-functional properties" of a system to convince him/herself that all these properties are just bad formulations of needs[58].

---

55 Since it also obviously does not directly refer to a property of the components of the system.

56 Strictly speaking, it indeed only refers to the system and not to its environment.

57 Which is now correctly written since "to maintain the system" is clearly a functional behavior of the maintenance teams.

58 Availability, operability, safety, reliability or security issues do, for instance, typically refer to expectations of customers, end-users and/or operators.

3.5. CESAM systems architecture matrix

We are now in position to introduce CESAM systems architecture matrix, which is presented in Table 3.6. This matrix is just a synthesis of the different architectural dimensions that we introduced within this chapter. It indeed presents all the types of views that allow us to exhaustively describe any system, classified according to:

– the first axis of classification corresponding to the three *architectural visions*, that is, the operational, functional and constructional vision;

– the second axis of classification corresponding to *behaviors*, that is, the conjunction of:

- *expected properties*,

- all types of *descriptions*, that is, states, static elements, dynamics and flows.

Mixing these two axes, one thus immediately gets the matrix of Table 3.6 where we listed the names of all different views that were introduced along the current section. As already stated above, the completeness of all these views in matter of system specification is an immediate consequence of all the material that we introduced along the previous pages.

Visions	Expected properties	Descriptions			
		States	Static elements	Dynamics	Flows
Operational vision	Needs	Operational contexts	Missions[59]	Operational scenarios	Operational flows or objects
Functional vision	Functional requirements	Functional modes	Functions[60]	Functional scenarios	Functional flows or objects
Constructional vision	Constructional requirements	Configurations	Components[61]	Constructional scenarios	Constructional flows or objects

Table 3.6. *The CESAM system architecture matrix*

59 Including descriptions of all integration mechanisms involving missions.

60 Including descriptions of all integration mechanisms involving functions.

61 Including descriptions of all integration mechanisms involving components.

As explained in section 3.4.3, one will of course always have to find a good balance between expected properties and descriptions when specifying a system. The CESAM system architecture matrix is thus only a help to ensure that all dimensions of a system were taken into account during its modeling, but it in no way provides – nor does the CESAM system architecting method – an automatic specification mechanism for systems. Systems architecture indeed remains an art where expertise, experience and competency of systems architects are clearly fundamental!

To concretely illustrate this last notion, let us now provide an example of a partially completed CESAM system architecture matrix for the electronic toothbrush.

Visions	Expected properties	Descriptions			
		States	Static elements	Dynamics	Flows
Operational vision	End-users want to have less than one cavity in average per 5 years due to teeth brushing	Teeth brushing	Brush teeth	Teeth brushing scenario	Toothpaste
Functional vision	The electronic toothbrush shall produce a brushing force of 0.5 N in automatic mode	Automatic mode	Produce a brushing force	Functional brushing force production scenario	Brushing force
Constructional vision	The electronic toothbrush shall have a removable head in children and adult configurations	Children configuration	Head	Constructional brushing force transmission scenario	Electricity

Table 3.7. *Example of a CESAM system architecture matrix for the electronic toothbrush*

One can now understand why system modeling is so unintuitive. If one completes a CESAM system architecture matrix by adding system abstraction/ integration levels, one may indeed understand that a system model looks much more like a cube than a matrix as depicted in Figure 3.20, which represents CESAM system architecture cube, the 3D-version of the 2D CESAM system architecture matrix. One can thus understand that it is easy to be lost in such a multi-dimensional world!

Note also that the three first descriptions types – that is, states, static elements and dynamics – are the most important since the last one – flows – is just a dedicated synthesis, focused on exchanges, which consolidates information that can already be found in the views corresponding to dynamics. Restricting the CESAM system architecture matrix to these three first descriptions types leads us thus to a simpler matrix – the so-called CESAM 9-views matrix[62] – which provides the minimal number of descriptions to construct when "modeling" a system[63]. An example of such CESAM 9-views matrix is provided below in the electronic toothbrush case study (see Figure 3.21).

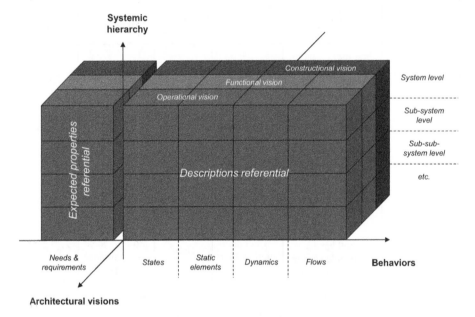

Figure 3.20. *CESAM system architecture cube. For a color version of this figure, see www.iste.co.uk/krob/systems.zip*

---

62 This terminology was invented by V. Vion from PSA Peugeot Citroën.

63 Beware that modeling is considered in this book in a broader way with respect to the usual meaning of this concept. Most authors, only refer to the construction of system descriptions, in the meaning of section 3.4.2.

At this point, note finally that the CESAM systems architecting method is nothing other than a certain way of moving in the CESAM system architecture matrix, starting from the knowledge of all use cases occurring in the system lifecycle, up to arriving at a precise vision on all constructional scenarios of the system. We will not develop this point here since the forthcoming chapters are dedicated to the presentation of the main deliverables of that architecting process.

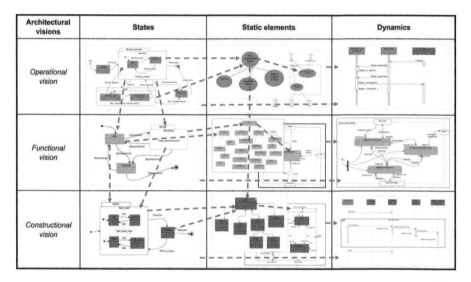

Figure 3.21. *Example of a CESAM 9-views matrix for an electronic toothbrush[64].*
For a color version of this figure, see www.iste.co.uk/krob/systems.zip

---

64 The example of the functional scenario, which is represented here, uses an activity diagram (see Booch *et al.* (2004)), which is an alternative to the mode of representation that we introduced and discussed previously for functional scenarios.

4

Identifying Stakeholders:
Environment Architecture

4.1. Why identify stakeholders?

Stakeholder identification, or equivalently environment architecture, is a key systemic analysis: each mistake in this analysis may indeed result in flaws in the product under design. We must indeed remember that a system is nothing other than a concrete answer to a series of needs[1] and that these needs are coming from external stakeholders. As an immediate consequence, forgetting important stakeholders, misevaluating their role and/or considering erroneous ones will result in missing needs and/or working with incorrect needs, and hence in missing requirements and/or working with wrong derived requirements, relatively to a given system. The resulting concrete system that might be developed on such a basis will therefore typically either miss the functions and components that are specifically addressing these missing needs, or have unnecessary functions and components that are associated with these incorrect needs. We can therefore easily understand the crucial importance of correctly identifying stakeholders – that is, the necessary and sufficient ones – since any system development process fundamentally relies on the quality of this identification.

To stress on this last point, we shall also have in mind the potential cost(s) of incorrect stakeholder identification which explain why we must put the necessary energy into this core initial analysis. In this matter, we commonly consider that such costs follow a geometric progression within the system lifecycle (see Figure 4.1): if

---

1 We recall that we are using here the term "need" in a technical way. A need indeed refers to any property expected (which would correspond to a need in the common sense) or imposed (which would rather correspond to a constraint in the common sense) by the environment of a given system (see section 3.4.2 for more details).

the correction of an error during stakeholder identification has cost 1 (i.e. typically adding a missing stakeholder or replacing an erroneous stakeholder in this analysis), we usually consider that correcting the consequence of that error will have cost 10 when done during system design, cost 100 when corrected during detailed design, cost 1,000 when discovered during integration and even cost 10,000 if managed when the system is in service. We must thus spend enough time initially in order to achieve an as-sound-as-possible environment architecture.

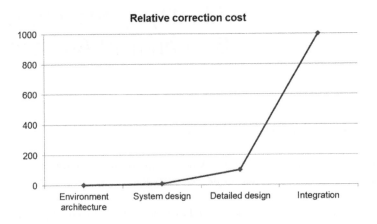

Figure 4.1. *Impact of an error in environment architecture. For a color version of this figure, see www.iste.co.uk/krob/systems.zip*

Any systems architect shall in particular always be highly anxious of being sure that stakeholders are correctly identified since the entire development process relies on that initial analysis!

Stakeholder identification may disrupt the nature of a design problem: the mobile industrial tool case

AVORE is an industrial company that produces heavy industrial electrical generators, each product having typically a weighfet of more than 100 tons. The average production duration of these electrical generators was unfortunately around one year, mainly a consequence of the absence of optimization of the industrial assembly lines of AVORE's plants.

An obvious reason for such a bad production delay was indeed related to the fact that the electrical generators were produced in an industrial chain, organized in three successive workshops where the generators were progressively assembled. Due to the huge weight of the generators, the logistical time required to move the generators from one workshop into the other represented 40% of the total construction time, which was not "lean" at all!

The method responsible of the Alsatian plant of AVORE had then a brilliant idea. Instead of moving the generators to the workshops, why not do the exact opposite and move the workshops to the generators, which would suppress a lot of stupidly lost time. Following this intuition, he launched a study for developing a mobile industrial tool – dedicated to the production activities of the second and third workshops of his plant – that would allow us to manage the construction of the generators without moving them.

The initial step of this study was logically dedicated to stakeholder identification. The first identified stakeholders were then naturally the plant, the industrial department of AVORE and the customers who would be the first beneficiaries of the new mobile industrial tool. In the second step, it was, however, understood that this tool had unfortunately a strong impact on another less important plant of AVORE, located in Normandy, which was dedicated to the absorption of the customer demands that the Alsatian plant could not manage. It indeed appeared that the increase of efficiency, brought by the mobile industrial tool, allowed the Alsatian plant to manage all customer requests, without any need of a supplementary plant.

The discovery of the Normandy plant as a new stakeholder radically changed the problem which was no longer a simple technical optimization question, but a deep political issue. Additional stakeholders emerged immediately: trade unions, local Norman politicians and finally AVORE's general direction who decided after two months of discussions to cancel the mobile industrial tool project in order to avoid any social trouble ...

Case study 4.1. *The mobile industrial tool case*

4.2. The key deliverables of environment architecture

For any system S, environment architecture has two core deliverables:

1) The *stakeholder hierarchy diagram* that hierarchizes all stakeholders associated with S – or equivalently external systems – according to an abstraction hierarchy (see below).

2) The *environment diagram* that describes the exchanges existing between S and its first-level stakeholders – or equivalently external systems – with respect to the above hierarchy.

These two deliverables are presented more in detail in the two below sections.

4.2.1. Stakeholder hierarchy diagram

Let S be a system and let Env(S) be its reference environment (see section 3.1). The *stakeholder hierarchy diagram* of S is then a hierarchical exhaustive representation of all stakeholders – or equivalently all external systems to S – that belong to Env(S), a stakeholder H1 being under another stakeholder H2 in this stakeholder hierarchy if and only if H1 is contained in H2 (simply viewed here as sets of elementary stakeholders), meaning that H1 is a special case of H2 or equivalently that H2 is more abstract than H1.

The project system is for instance a typical stakeholder, associated with any engineered system that is hierarchically abstract – in the above meaning – an engineering system, an industrialization system (including plants and industrial people), the supply chain and the delivery logistics. The engineering system may for instance be recursively hierarchically broken down into a project management team, a systems architecture team, different specialty engineering teams and a verification and validation team. The same type of recursive breakdown applies of course for all other first-order stakeholders.

Figure 4.2 below also provides an illustrative partial example of stakeholder hierarchy diagram for an electronic toothbrush, a stakeholder or equivalently an external system being – classically – represented here by a graphic depicting a person[2], when the inclusion or abstraction relationships on which this hierarchy relies are – also quite classically – represented by arrows.

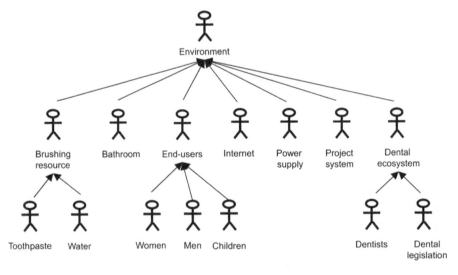

Figure 4.2. *Example of a stakeholder hierarchy diagram for an electronic toothbrush*

---

2 This is just a representation which may typically model any hardware, software or "humanware" system, as soon as they are part of the reference environment of the considered system.

When dealing with the stakeholder hierarchy diagram, the main standard difficulty is to find the "good" abstractions. We shall indeed avoid having too many first level stakeholders, as well as too many levels of abstractions, if we want to be able to efficiently use such a view. The 7x7x7 rule provides a simple trick to use in order to optimally organize this diagram. This ergonomic principle indeed claims that a human being can only holistically understand a maximum number of more or less 350^3 data, as far as they were hierarchically clustered into seven main groups of data, each of them again broken down into seven subgroups, each of them finally containing seven elementary data. The 7x7x7 principle is therefore a precious tool for organizing a stakeholder hierarchy diagram: the limitations of the human brain indeed oblige us to respect it when constructing such a diagram, as soon as we want to easily read and communicate with these diagrams. As a consequence, a typical "good" stakeholder hierarchy diagram has no more than seven high-level stakeholders, each of them broken down around seven medium-level stakeholders, refining finally into seven low-level stakeholders. Note of course that the number 7 shall just be taken as an order of magnitude. Obtaining up to 10–12 high-level stakeholders in a stakeholder hierarchy diagram would typically not be a heresy: however, we must not go further without at least checking whether this number is justified. Finally, we shall not hesitate to construct additional stakeholder hierarchy diagrams for refining such an initial analysis as soon as all relevant stakeholders are not captured.

4.2.2. Environment diagram

Again let S be a system and Env(S) be its reference environment (see section 3.1). The *environment diagram* of S is then a representation of:

– the system S and all the high-level stakeholders – or equivalently external systems to S – in the meaning of the stakeholder hierarchy introduced in the previous paragraph;

– all flows exchanged between the system and its stakeholders, that is, between S and the external systems of its reference environment.

Figure 4.3 gives an example of the environment diagram, here associated with an electronic toothbrush, taking the same representation for the stakeholders of Env(S) as in the previous stakeholder hierarchy diagram, when the system of interest S is modeled by a box.

---

3 We recall that 7 multiplied by 7, multiplied again by 7 makes 343.

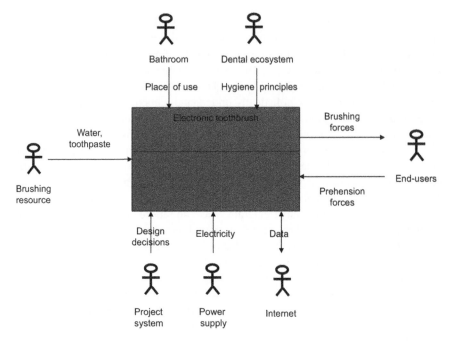

Figure 4.3. *Example of an environment diagram for an electronic toothbrush.
For a color version of this figure, see www.iste.co.uk/krob/systems.zip*

A classical way of organizing an environment diagram for a given system S consists of, respectively, positioning the following stakeholders, that is, external systems, in the four quadrants of the diagram:

– in the left hand-side of the diagram: key input systems of S;

– in the right-hand side of the diagram: key output systems of S;

– in the top of the diagram: key constraining systems with respect to S;

– in the bottom of the diagram: key resource systems with respect to S.

These key input, output, constraining and resource systems associated with S within the environment diagram will be, respectively, denoted below by I(S), O(S), C(S) and R(S).

Note that the environment diagram of Figure 4.3 is for instance typically organized in such a way. This mode of representation is useful since it equips such a diagram with a natural semantics. We may indeed automatically read the mission of the considered system on any environment diagram which is organized in such a way using the pattern given in Table 4.1.

Pattern of the mission statement of a system S
The system S shall transform inputs of I(S) into outputs of O(S) under constraints C(S) and with resources R(S).

Table 4.1. *Pattern of the mission statement of a system*

In a similar way, functional analysis is also naturally oriented by such a representation mode. The core functions of a system S are indeed then the functions that are connecting the input systems I(S) to the output systems O(S), when the piloting and the support functions of S are the functions that are mainly exchanging with, respectively, the constraining systems C(S) and the resource systems R(S).

The environment diagram is thus a very important diagram which induces structuring architectural orientations for a system. It can also be used for monitoring the first systems architecting activities. A good environment architecture shall indeed fundamentally always be well balanced: the number of lower-level stakeholders or of needs per high-level stakeholder shall typically be more or less the same. Any difference of balance in these numbers shall therefore necessarily puzzle the good systems architect who must question it, in order to find whether there is a rational explanation for it, which of course is the case (see Appendix 2 for an example of this situation). As we can see, the environment diagram is a very rich diagram and a precious tool for the systems architect!

5

Understanding Interactions with Stakeholders: Operational Architecture

5.1. Why understand interactions with stakeholders?

Operational architecture, or equivalently operational analysis, intends to precisely understand the interactions over time between the system of interest and the external systems of its reference environment, or equivalently of its stakeholders. Motivations of environment architecture, as already discussed in section 4.1, also apply in exactly the same terms – *mutatis mutandis* – to operational architecture. As for stakeholder identification, any forgetfulness, misunderstanding or error that could occur during the operational architecture process may indeed have disastrous – and usually costly – consequences on a system under development.

As previously pointed out in section 4.1, we must indeed understand that any function and any component of a system ultimately intend to provide an answer to a stakeholder and thus are always involved in the different interactions that are taking place between the system and its environment (of reference). We can therefore just not design – at least with a reasonable level of confidence – the different functions or components of a system without understanding the missions to which they contribute. Many design mistakes are typically done when designers do not have any precise idea of the various operational contexts in which the system they are developing will be used. We can thus only stress here the imperious necessity of always managing operational architecture in any systems architecting process, which will moreover allow us to bring back "meaning" to the end-engineer who is working on a little part of a large system. Medieval cathedrals – whose construction took centuries – would probably never have been built if all involved workers had not had a deep understanding of the global target to which they were contributing….[1]

The decoupling between operational architecture and both functional and constructional architecture is also fundamental. This apparently simple principle is in fact much more subtle than it seems. It typically allows us to develop systems that have very different operational architectures, but similar functional and constructional architectures. This is the principle of product lines where we construct "flexible" systems which have a very large customer diversity – in order to fit as closely as possible to the needs of the market – but with a very low technical diversity[2]. The idea is to develop a family of systems with a very large number of operational architectures, corresponding to different customer needs, on the basis of, on the first hand, standard functional and constructional elements (usually corresponding to everything that the customer does not see) and, on the second hand, a limited number of additional specific functional and constructional elements that are capturing the operational – or equivalently here the customer – diversity (and thus the business value which is perceived by the customer). Such an approach allows us to deliver highly customized products to the customer that are constructed using only standard modules. Many industries – automotive, consumer electronics and even food and beverage[3] – are using with success this type of architecture for their products.

Despite its core importance as stressed above, operational architecture is unfortunately still an analysis which is not well known and often not practiced at all, probably since it may be considered as not sufficiently technical and concrete (engineers usually like to quickly jump into technique …). We thus must emphasize

---

1 In "The announcement to Mary", a play written by the French writer P. Claudel whose action takes place in the Middle-Age during the construction of the Saint-Rémi church in Reims – France, two sculptors are working on a little statue located in the front of the church. One asks them what they are doing and they are answering: "we are building a cathedral"!

2 This last principle is the basis of *diversity management* whose purpose is to maintain in configuration among time such flexible architectures.

3 All types of Danone or Nestlé yoghurts are for instance made using the same white mass (standard module #1) and the same preforms, that is, tubes from which different types of cups are produced through adapted blowing (standard module #2). When making a yoghurt, the industrial process begins by creating a "generic" type of yoghurt, before adding the specific additives (or specific modules) that are given various flavors to yoghurts. This principle is called *late differentiation*: it allows us to quickly react when a competitor launches a new product or when the customer taste evolves, since we just need changing the last machines of the industrial chain to adapt, without reorganizing, the full chain (which takes time and money).

the value of operational architecture which is – even if apparently not too technical[4] – a core technical analysis that can only be done by a systems architect. We shall indeed understand that operational architecture deliverables are structured in order to be easily mapped with functional and constructional deliverables. Thus, it is just impossible to perform any operational architecting without precisely understanding its functional and constructional consequences, which can only be done by a technical-minded person, typically a systems architect.

A typical lack of operational architecture: the Airbus A400M Atlas Case

The Airbus A400M Atlas is a multi-national, 4-engine turboprop, military transport aircraft. It was designed by Airbus in order to replace older transport aircrafts, such as the Transall C-160 and the Lockheed C-130 Hercules. The project initiated in the early 1982, within the Future International Military Airlifter (FIMA) group which was set up jointly by Aérospatiale (France), British Aerospace (Great-Britain), Lockheed (USA) and Messerschmitt (Germany), when the first flight of the A400M took only place on December 2009 in Seville, Spain, as a result of a tremendous number of development program delays (that moreover also lead to huge cost overruns, as we could have expected).

The root cause of these problems can probably be traced back to the requested operational architecture for this aircraft. The A400M was indeed requested to support both tactical (i.e. managing supplies and equipment transportation to a theater of military operations) and strategic (i.e. transporting material, weaponry or personnel over long distances) missions. But it happens that these two operational contexts are radically different: on the one hand, the tactical context requires the aircraft to manage short landing and take-off distances and to have low-pressure tires allowing operations from small or poorly prepared airstrips; on the other hand, the strategic context is characterized by long landing and take-off distances and by high-pressure tires for moving heavy charges at normal military airports. We could also of course observe similar discrepancies at the level of the aircraft control logics. Thus, as we can easily guess, implementing these two very different opposite use cases in the same constructional architecture is not a "piece of cake"[5].

Case study 5.1. *The Airbus A400M Atlas Case*

---

4 Operational architecture can indeed be seen as an interface between the stakeholder and the engineer worlds, since it offers a language that can be understood both by stakeholders and engineers, which explains its apparent simplicity.

5 This case study also illustrates that the operational architecture cannot be done in isolation. We must always understand and validate its functional and constructional consequences before freezing an operational architecture.

5.2. The key deliverables of operational architecture

For any system S, operational architecture has five core types of deliverables:

1) The *need architecture diagram* that hierarchically organizes all needs – with respect to S – according to a refinement hierarchy (see below).

2) The *lifecycle diagram* that describes how S passes – with indication of the associated events – from an operational context to another one, starting from its birth up to its death.

3) The *use case diagrams* that are describing – in a purely static way – the missions of S that are contributing to a given operational context.

4) The *operational scenario diagrams* that are describing – in a dynamic way – the interactions taking place between S and its stakeholders[6] in a given operational context.

5) The *operational flow diagrams* that synthetize all flows – with their logical relationships – exchanged between S and its reference environment during the lifecycle of S.

These different types of deliverables are presented in more detail below.

5.2.1. *Need architecture diagram*

Let S be a system. The *need architecture diagram* of S is then a hierarchical exhaustive representation of all needs with respect to S, a need N1 being under another need N2 in this hierarchy if and only if we can logically deduce N1 from N2[7]. In this last situation, we say then more precisely that N2 refines into N1, which explains why we speak of a need refinement hierarchy[8].

Figure 5.1 below shows a (partial) need architecture diagram for an electronic toothbrush, a need being – classically – represented by a two-part box, whose first top part is a short name summarizing the need scope and whose second bottom part is the need statement, when the refinement relationships on which the need hierarchy relies are – also classically – represented by arrows.

---

6 Or equivalently external systems.

7 Remember that needs are logical predicates (see section 3.4.2).

8 An additional important property of a need architecture is *coverage*: we shall try to construct the need architecture diagram in order to maintain the coverage logical property which states that $N1 \land ... \land Nn \rightarrow N0$ for all needs N1, ..., Nn which are under a given need N0 in such a hierarchical diagram.

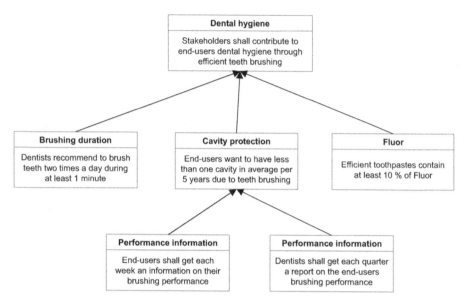

Figure 5.1. *Example of a need architecture diagram for an electronic toothbrush. For a color version of this figure, see www.iste.co.uk/krob/systems.zip*

The same issue that was already pointed out in the first part of section 4.2 when dealing with the stakeholder hierarchy diagram can also be expressed – more or less in the same terms – with the need architecture diagram: organizing a need refinement hierarchy is indeed always difficult since we shall avoid having too many first level needs, as well as too many levels of refinements if we want to be able to efficiently use such a view. The 7x7x7 rule (see the first part of section 4.2) is again precious to handle this real difficulty. As a consequence, a typical "good" need architecture diagram associated with a given system shall have no more than seven high-level needs, each of them refined in around seven medium-level needs, finally also refining in the same way into seven low-level needs. Note again that the number 7 shall of course be just taken as an order of magnitude. Obtaining up to 10–12 high-level needs in a need architecture diagram could of course work: however, we must probably not go further without analyzing whether this number is justified. Finally, we shall not hesitate to construct additional need architecture diagrams for refining such an analysis as soon as all relevant needs are not captured.

5.2.2. *Lifecycle diagram*

Again let S be a system. The *lifecycle diagram* of S is then a representation of:

– the operational contexts of S, with their relative temporal relationships, that is, consecutiveness, inclusion or simultaneity[9];

– the events that cause the different transitions between each operational context of S and the immediately consecutive ones.

To draw such a diagram, we shall give the standard representations of the three temporal relations between operational contexts that we introduced above, which are provided by Table 5.1, where C and D stand for generic operational contexts. Remember here that operational contexts are modeled by ovals, as introduced in the first paragraph of section 3.4.2.

Temporal relation	Semantics	Graphic representation
Consecutiveness	D is consecutive to C when a termination event of C is exactly equal to an initiation event of D	
Inclusion	D is included in C when the period of time underlying D is contained in the period of time underlying C	
Simultaneity	D is simultaneous to C when the periods of time underlying C and D are exactly equal	

Table 5.1. *Graphic representations of temporal relationships between operational contexts. For a color version of this table, see www.iste.co.uk/krob/systems.zip*

Figure 5.2 below provides an illustrative lifecycle diagram associated with an electronic toothbrush, taking here the standard representation of operational contexts and of their temporal relationships that we introduced. Events – that induce operational context transitions – are modeled by arrows labeled with the name of the relevant event. Note, however, that the initial (respectively, termination) events in each operational context do not respect this rule since they are conventionally

---

9 These three temporal relations are necessary and sufficient to model any temporal relationships between operational contexts among a system lifecycle. To be convinced of that claim, let us analyze the only embarrassing situation of two intervals of times P and Q that overlap, that is, such that P = [s, t] and Q = [u, v] with u < t. We can model such a situation with our temporal relations by first breaking down P into P1 = [s, u] and P2 = [u, t] and Q into Q1 = [u, t] and Q2 = [t, v], and observing then that P2 is consecutive to P1, Q1 is simultaneous to P2 and Q2 is consecutive to Q1.

modeled by small black circles (respectively, by white circles containing a black circle).

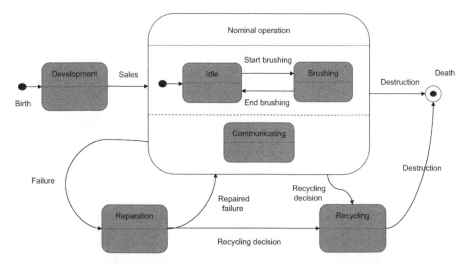

Figure 5.2. *Example of the lifecycle diagram for an electronic toothbrush. For a color version of this figure, see www.iste.co.uk/krob/systems.zip*

We may finally notice that there is a perfect symmetry between the environment diagram, which models the space in which evolves a system, and the lifecycle diagram, which models the periods of time through which a system passes. Since both space and time are always required to specify any system behavior (that necessarily takes place somewhere during a certain period of time), we can easily see that these two diagrams are equally important to specify any system.

5.2.3. *Use case diagrams*

Let S be a system, let Env(S) be its reference environment and let q(S) be an operational context of S. A *use case diagram* associated with S and q(S) is then a static representation of the missions achieved through the collaboration of S and its external systems within Env(S), during the period of time that is modeled by q(S), which explicitly specifies:

1) the external systems of the environment of S that are contributing to each mission;

2) the missions that contribute to another mission.

Note that it is sometimes necessary, when modeling a use case diagram, to also represent behaviors of Env(S) in which the system S is not contributing at all. This is done by just indicating that S is not contributing to such a function of Env(S).

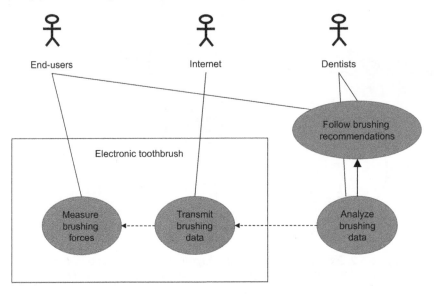

Figure 5.3. *Example of a use case diagram for an electronic toothbrush. For a color version of this figure, see www.iste.co.uk/krob/systems.zip*

Figure 5.3 that follows provides an example of a use case diagram, associated with the "brushing data transmission" operational context of an electrical toothbrush. The square represents the system of interest, and we used again the "person" representation to model its stakeholders. A mission is (respectively, not) placed in the square when the system of interest contributes (respectively, does not contribute) to it. In the same way, we put a line between a stakeholder and a mission when the considered stakeholder contributes to such a mission[10]. We also indicate using a rigid arrow when a mission contributes to another mission and using a dashed arrow when a given mission M_1 is mandatory to manage another one M_2. Beware at that last level since the standard convention in this matter is highly counter-intuitive: we indeed model such a situation by putting a dashed arrow from M_2 to M_1 and not the converse. Note finally that it is interesting to observe in that example that the motivation of the "brushing data transmission" cannot be found in

10 Let UC(S) be a use case diagram associated with a given system S. A mission which is put in the square part of UC(S) and which is connected through lines to stakeholders $S_1, \ldots, S_n$ within UC(S) is then formally a function of the system resulting from the integration of S with S_1 up to S_n.

a mission of the electronic toothbrush, but rather in the "follow brushing recommendations" which is an environment function involving only end-users and dentists, but not the electronic toothbrush. We can then easily understand the value of a use case diagram on such a situation since it would clearly not be possible to describe, without a specific environment-oriented formalism, such a situation.

It is interesting to point out that if we consider the special – limit – case of the operational context equal to the complete lifecycle of a given system S, the associated use case diagram would especially provide a hierarchical representation of all missions of S, jointly with the indication of the different stakeholders that are contributing to each mission of the system. For the sake of readability, we can of course break down that last use case diagram into the two following use case diagrams:

1) The first provides a hierarchical representation of all missions of S, which shall be naturally called the *Mission Breakdown Structure* (MBS) of S[11].

2) The second provides the indication of the stakeholders that contribute to each mission of the system, whose semantics is equivalent to a *mission to stakeholder allocation matrix*.

Note finally that if no hierarchically related missions occur when modeling a given use case diagram, the semantics of such a diagram is completely contained within the associated operational scenario diagram (see the next section). We shall in particular notice that a use case diagram is useless when we have the associated operational scenario diagram (the converse being not true).

5.2.4. *Operational scenario diagrams*

Let again S be a system, Env(S) be its reference environment and q(S) be an operational context of S. An *operational scenario diagram* associated with S and q(S) is then a dynamic representation of the missions achieved through the collaboration of S and its external systems within Env(S), during the period of time modeled by q(S), which explicitly specifies all interactions occurring between S and the stakeholders – or equivalently the external systems – of its reference environment.

---

11 If one decides to model such a mission breakdown structure (MBS), one must beware to the readability of such a view. All the recommendations based on the 7x7x7 rule that we previously gave for the stakeholder and the need architecture diagrams will then of course also apply – *mutatis mutandis* – in order to efficiently model the MBS.

Figure 5.4 shows an example of an operational scenario diagram, associated with the "reparation" operational context of an electrical toothbrush. We refer to the suitable paragraph of section 3.4.2 for all details on the semantics of the below representation.

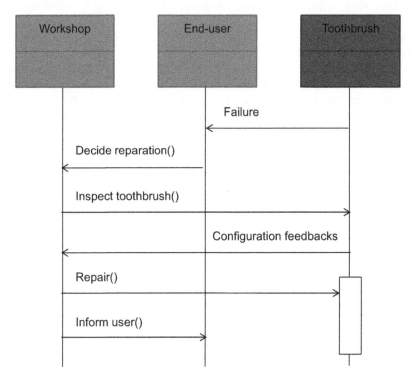

Figure 5.4. *Example of operational scenario diagram for an electronic toothbrush. For a color version of this figure, see www.iste.co.uk/krob/systems.zip*

An operational scenario diagram provides, therefore, an explicit algorithmic description which models the behavior of the environment of a given system during a given operational context. As already stated in the last paragraph, we must always choose whether to use either a use case diagram or an operational scenario diagram, to specify an operational context, when no hierarchically related missions occur within the use case diagram, since this last diagram will not add any semantics to the corresponding operational scenario diagram.

5.2.5. *Operational flow diagram*

Let S be a system. The *operational flow diagram* associated with S is a consolidated description of all operational flows associated with S and of:

1) their logical relationships;

2) their abstraction relationships[12].

This new diagram thus plays the role of the operational "data model"[13] of the system. Note that we may also split this diagram into two diagrams, each of them covering the two above points.

Figure 5.5 below shows an example of (partial) operational flow diagram, associated with an electrical toothbrush. The different logical relationships, which exist between the various operational flows (or objects) represented in that diagram, are modeled by rigid lines (without any arrow) labeled with the denomination of the corresponding relationship. Note that we usually use a verb – in the third form of singular – to name such a logical relation: in an operational flow diagram, the line connecting a flow of type A with a flow of type B that represents a logical relation between A and B is typically labeled by a verb such as "is related to" in order to express that "A is related to B" or that "B is related to A". To avoid ambiguity, we place the relationship denomination closer to the first term of such a logical relationship[14].

We may also put on the extremity of these lines an indication of the *arity* of the relationships: if n operational flows of type A can be associated with m operational flows of type B within a given logical relation, we just put a label with "n" (respectively, "m") at the A-extremity (respectively, B-extremity) of the line put between A and B that models the corresponding relation (we recall that (n,m) is called the arity of such a logical relationship). Note also that, by convention, we put "*" instead of a natural number when there are no known limits to the number of involved elements.

---

12 We recall that a flow A is abstracted by a flow B if and only if A is a special instance of B. As an example, matter is for instance abstracted by energy in relativist mechanics.

13 Beware that, even if we use the syntax of a data model for the operational flow diagram, this last diagram is not really a data model since it does not represent (only) data, but also physical objects, business objects or even informal information that may be exchanged by "humanware" stakeholders of a given system.

14 Strictly speaking, we should put two labels on each line between any flow A and any flow B in order to express both the logical relations between A and B and between B and A. However, this would be too heavy which explains our convention.

Finally, on another totally different hand, the possible abstraction relationships that are provided in the above diagram are modeled – according to a classical convention – by squared arrows.

As already stated, the operational flow diagram defines the operational flow or object model of a given system. It is completely "dual" to the environment, use case or operational scenario diagrams since it focuses on flows, and not on the different functions, either of the system or of its reference environment, that are producing these flows. Unfortunately, most of the engineers, who usually do not have any computer science or software engineering background, do not understand the importance and the value of this new type of flow-oriented diagram …

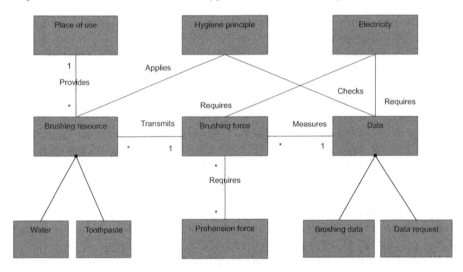

Figure 5.5. *Example of operational flow diagram for an electronic toothbrush.*
For a color version of this figure, see www.iste.co.uk/krob/systems.zip

We must therefore emphasize that such a diagram is of high importance since it rationally describes in a consolidated and organized way all inputs and all outputs of a given system. Hence, it gives the operational "dictionary" of the system, that is, the list of all the objects that are operationally manipulated by the system. This dictionary is of high value for ensuring a common vision between all project actors involved in the operational architecting process: these actors shall normally – in an ideal world – only use the terms of that dictionary when discussing an operational object. We may easily understand that such a principle allows us to avoid any ambiguity between the system designers and the project system stakeholders, as well as within the different specialty engineers. It is thus key for ensuring a good collaboration between all these actors.

6

Defining What the System Shall Do: Functional Architecture

6.1. Why understand what the system does?

Functional architecture, or equivalently functional analysis, intends to precisely describe the different functions of a system and their relative interactions[1]. The core motivation of functional architecture is to start understanding and specifying in detail the system, but only in terms of behaviors – that is, in other terms, to understand and specify what the system does – and not concrete structure, that is, its functional nature ... as we would have easily guessed!

It is indeed important to have first a functional description of a system, and not to immediately dig into the technique, if we want to be able to rationally manage trade-offs between different options[2]. Functional architecture is indeed usually independent of the technological choices[3] at least at some level of abstraction,

---

1 And also, how these functions are connected to missions. This point – even if important – will, however, not be addressed in this book since it can be easily addressed through a suitable mission to function allocation matrix.

2 Functional architecture allows in particular us to make early cost analysis, as soon as we have an idea of the average cost of an elementary function (see also the Constructive Cost Model for Systems – COSYSMO – Valerdi (2008)). Such a feature is especially interesting for trade-offs that may also be done at the functional level (typically in order to choose between two competing functional architectures for a given system).

3 The "produce torque" car function is for instance totally independent of the technology: it exists in any car, either with a thermic, or an electrical engine.

which means that functionally reasoning – of course at the good level of abstraction[4] – on a system allows us to reason at the same time on many different constructional options that we will be able to compare and to evaluate later (for more details, see Chapter 9 which is dedicated to trade-off analyses). We must indeed understand that skipping functional analysis by directly going to technical design is usually a very bad practice, even if widespread in engineering organizations, since it just means that we are making a very strong design choice without even being conscious of that choice. As a consequence, we will just be glued in that choice, without being able to move to radically different options that might be more adapted.

We must also stress that functional architecture is absolutely fundamental to capturing emergence and transversal behaviors that can only be modeled using its tools. By definition, all emergent behaviors can indeed not be captured by constructional architecture since they are functional properties of an integrated system (we refer to section 1.2 for more details). We must hence use functional architecture to describe and model such properties. As an immediate consequence, functional architecture is a key tool to structure transversal collaboration in an engineering organization whose purpose is indeed to efficiently manage the emergent transversal behaviors of a system.

Last, but not least, functional architecture also allows us to organize a system in functionally decoupled – as much as possible – sub-systems. This is very important if we want to avoid too many impacts when there is a change in a system design[5]. As already pointed out previously, this idea gives rise to layered functional architectures where each functional layer is strictly functionally segregated from the other ones by fixed standard functional interfaces that are managed in configuration. This architectural functional segregation/decoupling principle provides huge flexibility: in an ideal world, we will indeed be able to change a function in one layer without any impact on the other layers, as soon as the functional interfaces between layers are respected. We refer to the concrete examples of systems organized according to such a principle that are provided in the example section of Introduction and in the functional architecture subsection of section 3.2.

---

4 As a consequence of that simple remark, functional architecture is absolutely of NO USE if its analyses go into too much detail. A detailed functional architecture indeed usually either 1) overlaps with constructional architecture, as soon as the detailed functions identify with the high-level functions of the components of the system of interest, or 2) is totally misaligned with the constructional architecture (which means that the identified functions do not naturally map with the components). In the first case, functional architecture overlaps with constructional architecture since the two analyses provide exactly the same semantics. In the second case, functional architecture is dangerous since its results – which have here no concrete value – may mislead the system designers. In the two cases, it is therefore a waste of time and money.

5 See the case study 7.1 in the next chapter to see what can unfortunately happen in the case of a design evolution …

Transversal behaviors are crucial to master: the airport radar case

ALTHEIS is a leading airport radar company in the world. They developed a new airport radar on the basis of a modular generic functional architecture, each generic functional module being allocated to a certain part of a radar processing chain and managed by a dedicated engineering team. The idea was to replace development, when dealing with a specific radar deployment, by parameterization. Each generic functional module had thus to be specifically parameterized when instantiated on a given concrete airport application.

However, the overall number of parameters to manage was quite high: around 1 million elementary parameters that could be organized in around 50,000 high-level parameters, each of them with a specific business meaning, were indeed managed by the development engineers. This huge complexity led initially to what could have become a real industrial disaster: when an airport radar was parameterized and put in service, it happened that the radar never stabilized, since bugs were permanently appearing on the field, which regularly obliged the radar to go back to the factory to be reparameterized, which could only be done by development team experts due to the technicity of the parameterization. This situation was terribly uncomfortable and clearly economically not sustainable[6].

CESAMES was appointed to analyze and to try to solve that issue. It appeared that its root cause was connected to the lack of a shared and explicit radar functional architecture. When the parameterization was initially done, each team in charge was indeed not conscious at all of its functional interdependence – through transversal functions – with the other teams. As a consequence, each parameterization done locally, at the level of one single team, was in conflict with the other parameterizations, which lead to the observed problems.

The solution – provided by CESAMES – was to architect all parameters in alignment with the radar functional breakdown structure (FBS), by clustering the parameters according to the different functions of the FBS. A parameter architecture team – managed by a functional architect – was then created to manage, guarantee and maintain among time the functional coherence of each of all these parameter clusters.

Case study 6.1. *The airport radar case*

6.2. The key deliverables of functional architecture

For any system S, functional architecture has five core types of deliverables:

---

6 A radar business model is indeed based on, first, a fixed initial price that just covers development costs and, secondly, a yearly maintenance fees on which the radar constructor is making its benefit. We can therefore easily understand that permanent bugs are just destroying such a radar business model.

1) The *functional requirement architecture diagram* that hierarchically organizes all functional requirements – with respect to S – according to a refinement hierarchy.

2) The *functional mode diagram* that describes how S passes – with indication of the associated events – from a functional mode to another one, starting from its birth up to its death.

3) The *functional breakdown and interaction diagrams* that are describing – in a purely static way – the functions of S with their internal and external interactions[7].

4) The *functional scenario diagrams* that are describing – in a dynamic way – the interactions between the functions of S and possibly the environment, in a given functional mode.

5) The *functional flow diagrams* that synthetize all flows – with their logical relationships – absorbed or produced by the functions of S during the "functional mode cycle"[8] of S.

These different types of deliverables are presented more in detail below.

6.2.1. *Functional requirement architecture diagram*

Let S be a system. The *functional requirement architecture diagram* of S is then a hierarchical exhaustive representation of all functional requirements of S, a functional requirement R1 being under another functional requirement R2 in this hierarchy if and only if we can logically deduce R1 from R2[9]. In this last situation, we say then more precisely that R2 refines into R1, which explains why we speak of a functional requirement refinement hierarchy[10].

Figure 6.1 illustrates here a (partial) functional requirement architecture diagram for an electronic toothbrush, a functional requirement being – classically and similarly to a need – represented here by a 2-part box, whose first top part is a short name summarizing the functional requirement scope and whose second bottom part is the functional requirement statement, the refinement relations, on which relies the functional requirement hierarchy, being – also classically – represented by arrows.

---

7 Usually, only at the global level, as well as possibly in only a given functional mode.

8 That is, the period of time modeled by the functional mode diagram.

9 Remember that functional requirements are logical predicates (see section 3.4.2).

10 An additional important property of a functional requirement architecture is *coverage*: we shall try to construct the functional requirement architecture diagram in order to maintain the coverage logical property $FR1 \wedge ... \wedge FRn \rightarrow FR0$ for all functional requirements FR1, ..., FRn which are under a given functional requirement FR0 in such a diagram.

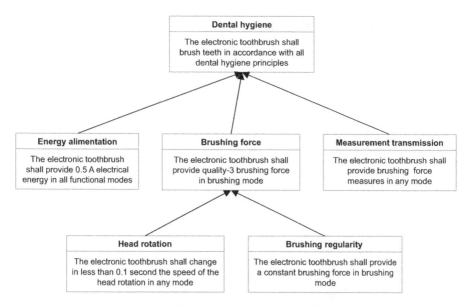

Figure 6.1. *Example of a functional requirement architecture diagram for an electronic toothbrush*

Note that the same issue, already pointed out for the need requirement architecture diagram, also takes place with the functional requirement architecture diagram: organizing a functional requirement refinement hierarchy is indeed always difficult since we shall avoid having too many first level functional requirements, but of course also too many levels of refinements, if we want to be able to efficiently use such a view. The 7x7x7 rule (see the first part of section 4.2) is again a precious tool to handle this real difficulty. As a consequence, a typical "good" functional requirement architecture diagram associated with a system shall have no more than seven high-level functional requirements, each of them refined in around seven medium-level functional requirements, finally also refining in the same way into seven low-level functional requirements. Note again that the number 7 shall just be taken as an order of magnitude. Obtaining up to 10–12 high-level functional requirements in a functional requirement architecture diagram could of course work: however, we must not go further without analyzing whether this number is justified. Finally, we shall not hesitate to construct as many additional functional requirement architecture diagrams as necessary, for refining such an analysis as soon as all relevant functional requirements are not derived and/or captured.

6.2.2. *Functional mode diagram*

Let S be again a system. The *functional mode diagram* of S is then a representation of:

– the functional modes of S, with their relative temporal relationships, that is, consecutiveness, inclusion or simultaneity[11];

– the events that cause the different transitions between each functional mode of S and the immediate consecutive ones from a temporal perspective.

The standard representations of the temporal relations between functional modes introduced above are given – *mutatis mutandis* – by Table 5.1, if we now interpret C and D as functional modes.

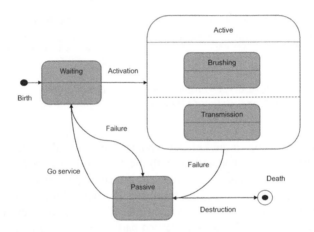

Figure 6.2. *Example of functional mode diagram for an electronic toothbrush*

The above Figure 6.2 provides in particular an illustrative functional mode diagram associated with an electronic toothbrush, taking here the standard representation of functional modes and of their temporal relationships that we introduced, when events – that induce functional mode transitions – are modeled by arrows labeled with the name of the relevant event. Note also that the initial (respectively, termination) events in each functional mode do not respect this rule since they are conventionally modeled by small black circles (respectively, by white circles containing a black circle).

It is finally important to understand that the functional mode diagram is key since it models – from a functional perspective – time. Following the intuition that

---

11 We refer to the second paragraph of section 5.2 in this matter.

we developed at the end of the second paragraph of section 5.2, we could say that the next diagrams – that is, the functional breakdown and interaction diagrams – are modeling the "functional space" in which functions are evolving. Since space and time are always required to specify any functional behavior (that takes place "functionally somewhere" at a certain time), these two diagrams are completely complementary.

6.2.3. *Functional breakdown and interaction diagrams*

Let S be a system. The *functional breakdown diagram* associated with S is then a hierarchical representation of the functions of S, a set F1, F2, …, FN of functions being under another function G in this hierarchy if G is the result of the integration – in the meaning of Definition 1.5[12] – of the functions F1, …, FN[13] (F1, …., FN are then classically called "sub-functions" of G). The *functional interaction diagrams* associated with S are then just the different representations – there is one functional interaction diagram per integration relationship involved in the functional breakdown diagram – of each such integration relationship that exists between the different functions appearing in the hierarchy modeled by the functional breakdown diagram.

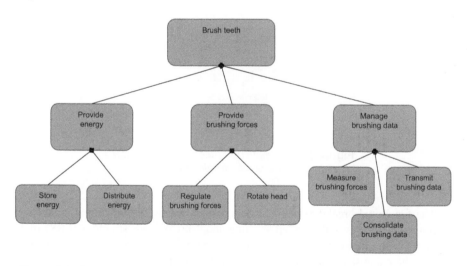

Figure 6.3. *Example of a functional breakdown diagram for an electronic toothbrush*

---

12 Considered here uniquely for its functional scope.

13 Due to our definition of the integration operator, this hierarchy is therefore an abstraction hierarchy.

Figure 6.3 above now provides an illustrative partial example of the functional breakdown diagram for an electronic toothbrush, where the integration relationships on which this hierarchy relies are – quite classically – represented by squared arrows.

We also give an example of a functional interaction diagram for an electronic toothbrush that can be found in Figure 6.4. In this example, we modeled the integration relationship existing between the global function of the toothbrush and its first "sub-functions" (using the formalism of a classical "activity diagram" in the UML or SysML meaning; see Booch *et al.* (2004) or Friedenthal *et al.* (2012)). Note also that external interfaces are here – quite classically – represented by white squares at the border of the external oval that is representing the integrated function (here the global function of an electronic toothbrush).

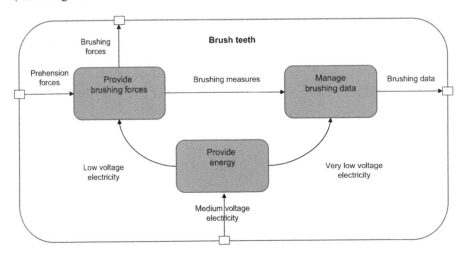

Figure 6.4. *Example of a functional interaction diagram for an electronic toothbrush*

The functional breakdown of a system S modeled by the functional breakdown diagram is also classically called the functional breakdown structure (FBS) of S. Similarly to the mission breakdown structure that we introduced in the last chapter, it gives the exhaustive dictionary of the functions of the system and thus has a key role in guaranteeing a common understanding on the functional scope of a system, which is mandatory for an efficient transversal collaboration between the different actors and stakeholders of a system development project.

We must, however, be aware of the readability of such a view. All the recommendations based on the 7x7x7 rule that we previously gave for the stakeholder and need architecture diagrams of course also apply – *mutatis mutandis* – to efficiently model the functional breakdown structure of a system.

Last, but not least, we refer to Figure 1.9 in Chapter 1 for a concrete functional interaction diagram associated with an aircraft: it represents how all first-level sub-functions may be integrated to obtain the high-level global function of an aircraft. Other examples of concrete functional interaction diagrams may also be found in the example section of Introduction.

6.2.4. *Functional scenario diagrams*

Let S again be a system and q(S) a functional mode of S. A *functional scenario diagram* associated with S and q(S) is then a dynamic representation of the interactions that are taking place between the functions of S, and possibly the environment, during the period of time which is modeled by q(S).

The below Figure 6.5 shows an example of functional scenario diagram, associated with the "active" functional mode of an electrical toothbrush. We refer to the suitable paragraph of section 3.4.2 for the fundamentals of the semantics of this representation. However, we are obliged to introduce richer semantics with respect to the one that was introduced in section 3.4.2. The below diagram indeed expresses that, as far as the electronic toothbrush is in an active mode (which was modeled by the big box with "loop" on its top left and the "[active mode]" indication[14] in its top middle), it shall do in parallel (which was modeled by the big box with "par" on its top left), that is, at the same time, three types of operations (that are separated by dashed lines in the "par" big box): the first one being brushing force management, the second one being brushing data management and the third one being energy management. For the sake of completeness, we shall also know that there exists an "alt" (for alternative) box which allows us to express "if then otherwise" situations[15].

A functional scenario diagram provides the explicit "algorithm" which is underlying to the functional behavior of the system in a given functional mode. This is key to finally understanding what – at least functionally – happens during a given

---

14 This indication means "as soon as". Hence, we meant here "as soon as the system is in active mode".

15 The "if then else" situation is expressed by a big box labeled "alt" on its top right, split into two parts – Part 1 (top) and Part 2 (bottom) – separated by a dashed line, with a "condition" statement at its top middle. Its semantics is that when the "condition" is satisfied (respectively, not satisfied), the system shall do the instructions of Part1 (respectively, Part 2).

functional mode. The enriched semantics that we introduced indeed allows us to express any distributed algorithmic property of a system[16].

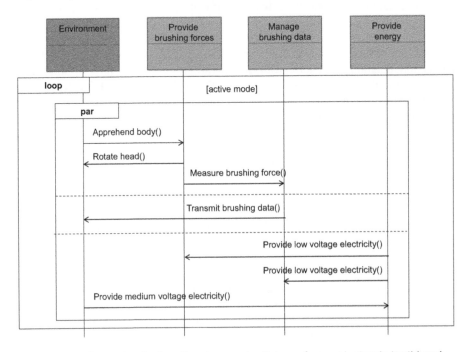

Figure 6.5. *Example of a functional scenario diagram for an electronic toothbrush. For a color version of this figure, see www.iste.co.uk/krob/systems.zip*

6.2.5. *Functional flow diagram*

Let S be a system. The *functional flow diagram* associated with S is a consolidated description of all the functional flows associated with S and of:

1) their logical relationships;

2) their abstraction relationships (see the last paragraph of Chapter 5).

---

16 This comes from the fact that the usual algorithms only require the "while" (modeled by the "loop" box) and the "if then else" (modeled by the "alt" box) operators. When we pass to distributed – that is, parallel – algorithms, it is then sufficient to add the "parallel" operator (modeled by the "par" box) to get full expressivity.

Hence, it plays the role of the functional "data model"[17] of the system. Note that we also may split this diagram into two diagrams, each of them covering the two above points.

Figure 6.6 below shows an example of (partial) functional flow diagram, associated with an electrical toothbrush. Its syntax exactly follows the same principles as the operational flow diagram (see the last section of Chapter 5).

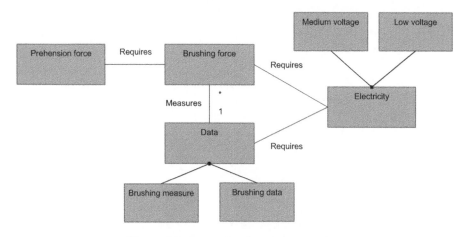

Figure 6.6. *Example of the functional flow diagram for an electronic toothbrush*

As already stated, the functional flow diagram defines the functional flow or object model of a given system. It is completely "dual" to the functional breakdown, interaction or scenario diagrams since it focuses on flows and not on the functions of the system that are producing these flows.

We must thus again emphasize that such a diagram is of high importance since it rationally describes in a consolidated and organized way all inputs and all outputs of the functions of a given system. Hence, it gives the functional "dictionary" of the system, that is, the list of all objects that are functionally manipulated by the system. This dictionary is of high value for ensuring a common vision between all project actors involved in the architecting process: these actors shall normally – in an ideal

---

17 Beware that, even if we use the syntax of a data model for the functional flow diagram, this last diagram is not really a data model in the usual way, since it does not represent (only) data, but also physical objects, business objects or even informal information that may be functionally exchanged with "humanware" stakeholders of a given system.

world – only use the terms of that dictionary when discussing a functional object. We may easily understand that such a principle allows us to avoid any ambiguity between the different project actors. It is thus again key for ensuring a good collaboration between these actors.

Deciding How the System Shall be Formed: Constructional Architecture

7.1. Understanding how the system is formed?

Constructional architecture, or equivalently constructional analysis, intends to precisely describe the different components of a system, as well as all their relative interactions[1]. The core motivation of constructional architecture is to concretely understand and specify in detail the system, in terms of structure – that is, in other terms, to understand how the system is formed – and not of behaviors, that is, in its constructional nature ... as we would have naturally guessed!

Constructional architecture is key since it consolidates all architectural analyses into a concrete vision of the considered system. It makes in particular the synthesis between a top-down design approach, as provided by the systems architecting process, and a bottom-up one, which is typically induced by the constraints due to an existing product architecture or by the new possibilities brought by the advances of technology. The entire idea of constructional architecture is thus to find the best possible balance between these two apparently contradictory, but, in reality, completely complementary, approaches. As a consequence, constructional architecture intends to solve a "simple" – to state, but not to solve – multi-dimensional optimization problem: "what is the best concrete architecture – that is, what are the suitable components with their organization – which answers to the

---

1 And also, how these components are connected both to missions and functions. This point – though important – will not be addressed here since it can be easily managed via suitable mission and function to component allocation matrices.

stakeholder needs (top-down approach) while integrating all industrial and technological constraints and opportunities (bottom-up approach), within classical cost, quality, delay and performance objectives?"[2] This problem is of course highly non-trivial and highly complex in practice due to its large number of parameters and variables. The motivation of constructional architecture is – quite modestly – to propose some key tools that may contribute to that objective.

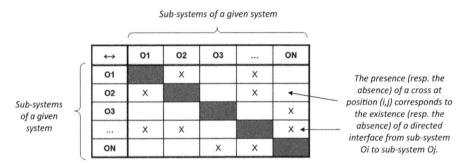

Figure 7.1. *Design structure matrix (DSM) of a system*

Constructional architecture also allows us to integrate "by design" some important key architectural principles within a system. The best way to prevent the propagation of a local problem throughout a system and its transformation into a global problem is for instance to organize the system as an integration of decoupled sub-systems, that is, with minimal mutual interfaces. This property can be easily depicted on the design structure matrix (DSM) associated with a given system S – see Figure 7.1 – where we indicate a connection from a sub-system Oi of S to another sub-system Oj of S if and only if there is a directed interface from Oi to Oj: minimizing the interfaces of S therefore means finding a constructional implementation minimizing the number of elements of such a matrix.

Last, but not least, we must point out that constructional architecture is the main input of a series of important engineering activities such as specialty engineering analyses, safety analyses, verification and validation (see IEEE (2005), INCOSE (2011), ISO (2018) or NASA (2016) for more details on these activities).

---

2 It is always important to be able to properly state any constructional architecture problem using such a pattern.

**What happens when a system has not a decoupled constructional architecture:
the Fighter Aircraft F/A-18 case[3]**

The standard aircraft F/A-19 is a fighter and attack aircraft that was developed by McDonnell Douglas for the US Army in the late 1970s. It was designed as a carrier-based aircraft, supporting 3,000 flight hours, 90 minutes of average sorties and 7.5 g of positive maximal accelerations with a 15-year useful lifespan.

In the early 1990s, the Swiss Army decided to acquire this aircraft. However, due to its geographic and politic specificities, Switzerland had very different requirements. First, due to their neutrality policy, they did not want a fighter, but rather an interceptor aircraft. Since Switzerland does not have any sea (Leman Lake does not count as one …), there was a demand for land-based aircraft. Swiss people also like their belongings to last a long time, so they requested their aircrafts to support 5,000 flight hours with a 30-year useful lifespan. Finally, we shall remember that Switzerland is a very small country with mountains to avoid during each sortie, which led to the need for, on one hand, 40 minutes of average sorties and, on the other hand, 9 g of positive maximal accelerations.

When McDonnell Douglas engineers analyzed these demands, it was quickly understood that the US version of the F/A-18 could easily respect the Swiss requirements as soon as its less resistant fatigue components were replaced. A deeper analysis showed them that it was even sufficient to replace a few – weighting around 500 grams – structural aircraft parts made in aluminum with equivalent components made in titanium (which is more robust).

Unfortunately, when this – apparently quite small – change was done, the center of gravity changed, which required stiffening the fuselage and increasing the gross takeoff weight to rebalance the aircraft. Due to those various changes, the weight distribution evolved within the aircraft, impacting the flight control software which it was necessary to redesign. Various other changes occurred and, at the very end, the industrial manufacturing processes and the associated plant were even highly impacted, leading to a 10 million dollars overall overcost for a little initial change of less than 1 kg …

Well decoupling a system's constructional architecture is therefore crucial!

Case study 7.1. *The Fighter Aircraft F/A-18 case*

7.2. The key deliverables of constructional architecture

For any system S, constructional architecture has five core types of deliverables:

---

3 The author is grateful to O. de Weck (MIT, USA) who introduced him to this case study.

1) The *constructional requirement architecture diagram* that hierarchically organizes all the constructional requirements – with respect to S – according to a refinement hierarchy.

2) The *configuration diagram* that describes how S passes from a configuration to another – with indication of the associated events – from its birth up to its death.

3) The *constructional breakdown and interaction diagrams* that are describing – in a purely static way – the components of S with their internal and external interactions[4].

4) The *constructional scenario diagrams* that are describing – in a dynamic way – interactions involving the components of S, and possibly the environment, in a given configuration.

5) The *constructional flow diagrams* that synthetize all flows – with their logical relationships – absorbed or produced by the components of S during the "configuration cycle"[5] of S.

These different types of deliverables are presented more in detail below.

7.2.1. *Constructional requirement architecture diagram*

Let S be a system. The *constructional requirement architecture diagram* of S is then a hierarchical exhaustive representation of all constructional requirements of S, a constructional requirement R1 being under another constructional requirement R2 in this hierarchy if and only if we can logically deduce R1 from R2[6]. In this last situation, we say then more precisely that R2 refines into R1, which explains why we speak of a constructional requirement refinement hierarchy[7].

The above Figure 7.2 shows a (quite partial) constructional requirement architecture diagram for an electronic toothbrush, a constructional requirement being – classically and similarly both to a need and to a functional requirement – represented here by a 2-part box, whose first top part is a short name summarizing the constructional requirement scope and whose second bottom part is devoted to the

---

4 Usually, only at the global level, but also possibly in only a given configuration.

5 That is, the period of time modeled by the configuration diagram.

6 Remember that constructional requirements are logical predicates (see section 3.4.2).

7 An additional important property of a constructional requirement architecture is *coverage*: we shall try to construct the constructional requirement architecture diagram in order to maintain the coverage logical property $CR1 \land \ldots \land CRn \to CR0$ for all constructional requirements CR1, …, CRn which are under a given constructional requirement CR0 in such a diagram.

constructional requirement statement, when the different refinement relationships on which relies the constructional requirement hierarchy are – also classically – represented by arrows.

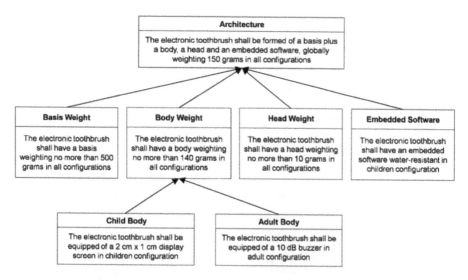

Figure 7.2. *Example of a constructional requirement architecture diagram for an electronic toothbrush*

The same issue that was already pointed out, both for need and functional requirement architecture diagrams, also happens in the same terms for the constructional requirement architecture diagram: organizing a constructional requirement refinement hierarchy is indeed always difficult since we shall avoid having too many first level constructional requirements, but of course also too many levels of refinements, as soon as we want to be able to efficiently use such a view. The 7x7x7 rule (see the first part of section 4.2) is again precious to handle this real difficulty. As a consequence, a typical "good" constructional requirement architecture diagram associated with a given system shall have no more than seven high-level constructional requirements, each of them being refined in around seven medium-level constructional requirements, finally also refined in the same way into seven low-level constructional requirements. Note again that the number 7 is just an order of magnitude. Obtaining up to 10–12 high-level constructional requirements in a constructional requirement architecture diagram could of course work: however, we must probably not go further without analyzing whether this number is justified. Finally, we shall not hesitate to construct as many additional constructional requirement architecture diagrams as necessary, for refining such an analysis as soon as all relevant constructional requirements are not derived and/or captured.

7.2.2. Configuration diagram

Again let S be a system. The *configuration diagram* of S is then a representation of:

– the configurations of S, with their relative temporal relationships, that is, consecutiveness, inclusion or simultaneity[8];

– the events that cause the different transitions between each configuration of S and the immediately consecutive ones.

The standard representations of the temporal relations between configurations introduced above are given – *mutatis mutandis* – by Table 5.1, if we now interpret C and D as configurations.

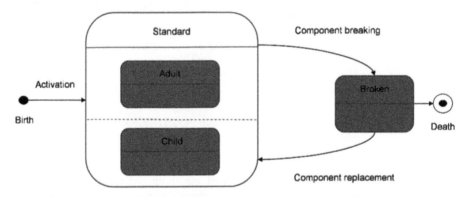

Figure 7.3. *Example of configuration diagram for an electronic toothbrush. For a color version of this figure, see www.iste.co.uk/krob/systems.zip*

The above Figure 7.3 provides an example of configuration diagram associated with an electronic toothbrush, which is here quite simple, taking the standard representation of configurations and of their temporal relationships that we introduced, when events – that induce configuration transitions – are modeled by arrows labeled with the name of the relevant event. Note also that the initial (respectively, termination) events in each configuration do not respect this rule since they are conventionally modeled by small black circles (respectively, by white circles containing a black circle).

The configuration diagram is key since it models – from a purely constructional perspective – time, even if it is not immediately obvious to see here. Following the

8 We refer to the second paragraph of section 5.2 in this matter.

intuition that we developed at the end of the second paragraphs of sections 5.2 and 6.2, we could consider that the next diagrams – that is, the constructional breakdown and interaction diagrams – are modeling the "constructional space" in which components are evolving. Since both space and time are always required to specify any constructional reality (that takes place somewhere at a certain time), we can easily see that these two diagrams are again completely complementary.

7.2.3. Constructional breakdown and interaction diagram

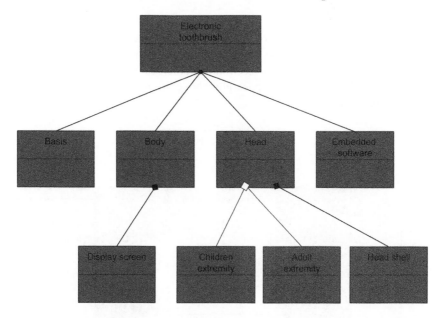

Figure 7.4. *Example of a constructional breakdown diagram for an electronic toothbrush. For a color version of this figure, see www.iste.co.uk/krob/systems.zip*

Let S be a system. The *constructional breakdown diagram* associated with S is then a hierarchical representation of the components of S, a set C1, C2, ..., CN of components being under another component D in this hierarchy if D is the result of the integration – in the meaning of Definition 1.5 – of the components C1, ..., CN[9] (C1, ..., CN are then classically called "sub-components" of D). The *constructional interaction diagrams* associated with S are then just the different representations – there is one constructional interaction diagram per integration relation involved in the constructional breakdown diagram – of each such integration relationship that

---

9 Due to our definition of the integration operator, this hierarchy is therefore again an abstraction hierarchy.

exists between the different components appearing in the hierarchy modeled by the constructional breakdown diagram.

The previous Figure 7.4 now provides an illustrative partial example of constructional breakdown diagram for an electronic toothbrush, where the integration relationships on which such an hierarchy relies are – quite classically – represented by black-squared (respectively, white-squared) arrows when the low-level component is mandatory (respectively, optional, which allows us to model product options using this last syntax), with respect to the depicted integration relationship.

We also give an example of a constructional interaction diagram for an electronic toothbrush that can be found in Figure 7.5. It provides the integration relationship existing between the electronic toothbrush in its whole and its first "sub-components" as they are appearing above in the previous constructional breakdown diagram.

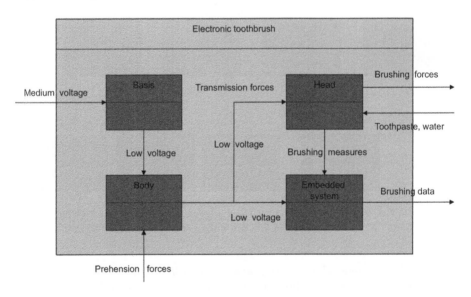

Figure 7.5. *Example of a constructional interaction diagram for an electronic toothbrush. For a color version of this figure, see www.iste.co.uk/krob/systems.zip*

The constructional breakdown of a system S modeled by the constructional breakdown diagram is also classically called the product breakdown structure (PBS) of S. Similarly to the mission or the functional breakdown structures that we introduced in the two last chapters, it provides the exhaustive dictionary of components of the system and has a key role in guaranteeing a common understanding on the constructional scope of a system, which is mandatory for efficient transversal collaboration between the different actors and stakeholders of a system development project.

We must, however, be aware of the good readability of such a view. Just observe in this matter that all the recommendations based on the 7x7x7 rule that we previously gave for the stakeholder and the need architecture diagrams of course also apply – *mutatis mutandis* – for efficiently modeling the PBS of a given system.

Note also that Figure 1.9 in Chapter 1, even if formally functionally oriented, can also be easily re-interpreted as a constructional interaction diagram, here associated with an aircraft: each "box" of this diagram, even if, strictly speaking, representing a first-level sub-function of an aircraft, may indeed also naturally be interpreted as a first-level sub-system of an aircraft. The same remark does not, however, apply – *mutatis mutandis* – for the functional architectures discussed in Introduction since the functional and constructional architectures are not fully aligned for these examples.

7.2.4. Constructional scenario diagram

Let again S be a system and q(S) a configuration of S. A *constructional scenario diagram* associated with S and q(S) is then a dynamic representation of the interactions that are taking place between the components of S, and possibly the environment, during the period of time modeled by q(S).

The following Figure 7.6 shows an example of the constructional scenario diagram, associated with the "children" configuration of an electrical toothbrush. It shows how the electronic toothbrush sends an encouraging message to the end-user, when in a children configuration (see Table 3.5 for the corresponding illustration). We refer to the suitable paragraph of section 3.4.2 for all the details on the semantics of the below representation.

A constructional scenario diagram provides therefore the explicit "algorithm" which is underlying to the constructional interactions of the system that occur in a given configuration. This is key to finely understand what concretely happens during a given configuration.

Observe finally that this last diagram has also a functional nature since it models in a certain way a "constructional behavior": we shall thus always be aware, on the first hand, not to overlap at this level with functional architecture in order to avoid making two times similar analyses and, on the second hand, to be fully consistent with the already constructed functional scenario diagrams.

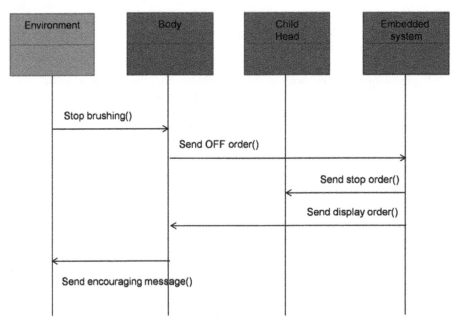

Figure 7.6. *Example of a constructional scenario diagram for an electronic toothbrush. For a color version of this figure, see www.iste.co.uk/krob/systems.zip*

7.2.5. Constructional flow diagram

Let S be a system. The *constructional flow diagram* associated with S is a consolidated description of all constructional flows associated with S and of:

1) their logical relationships;

2) their abstraction relationships (see the last section of Chapter 5).

Hence, it plays the role of the constructional "data model"[10] of the system. Note that we may also split this diagram into two diagrams, each of them covering the two above points.

Figure 7.7 that follows shows an example of a (partial) constructional flow diagram, associated with an electrical toothbrush. It can be constructed by

---

10 Beware that, even if we use the syntax of a data model for the constructional flow diagram, this last diagram is again not really a data model since it does not represent (only) data, but also physical objects, business objects or even informal information that may be exchanged with "humanware" stakeholders of a given system.

consolidating all the constructional flows that are appearing in the high-level constructional interaction diagram which is provided in Figure 7.5 for an electronic toothbrush. Its syntax exactly follows the same principles than for the operational and functional flow diagrams (see the last paragraph of the last two previous chapters).

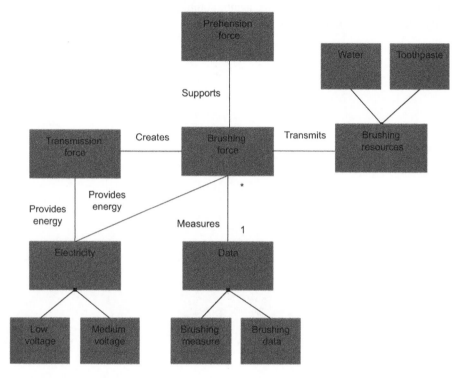

Figure 7.7. *Example of a constructional flow diagram for an electronic toothbrush. For a color version of this figure, see www.iste.co.uk/krob/systems.zip*

As already stated, such a constructional flow diagram defines the constructional flow or object model of a given system. It is therefore completely "dual" to the constructional breakdown, interaction or scenario diagrams since it focuses only on flows and absolutely not on the different components of the system that are producing these flows.

We must therefore emphasize that such a diagram is of high importance since it rationally describes in a consolidated and organized way all inputs and all outputs of the components of a given system. Hence, it gives the constructional "dictionary" of the system, that is, the list of all objects that are constructionally – that is, concretely – manipulated by the system. Hence, this dictionary is of high value for ensuring a common constructional vision between all project actors involved in the architecting process: these actors shall normally – in an ideal world – only use the terms of that dictionary when discussing a constructional object. We may therefore easily understand that such a principle allows us to avoid any ambiguity between the different project actors. It is thus again completely key for ensuring a good collaboration between these actors.

Taking into Account Failures: Dysfunctional Analysis

8.1. Systems do not always behave as they should

Despite the fact that a given system was well architected, internal and external hazards, dysfunctions and failures may unfortunately always occur and lead to unexpected consequences, either on the system and or on its environment[1]. Systems are indeed not always behaving as they should!

Due to the potential severity of such consequences, there is a specific domain within engineering – safety, or dysfunctional, analysis – which is especially dedicated to the study of failures, that is, of what the system shall normally not do, in order to be able to design and define the best mitigation strategies in such situations. Any systems architect shall therefore know how to interact with safety experts, which is the purpose of the current chapter. The point is not to become a safety specialist, but to know the basic concepts of safety and to efficiently manage the interface[2] between systems architecting and safety, which is key, due to the core importance of this last domain.

In this matter, the safety/dysfunctional analysis process can in particular be defined as the systems engineering process which is dedicated to the analysis of the potential risks to which may be exposed a given system. Safety/dysfunctional

---

1 The worst consequences being the death of people.

2 Which is not easy at all, since all safety industrial standards are imposing a Chinese wall between designers and safety engineers. In other words, safety engineers shall not be involved in design, while designers shall not be involved in safety analysis. The key point is thus to find the right way of managing the necessary interactions between these two worlds, while respecting safety standards (see the end of this section for more details).

analysis especially intends to identify, classify and quantify the risks associated with a given system and to define the safety requirements that this system will have to respect in order to be able to normally work in the presence of risks. The safety/dysfunctional analysis process shall especially perform two major complementary missions:

– An *internal mission* whose objective is to analyze the safety of a given system design in order to provide safety/dysfunctional-oriented feedbacks to the system design teams, through risk assessment techniques that identify accident and incident scenarios, assess their probability and the severity of their consequences, and to propose safety requirements to fulfill and mitigation mechanisms or safety barriers, in order to reduce the likelihood of an accident occurring and/or to minimize its impact on the system and its environment.

– An *external mission* whose objective is to convince stakeholders that the designed system is safe, which requires to implement activities such as system certification, that shall prove to stakeholders – including safety authorities – that everything has been done in order to make the system safe, and system insurance, where mechanisms are put in place to compensate stakeholders (customers, users, community, etc.) in the event of an accident.

Note that safety has also a legal dimension: the safety officer of a complex system development company is usually legally responsible before courts, in case of a trial due to a safety issue.

How a system can collapse: the Chernobyl case

Chernobyl is a major industrial accident that allows us to understand the systemic nature of failures. In this matter, we shall first recall that Chernobyl nuclear reactor was very stable by design in nominal mode due to two physical effects that compensate then each other: the increase of temperature decreases the nuclear reaction, but increases the vacuum coefficient, which as a consequence increases the nuclear reaction. But the vacuum coefficient prevails in reduced operation and the reactor is then unstable.

It happened that the Chernobyl operator wanted to test whether it was possible to supply the pumps, ensuring the circulation of water, with the residual power generated by the turbo-alternators during the plant shutdown phase. Before the accident, this experiment had already been attempted twice without success at Chernobyl.

By April 25, 1986, unit 4 of Chernobyl power plant had to be shut down for normal periodic maintenance. Operator therefore prepared the experiment.

By April 25, 1986 – afternoon, setback because the Leningrad region needs electricity. As a consequence, the reactor will operate for nine hours at half power (which is contrary to safety rules). The reactor core is gradually "poisoned-born" by the creation of Xenon (which is usually destroyed at full power). To compensate for the loss of power which is induced by this poisoning, the control bars are raised one after the other.

By April 25, 1986 – 23:00–1:00: the power decreases again and drops at 30 MWth at 0:30. Xenon heart poisoning continued. To compensate it, almost all of the control bars were raised by the operators at 1:00. The power is then manually stabilized around 200 MWth.

By April 25, 1986 – 1:03–1:22: as scheduled in the experiment, additional pumps were started, which causes a very large increase in water circulation. But the power is not what was expected: the reactor is unstable. The staff disconnects then all the alarms one by one!

By April 25, 1986 – 1:23:00: the power to the pumps was supplied by the inertia of the turbo-alternators as expected. But the flow of water passing through the reactor causes the formation of bubbles in the coolant. Due to the positive vacuum coefficient, the nuclear reactor enters into a positive feedback, which results in a rapid increase in reactor power.

By April 25, 1986 – 1:23:40: the chief operator orders the emergency stop. However, the reactor is already too hot, which has distorted the channels for the control rods. The control bars can therefore only be lowered to 1.50 meters instead of the normal 7 meters.

By April 25, 1986 – 1:23:43: the radiolysis of water leads to the formation of a detonating mixture of hydrogen and oxygen. In three to five seconds, the power of the reactor increases 10 times. The 1,200 tons of the concrete slab covering the reactor are thrown into the air and fall with an angle on the reactor core, which is fractured by the impact!

As we can see, the root causes of the Chernobyl accident are multiple and not at all only technical: political pressure to succeed the experiment that provoked the accident, change of mission during the day preceding the accident, stress of the operators after a long day of work and night period of the accident were key risk factors that aligned to lead to this huge catastrophe. We shall therefore remember that risk is of systemic nature.

Case study 8.1. *The Chernobyl case*

As we can see, safety/dysfunctional analysis is fundamentally dealing with risks in systems contexts. Let us therefore precisely introduce first the definition of what is a risk.

Let S be a system. A *risk* r(S) related to S is then defined as the combination r(S) = (e(S), q(S)) of:

– an *initiating event* e(S) – also usually called a hazard – that is, the initiating factor of the risk r(S) and that may lead to an impact on the system S;

– a *degraded situation* q(S) of the system S – also usually called a failure – which results, or equivalently is a consequence, of the initiating event e(S) and in which the integrity of the system S and/or of its environment is more or less seriously impacted.

These two dimensions of a risk are illustrated on the below Figure 8.1.

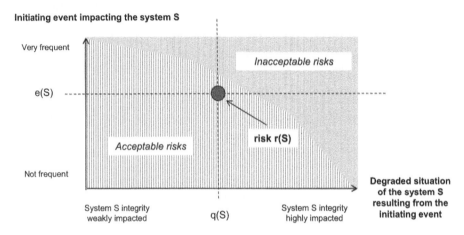

Figure 8.1. *The two dimensions of a risk. For a color version of this figure, see www.iste.co.uk/krob/systems.zip*

The key point is that any system will always have to deal with risks. The question is thus whether these risks are acceptable, that is, whether the most severe risks are sufficiently unlikely and whether the most frequent risks are sufficiently insignificant. Hence, from a safety/dysfunctional perspective, it is of key importance to classify risks from the negligible up to the unacceptable ones. This is usually done, based on the definition of a risk, by classifying each risk depending on values associated with the two features that are defining it, that is, the frequency of the initiating event of a risk and the degree of severity of the degraded situation, resulting from the initiating event, involved in a risk. The below Figure 8.2 provides for instance a generic pattern for such a classification.

We shall also notice that the key concepts that are involved in the definition of a system risk can typically be interpreted using the following classical concepts coming from the probability theory:

– The initiating event of a risk has a *probability of occurrence* during a given period of time (this probability shall therefore be measured per suitable unit of time).

– A degraded situation is a *random variable* to which we can associate many other random variables measuring its level of degradation in terms of severity (e.g. cost, duration, etc.).

		Severity of degraded situation resulting from the initiating event			
		Insignificant	Marginal	Critical	Catastrophic
Frequency of the initiating event	Frequent	Undesired	Unacceptable	Unacceptable	Unacceptable
	Probable	Acceptable	Undesired	Unacceptable	Unacceptable
	Occasionnal	Acceptable	Undesired	Undesired	Unacceptable
	Unlikely	Negligible	Acceptable	Undesired	Undesired
	Improbable	Negligible	Negligible	Acceptable	Acceptable
	Eliminated	Negligible	Negligible	Negligible	Negligible

Figure 8.2. *Example of a risk classification grid. For a color version of this figure, see www.iste.co.uk/krob/systems.zip*

As a consequence, a risk can therefore be analyzed in terms of mathematical expectation, that is, the product of the probability of occurrence of its initiating event multiplied by the measurement of its degraded situation on a chosen severity scale (cost, duration, etc.).

Based on these fundamentals, the core activity of safety/dysfunctional analysis is risk assessment: it consists of analyzing how a system achieves a given safety goal and identifying the safety requirements that the system shall fulfill in order to meet the safety goal. In this matter, we shall observe that a safety goal can, however, only be stated in terms of the probability of failure, due to the intrinsic random nature of a risk-initiating event. A typical safety goal has for instance the following standard form:

> *The system S shall work with a probability of failure of less than p when event e occurs*[3].

In the same way, a typical safety requirement is of similar probabilistic nature (see next sections).

As a consequence, safety/dysfunctional analysis deeply relies on probability theory that can be seen as the key mathematical background of this engineering

---

3 Or, if we are taking a stakeholder's perspective: *The stakeholders of S shall be impacted by S with a probability of less than p when event e occurs.*

discipline[4]. We shall here especially refer to Rauzy (2008), Leveson (2012, 2020), Smith (2017) or Smith and Simpson (2020) for more details on that domain.

We shall also finally recall that, in safety matters, most of industrial domains have structured their doctrine through safety standards that are mandatory to follow when engineering a system (see for instance Smith and Simpson (2020) for a detailed survey on these standards). These safety standards usually explain the main safety concepts, discussing how to classify risks, presenting the main steps of the safety analysis process to follow and eliciting engineering activities to do, depending on the classification of a risk. Examples of such standards are provided by the below Table 8.1 for various industries.

Sector	Standard	Name
Aeronautics	ARP 4754A	Guidelines for development of civil aircraft and systems
	DO-178C/ED-12C	Software considerations in airborne systems and equipment certification
Automotive	ISO 26262	Road vehicles - functional safety
	SOTIF ISO21448	Road vehicles - safety of the intended functionality
Railway	EN 50129	Railways applications - communications, signaling and processing systems - safety-related electronic systems for signaling
	EN 50126	Railways applications - the specification and demonstration of reliability, availability, maintainability and safety
Nuclear	IEC 61513	Nuclear power plants – instrumentation and control for systems important to safety – general requirements for systems

Table 8.1. *Examples of safety standards in various industries*

The connection between systems architecting and safety is thus highly structured by these standards. The key principle on which safety/dysfunctional analysis relies in practice – due to these standards – is in particular a *very strict separation between*

---

4 This remark also explains why safety analysis is such a different discipline compared to systems architecting which, on the other hand, relies on mathematical logic, as we have already discussed in this book (see Chapter 1).

design activities and safety/dysfunctional analysis activities, that is, that these activities shall be managed by two different teams:

– the design activities shall be achieved by a design team;

– the safety activities shall be achieved by an independent safety team.

This separation is key since trust comes from the fact that there exists a design-independent team that will regularly assess the design from a safety/ dysfunctional perspective.

A typical design process that integrates safety is illustrated in Figure 8.3. The typical usual steps of such a safety-oriented design process are the following:

1) The design team proposes an initial system design.

2) The safety team evaluates this initial system design from a safety/ dysfunctional perspective.

3) The safety team tells then to the design team whether the proposed system design meets the safety goals to be achieved, which is rarely the case for the initial design, and what are the safety requirements to fulfill in order to obtain a safety-acceptable system design.

4) The design team shall then propose a new version of the system design that will achieve these safety requirements.

5) The new version of the system design is then again evaluated by the safety team.

This iteration process between the design and safety teams continues then up to achieving a system design which is validated by the safety team. In this matter, note as illustrated in Figure 8.3, that the safety team will develop – especially for computational purposes[5] – its own safety model, which is correlated, but independent of the system model defined by the design team. In this last matter, a key non-obvious problem is always to maintain the alignment between these two types of models.

Last, but not least, note that from now on, we will only speak of *dysfunctional analysis*, rather than of safety, in order to denote the large domain that we introduced, since other key system dimensions – such as for instance reliability, availability or maintainability – can be addressed – *mutatis mutandis* – by exactly the same mathematical and engineering frameworks and techniques.

---

5 In order to be able to compute the various probabilities of failure involved in dysfunctional analyses.

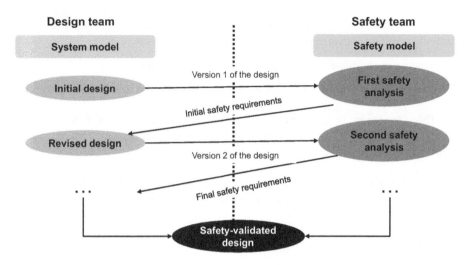

Figure 8.3. *Typical interface between design and safety teams according to safety standards. For a color version of this figure, see www.iste.co.uk/krob/systems.zip*

8.2. The key deliverables of dysfunctional analysis

For any system S, the key deliverables – from the specific perspective of the systems architect[6] – of dysfunctional analysis, classified per architectural vision, are the following:

1) At the **operational level**, the main deliverable is the *list of external hazards* that organizes all the external initiating events of a risk with respect to S, per lifecycle phase and stakeholder.

2) At the **functional level**, there are two main deliverables:

– the *list of functional hazards* that organizes all the internal initiating events of a risk with respect to S that are related to a function of S, per functional mode;

– the *list of functional safety requirements* associated with S.

---

6 These deliverables are the only ones that are exchanged between the safety team and the design team, as explained in the last section. Many more intermediate deliverables (e.g. failure modes, effects and criticality analyses, failure tree analyses, safety models, etc.) are of course managed and achieved by the safety team. But we will not discuss them here since we shall only take the perspective of the systems architect within this book.

3) At the **constructional level**, there are two main deliverables:

– the *list of constructional hazards* that organizes all the internal initiating events of a risk with respect to S that are related to a component of S, per configuration;

– the *list of constructional safety requirements* associated with S.

These different types of deliverables are presented more in detail below.

8.2.1. *Dysfunctional analysis from an operational perspective*

Let S be a system. An *external hazard* of S is any abnormal event, coming from or initiated by a stakeholder of S, that may be the initiating event of a risk, that is, that may lead to a dysfunction of the considered system (typically in terms of reliability, availability, safety or security).

The *list of external hazards* associated with S is then a table where the external hazards are classified according to the stakeholder that initiates them and the lifecycle phase in which they occur[7].

The below Table 8.2 illustrates a partial list of external hazards in an electronic toothbrush case. In this example, we only considered two lifecycle phases, with a limited number of stakeholders and a very limited list of identified external hazards. Note also that we here introduced several categories of external hazards in order to avoid a flat list of external hazards: this is a good practice that shall be generalized – and recursively extended to categories of categories, as soon as it is useful – in order to hierarchically organize the list of external hazards for a better understanding of that list, which is often mandatory in practice due to the quite large number of such external hazards that are naturally associated with any system.

Note finally that the external hazards, as provided by the list of external hazards, shall of course be used within the various operational analyses managed by the systems architect. They shall typically impact the lifecycle diagram that shall integrate them, when relevant, since external hazards are events that may lead to a change of lifecycle phase. Moreover, we shall usually also increase the scope, on one hand, of the use case diagrams and of the associated operational scenario diagrams and, on the other hand, of the needs, in order to take into account all the dysfunctional information provided by the list of external hazards of a given system.

---

7 Note that a lifecycle phase where an external hazard may occur is called a *safety lifecycle phase*.

Lifecycle phase	Stakeholder	Categories of external hazards	External hazards
Development	Project system	Malicious attempts	Virus implementation
			Backdoor reservation
		Incomplete specifications	Need misunderstanding
			Wrong safety goal
Nominal operation	End-users	Misuses	Use with baby teeth
			Lack of maintenance
	Power supply	Malfunctions	Wrong voltage
			Bad frequency
	Internet	Errors	Erroneous request
		Malfunctions	Loss of network

Table 8.2. *Example of a partial list of external hazards for an electronic toothbrush*

8.2.2. *Dysfunctional analysis from a functional perspective*

Let S be a system. A *functional hazard* of S is any abnormal event, coming from or initiated by a function[8] of S, that may be the initiating event of a risk, that is, that may lead to a dysfunction of the considered system (typically in terms of reliability, availability, safety or security).

Functional mode	Function	Categories of functional hazards	Functional hazards
Brushing	Provide brushing forces	Malfunctions	Loss of function
			Weak brushing
	Provide energy	Malfunctions	Loss of energy
			Bad transmission
Transmission	Manage brushing data	Losses	Loss of network
		Errors	Error in transmission
			Erroneous data
	Provide energy	Malfunctions	Loss of energy
			Bad transmission

Table 8.3. *Example of a partial list of functional hazards for an electronic toothbrush*

---

8 Note that functions that are at the source of functional hazards are called *safety functions* and that a functional mode in which a functional hazard may occur is called a *safety functional mode.*

The *list of functional hazards* associated with S is then given in a table where the functional hazards are classified according to the function that initiates them and the functional mode in which they occur.

Functional hazards shall of course focus on dysfunctional functional properties of the system. The dysfunctional operational properties of the system shall then be covered by external hazard analysis as introduced in the last section. Note also that the root cause of a functional hazard may be purely internal (bug, loss of a function, etc.) or external (typically initiated by an external hazard).

Table 8.3 illustrates a partial list of functional hazards for an electronic toothbrush case. In this example, we only considered two functional modes, with a limited number of functions and a very limited list of identified functional hazards. Note also that we can introduce – as we sketched it here above – categories of functional hazards in order to hierarchically organize the list of functional hazards for a better understanding of that list, which is often mandatory in practice due to the quite large number of such functional hazards that are naturally associated with any system.

Note finally that the functional hazards, as provided by the list of functional hazards, shall of course be used within the various functional analyses managed by the systems architect. They shall typically impact the functional mode diagram that shall integrate them, when it is relevant, since functional hazards are events that may lead to a change of functional mode. Moreover, we shall usually also increase the perimeter, on one hand, of the functional interaction diagrams and of the associated functional scenario diagrams and, on the other hand, of the functional requirements, in order to take into account the dysfunctional information provided by the list of functional hazards of a system. Last, but not least, we may also need to create specific protection or support functions, which may impact all aspects of functional architecture, in order to provide adequate mitigation answers to the functional hazards that were identified.

Again let S be a system. A *safety functional requirement* associated with a function F of S is then a functional requirement with a probabilistic performance that has the following form:

> *The system S shall do F with a probability of failure of*
> *less than p when functional hazard e occurs.*

The specificity of such a requirement is of course its probabilistic nature, but it is just a requirement like another. The point here is thus to take into account these functional safety requirements, first of all, within the functional requirement architecture diagram, and, then, to understand their consequences, more generally, in terms of the functional architecture of the considered system.

8.2.3. *Dysfunctional analysis from a constructional perspective*

Let S be a system. A *constructional hazard* of S is any abnormal event, coming from or initiated by a component[9] of S, that may be the initiating event of a risk, that is, that may lead to a dysfunction of the considered system (typically in terms of reliability, availability, safety or security).

The *list of constructional hazards* associated with S is then given in a table where constructional hazards are classified according to the component that initiates them and the configuration in which they occur.

Constructional hazards shall focus on dysfunctional constructional properties of a given system. The dysfunctional functional (resp. operational) properties of the system shall of course be covered by functional (resp. external) hazard analysis as introduced in the last sections. Note also that the root cause of a constructional hazard may in particular be either purely internal (misfunction or loss of a component, etc.), or external (i.e. initiated by an external hazard).

Configuration	Component	Categories of constructional hazards	Constructional hazards
Standard	Head	Physical damages	Corruption
			Partial destruction
		Errors	Wrong configuration
			Bad setting
	Body	Physical damages	Corruption
			Partial destruction
	Embedded system	Physical damages	Overvoltage
			Water leakage
	Base	Physical damages	Corrosion
			Partial destruction

Table 8.4. *Example of a partial list of constructional hazards for an electronic toothbrush*

9 Note that components that may be at the origin of constructional hazards are called *safety components* and that a configuration in which a constructional hazard may occur is called a *safety configuration*.

Table 8.4 illustrates a partial list of constructional hazards on an electronic toothbrush case. In this example, we only considered a single configuration, with all high-level components, but only a very limited list of identified constructional hazards. Note also that we can introduce – as we sketched it here above – categories of constructional hazards in order to hierarchically organize the list of constructional hazards for a better understanding of that list, which is often mandatory in practice due to the quite large number of such constructional hazards associated with any system.

Note finally that the constructional hazards, as provided by the list of constructional hazards, shall of course be used within the various constructional analyses managed by the systems architect. They shall typically impact the configuration diagram that shall integrate them, when it is relevant, since constructional hazards are events that may lead to a change of system configuration. Moreover, we shall usually also increase the perimeter, on one hand, of the constructional interaction diagrams and of the associated constructional scenario diagrams and, on the other hand, of the constructional requirements, in order to take into account the dysfunctional information which is provided by the list of constructional hazards of a system. Finally, we may also need to create specific protection components, which may globally impact a constructional architecture, in order to provide adequate mitigation answers to the constructional hazards that were identified.

Let S be again a system. A *safety constructional requirement* associated with a component C of S is then a constructional requirement with a probabilistic performance that has the following form:

The system S shall be formed of C which shall have a probability of failure of less than p when constructional hazard e occurs.

The specificity of such a requirement is of course its probabilistic nature, but it is just a requirement like any other. The point is thus to take into account these constructional safety requirements, first of all, within the constructional requirement architecture diagram, and, then, to understand what are their more general consequences in terms of the constructional architecture of the considered system.

9

Choosing the Best Architecture: Trade-off Techniques

9.1. Systems architecting does not usually lead to a unique solution

Systems architecting is not like mathematics since systems architecting issues have commonly never only fully true or false answers, which may be disorientating for the beginner. A systems architecture process indeed classically leads to many different possible and valuable solutions. So, the core questions in systems architecting are always choices and decisions among these various options. The key point is of course to be able to make these choices and decisions in the most rational possible way, which is the main purpose of systems architecting and of this book.

Note first that systems architecture options can occur in each architectural vision: there are usually lots of choices to make in terms of prioritization of needs or requirements, as well as of selection of missions, functions or components. We must in particular always arbitrate between performance and cost under quality and delay constraints, in any real system development context. These key indicators lead to make regular arbitrations relatively, either to the level of coverage both of stakeholder needs and of system requirements, or on the scope covered by a system's architecture.

Trade-offs – that is, the specific engineering activities that result in making a choice between various architectural options – are thus permanent within any systems architecting process where decision plays a key role. As a consequence, if we want these decisions to be as rational as possible, we need both to organize the trade-off processes in the most efficient way and to have rigorous methods for taking such decisions on the basis of explicit and shared decision criteria. The trade-off techniques presented in this current chapter try to propose a valuable answer to this reasonable and strategic objective of any system development process.

Trade-offs are, however, never easy. A trade-off is indeed a situation that involves losing one feature of a system in return for gaining another quality or aspect. More colloquially, if one thing increases, some other thing must decrease. Trade-offs can occur for many reasons, including simple geometry (into a given amount of space, we can fit, either many small objects, or fewer large objects). As already mentioned above, the idea of a trade-off always in a system development context implies a decision that has to be made with full understanding of both the upside and downside of a particular choice, such as when somebody decides whether to invest in stocks (more risky, but with a greater potential return) versus bonds (generally safer, but lower potential returns)[1].

Note finally that "human engineering" is a key point when managing trade-offs. As noticed above, making a trade-off in any systems architecting context means eliminating an architectural option for choosing another one, which means privileging some part of the organization against another one, due to the fact that we shall never forget that there are always people behind systems (see the last paragraph of section 3.3). As it can be imagined, these human and/or political issues are at the heart of the difficulties when managing architectural trade-offs in practice.

Prioritizing a system budget: the data warehouse case

TELBYTE is a leading communication company in Europe. In order to make offers – as well as possible – adapted to their customer needs, the general direction of TELBYTE decided to develop a data warehouse[2], where all existing customer information shall be stored in order to provide suitable data for a number of customer-oriented internal services.

A scoping study showed that around 1,500 data sources were to be connected to the data warehouse in order to be able to deliver the 300 internal services that were requested by around 10 marketing-focused teams within TELBYTE. A dedicated project – named APERO – was then launched on this basis in order to construct the corporate data warehouse for a budget of around 40 million euros.

Unfortunately, nine months after having started, APERO faced a severe budget restriction – due to bad market figures – of 20%. The project team did not have any idea on how to deliver the expected services to the marketing department within a reduced budget of 32 million euros. A trade-off was clearly required and APERO asked CESAMES to manage it.

CESAMES analyzed the situation and quickly understood that the complexity of the project was too high and that value was totally absent of the way the APERO project was

---

1 This paragraph was highly inspired by the Wikipedia article on "trade-off" (see Wikipedia 2021o).

2 A data warehouse is a huge data basis, constructed with specific technology to guarantee transactional performance.

working, which explained why the project was not able to manage alone the trade-off it was facing. Several activities were then managed in parallel by CESAMES, during around a month, for creating conditions of a successful trade-off through a collaborative prioritization workshop. The first one was to reduce the data source complexity: by clustering the initial 1,500 data sources according to their origins, it was possible to only handle 250 data clusters. The second one was to give 100 tokens to each marketing team and to ask them to distribute their tokens on the best services that they were requesting: as an immediate side-effect of putting value at the heart of the problem, the number of requested services diminishes from 85% to arrive to only 50 services. Each team indeed understood that it was necessary to concentrate their tokens on the services with the highest value if these services wanted to have a chance to be selected during a collective prioritization process[3].

As a consequence, the complexity of the trade-off problem to solve passed from 1,500 x 300 = 450,000 possible source/service to 250 x 50 = 12,500 possible cluster/service choices to arbitrate, that is, a 97% reduction of complexity which allowed us to successfully make a collective arbitration – both of the data clusters to interface with the data warehouse and on the precise service scope to offer – during a one-day collective prioritization workshop involving all concerned business actors. The result achieved during that workshop allowed covering 95% of the marketing demands within the new 80% restricted budget[4], which made everybody happy since renouncements were quite light at the very end.

Case study 9.1. *The data warehouse case*

9.2. Trade-off techniques

9.2.1. *General structure of a trade-off process*

The objective of any trade-off process is to help its involved stakeholders to make a rational choice among several possible architectural choices, based on shared decision criteria. As a consequence, any trade-off process shall consist of the following main steps:

1) Identify the set of stakeholders involved in the trade-off decision process.

---

3 We can easily understand that any team which would not have concentrated its tokens on a limited number of choices could not win in a collective prioritization as soon as another team decided to have such a strategy. Hence, the best strategy for everybody is concentrating the tokens, which is a classical Nash equilibrium in the meaning of game theory (see Wikipedia 2021e).

4 This illustrates another point that we shall have in mind when performing trade-offs. Costs are often distributed with respect to value according to Pareto laws: 20% of the costs usually allow offering 80% of the value, when 80% of the costs only deliver 20% of the value. This type of law explains why the arbitration could work in the data warehouse case and why it was – in some sense (this case indeed required a lot of work) – so easy to achieve.

2) Identify and share the architectures that shall be discussed.

3) Define and share the decision criteria to be used.

4) Evaluate each possible architecture according to the chosen decision criteria.

5) Prioritize the evaluated architectures.

Steps 1–3 can be typically prepared by the systems architect alone (or with a small team), without opening the circle of stakeholders too much. Steps 4 and 5 shall, however, necessarily be achieved through a collective decision process – typically managed in a collective prioritization workshop – as soon as we want the involved stakeholders to be part of the resulting decision in order for them to be collectively engaged in the decision (and respect it). Each of these steps is quickly described below.

The first step – stakeholder identification – is not the easier. We, however, will here only refer to the last paragraph of section 3.3 where this question was already discussed. The second step – that is, architecture identification – "just" consists of applying all the systems architecture techniques we presented from Chapter 4 up to Chapter 7 and tracing the valuable architectural options that occur during the systems architecting process. The third step – decision criteria identification – can then rely on the need and requirement architecture as discussed in the previous chapters: the "good" decision criteria are indeed typically structuring high-level needs and/or requirements. We thus see that these three first steps totally rely on the already discussed systems architecture techniques.

The fourth step – architecture evaluation – is quite easy since the only complementary technical ingredient that it requires is to provide an evaluation scale when defining the decision criteria. The main difficulty here lies, however, not in technique, but in the human dimension of that step, that is, in workshop facilitation, as soon as we use a collaborative prioritization workshop to achieve that evaluation, as we highly recommend.

The fifth and last step – prioritization – is more complex since we cannot apply any deterministic protocol to achieve it. Prioritization can only be obtained by a collective discussion, using the results of step 4 as an input, without, however, being prisoners of them, in order to collectively make the most rational choice, taking into account all the dimensions of the decision that will be brought by the different actors involved in a collective prioritization workshop.

We shall finally point out that such a technique is not making the decision, just helping to prepare it[5]. Ultimately, the real decision can indeed only be taken by a

---

5 This is why we also speak of decision-aid techniques for such trade-off techniques.

suitable system governance board. It is thus extremely important to integrate any trade-off technique within a shared governance process where roles are transparently distributed between the people involved in the trade-off protocol as presented above and the people involved in governance[6], who are the only ones habilitated to make the formal final decision, as already mentioned above.

9.2.2. *Managing trade-offs in practice*

As already discussed in the last section, it is a good practice – that we can only highly recommend – to manage trade-offs in practice through collaborative prioritization workshops, involving all key actors that may be impacted by the trade-off decision. We would therefore just like to conclude this short chapter dedicated to trade-off techniques by presenting some illustrations coming from a real collaborative prioritization workshop.

The first one is an example of evaluation that took place during such a workshop which is provided in Figure 9.1. Each sticker in this figure corresponds to an evaluation of 1 of the 45 domain experts who participated in this workshop. These experts were asked to evaluate nine architectural options (represented through columns in Figure 9.1, the seven first ones being prepared by the systems architect before the workshop, while the last two emerged through the collective discussion during the workshop) in order to know:

1) their value, measured through the covering of five structuring needs (in green in Figure 9.1);

2) their level of risk, measured through four risk factors (in red in Figure 9.1).

Each of these value/risk criteria was then evaluated by the involved experts on a low–medium–high scale, the evaluation being concretely achieved by putting a sticker on the relevant location of the evaluation 12 meters x 1.5 meters panel depicted in Figure 9.1.

---

6 It is in particular a key good practice to completely separate the roles and not to mix the people who are preparing the decision with the people who are taking – formally – the decision. Such a role separation indeed allows the governance body not to follow the recommendation brought by the trade-off process, which may happen – even if normally not, if the systems architect made a good job – if, for instance, some strategic decision criteria were not properly taken into account during the collective prioritization workshop.

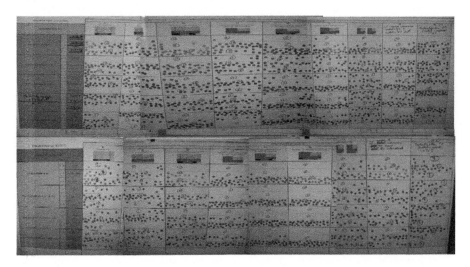

Figure 9.1. *Example of a collective vote during a prioritization workshop.
For a color version of this figure, see www.iste.co.uk/krob/systems.zip*

It is also interesting to share the synthetic final evaluation that was achieved during this collaborative prioritization workshop. The nine architectural options that were analyzed during the workshop were put on a value/risk matrix – each option being now represented by a simple dot in that matrix – where we can easily compare them (see below Figure 9.2). We can then easily see that:

– architectures S5 and S6 would lead to a project with the maximal level of risk;

– it is better to take S8 rather than S4 and S3, since S8 has more value and less risk than these two other variants, the same conclusion occurring for S7 with respect to S4;

– architectures S0, S1 and S2 have poor business value.

On the basis of that analysis, which was collectively shared during the corresponding prioritization workshop, the participants to the workshop proposed their governance body to launch a project oriented toward architecture S8, with architecture S7 as a fallback option. Their choice was fully confirmed by the governance committee that took place in the week following the workshop. As a matter of fact, this collaborative prioritization technique allowed us to successively achieve a complex arbitration on a 700 million euros budget dedicated to a strategic system development project!

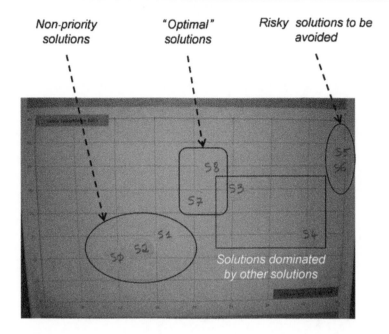

Figure 9.2. *Example of a collective evaluation during a prioritization workshop. For a color version of this figure, see www.iste.co.uk/krob/systems.zip*

Conclusion

C.1. The first journey in systems architecting

This book intends to offer to the reader the first journey through systems architecting and we hope that it was appreciated. We thus explored the following topics as provided in Table C.1.

Chapters	Topics covered
Introduction and 1	Systems Fundamentals
2	Systems Architecting Motivations
3	CESAM Framework Overview
4	Environment Architecture
5	Operational Architecture
6	Functional Architecture
7	Constructional Architecture
8	Dysfunctional Analysis[1]
9	Trade-off Techniques

Table C.1. *Systems architecting topics covered within this book*

However, we shall notice that our book does not, of course, cover the complete domain of systems architecting. We only focused on the fundamentals that every systems architect – even junior – shall know. Thus, we put an important stress on system modeling, since we just cannot do any systems architecting activity in practice without models. Models do indeed form the language of systems

---

1 The question is here absolutely not to become a safety specialist, which is a totally different type of expertise, but to be able to efficiently manage the interface between systems architecture and safety.

architecting: they can be used to analyze a problem, to describe a system, to elaborate a common vision, to communicate on a solution… The internal coherence of a system model – that leads to permanent cross-checking between the various diagrams that we introduced – is also a powerful tool for the systems architect in order to be confident in the robustness of a system architecture.

C.2. The other key systems architecting topics

We did not discuss in this book that was just intended to be an introduction to the huge domain[2] of systems architecting, of many other systems architecting topics – summarized in Table C.2 below, and that could be addressed by all people who want to specialize in systems architecting. Among them, we may cite the first group of three important topics – even if usually not the ones to learn on the first step – that should also be part of the common knowledge of any senior systems architect, that is:

– *verification and validation* (how to guarantee that a real system satisfies its needs and requirements and its descriptions?);

– *project architecture* (how to optimally structure a development project, taking into account the constraints coming from systems architecture?);

– *collaborative architecture* (how to efficiently organize the collaboration between the internal and external actors of a system development project?).

In the second group, we may also distinguish the following three quite specialized – and technically much more difficult – topics that may be typically reserved for expert systems architects:

– *system family architecture* (how to architecture a full family of systems?);

– *system of systems architecture* (how to architecture a system of systems?);

– *agile systems architecture* (how to quickly develop a systems architecture?).

Note finally that there are also some other classical topics such as needs capture techniques, advanced functional architecture, systems architecture simulation, interface architecture or design to X^3 techniques, which could also be placed in that second group.

---

2 Systems architecting is a "continent to explore", to rephrase an expression due to M.P. Schützenberger, one of the seminal fathers of modern computer science (personal communication).

3 X can mean cost (design to cost), value (design to value), maintainability (design to maintainability), etc.

Other core topics	Specialized topics
Verification and Validation	System Family Architecture
Project Architecture	Systems of Systems Architecture
Collaborative Architecture	Agile Systems Architecture

Table C.2. *Other systems architecting topics*

C.3. Systems architecting in practice

It is also important to quickly give some insights on the practical deliverable of a systems architecting activity related to a given system. In this last matter, the most important such deliverable is called a *system architecture file* (see Table C.3 for the generic structure of such a file). It consists of organizing in a reasoned way all systems architecture diagrams that are forming a given system model, with all required explanations and precisions, in order to achieve a complete and coherent system specification of the system of interest from all operational, functional and constructional perspectives.

The typical organization of such a system architecture file follows therefore the structure of this book by presenting, one after the other, the various systems architecture views that are describing a given system, according to the following structure (cf. Table C.3):

– The file starts with a short description of the system development project context, objectives, organization and agenda.

– The file presents then the environment architecture, by means of the stakeholder hierarchy diagram and of the environment diagram.

– The file describes then operational architecture, by discussing the need architecture diagram, the lifecycle diagram, the use case (if necessary) and operational scenario diagrams, the operational flow diagram and, if safety is involved, the list of external hazards[4].

– The file passes then to functional architecture, by introducing the functional requirement architecture diagram, the functional breakdown and interactions diagrams, the functional mode diagram, the functional flow diagram and, if safety is involved, the lists of functional hazards and of functional safety requirements.

– The file finally finishes with constructional architecture, by presenting the constructional requirement architecture diagram, the constructional breakdown and interactions diagrams, the configuration diagram, the constructional flow diagram

---

4 Or equivalently of environmental hazards.

and, if safety is involved, the lists of constructional hazards and constructional safety requirements.

A synthesis of the generic structure of such a system architecture file is provided in Table C.3. Note that we gave the meaning of each section of the system architecture file in its title: this is always a good practice that shall be followed, since systems architecting fundamentally deals with working with the right architectural semantics, as you could see throughout all this book.

- **0: Describing the System Development Project**
  - 0.1 – Presenting the system development project context & objectives
  - 0.2 – Presenting the system development project organization & agenda
- **1: Identifying Stakeholders: Environment Architecture**
  - 1.1 – Identifying Stakeholders – Stakeholder Hierarchy Diagram
  - 1.2 – Describing Interactions between the System and its Stakeholders – Environment Diagram
- **2: Understanding Interactions with Stakeholders: Operational Architecture**
  - 2.1 – Organizing stakeholder Needs – Need Architecture Diagram
  - 2.2 – Analyzing System Lifecycle Phases from the Stakeholders Perspective – Lifecycle Diagram
  - 2.3 – Describing Possible Uses of the System – Use Case & Operational Scenario Diagrams
  - 2.4 – Synthesizing Operational Objects – Operation Flow Diagram
  - 2.5 – Identifying External Hazards – List of External Hazards
- **3: Defining What the System Shall Do: Functional Architecture**
  - 3.1 – Describing System Behaviors – Functional Breakdown, Interactions & Modes Diagrams
  - 3.2 – Synthesizing Functional Objects – Functional Flow Diagram
  - 3.3 – Organizing System Functional Performances – Functional Requirement Architecture Diagram
  - 3.4 – Analyzing functional Failures – Lists of Functional Hazards & Safety Requirements
- **4: Deciding How the System Shall be Formed: Constructional Architecture**
  - 4.1 – Specifying System Structure – Constructional Breakdown, Interactions & Configurations Diagrams
  - 4.2 – Synthesizing Constructional Objects – Constructional Flow Diagram
  - 4.4 – Organizing System Technical Performances – Constructional Requirement Architecture Diagram
  - 4.4 – Defining How to Master Failures – Lists of Constructional Hazards & Safety Requirements

Table C.3. *Generic structure of a system architecture file*

In the same line, note that diagrams are not the most important material in such a file, even if they are of course very important since they do contain the main architectural artifacts that form a given system design and model: the most important lies indeed always in the architectural and business principles that guided the systems architect in doing his/her systems architecture choices and making his/her architectural decisions. The comments, remarks, explanations and motivations, which we shall necessarily find in a good systems architecture file, are thus always key in order to provide the system stakeholders with a full understanding of the proposed system architecture.

Note finally that a sketchy example of system architecture file is provided in Appendix 3 on a smart phone case study. Another example of such system architecture file can be seen in Figure C.1, here for the power sliding door of car (image was blurred for privacy reasons). In these two examples, we can observe that the architectural diagrams are never alone and that they are always accompanied by many explanations which are indeed fundamental for their good understanding.

 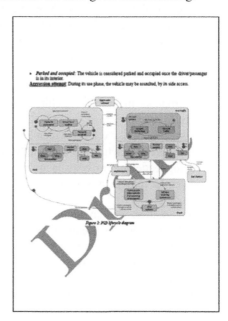

Figure C.1. *Example of a system architecture file for a power sliding door within a car (extract). For a color version of this figure, see www.iste.co.uk/krob/systems.zip*

C.4. How to develop a systems architecting leadership?

Mastering the modeling techniques contained in this book is clearly the first necessary important step for any systems architect. However, systems architecting cannot and shall not be reduced to systems modeling. The core of systems architecting indeed consists of helping system development teams to make rational and shared optimal choices in complex environments. As a consequence, the main difficulty of systems architecting is not to master modeling on its own, which by the way is not easy. The main difficulty of systems architecting is indeed to be able to create a common vision – involving all project actors – around the system in development with the help of system models.

This last point can only be approached through concrete development projects with real experiences of consensus building. Understanding the "theory" is clearly not enough, as soon as we are dealing with human relationship issues, which are in fact at the core of systems architecting practice. We shall indeed understand that we cannot manage a convergence protocol, in order to create a shared vision among project actors on a given topic, in the same way as a technical study or a prototype development. When dealing with people, mistakes or bugs are typically forbidden[5]: contrarily to a purely technical problem, human issues shall always be managed with great care. The complexity of the systems architect job is in particular to be able to manage convergence protocols – with their inherent socio-dynamic difficulties – in complex technical environments[6].

To progress in systems architecting, the systems architect shall thus clearly develop its non-technical competency (consensus creation, workshop animation, meeting facilitation, etc.), but which has to be applied in technical complex contexts. In this matter, practice is absolutely fundamental. We can just not achieve developing leadership in systems architecting without confronting the complexity of real-system development situations.

In this matter, we may note that CESAMES is offering a dedicated 6–10 month on-the-job training in systems architecting. Such trainings are especially devoted to that leadership construction through the concrete application of a full systems architecting process on a real system and the achievement of a complete systems architecture specification file (see the previous section). For more details, we refer to the corresponding item in the training section on our website: www.cesames.net.

C.5. Towards a new systems architecture modeling language

Last, but not least, we would like to point out that the different diagrams we introduced in this book were all constructed on the basis of a SysML syntax (see for instance Friedenthal *et al.* (2012)) in order both to avoid disorienting the reader and to let him/her able to use standard modeling tools to practically apply the material he/she will find in this book. In this matter, note that the specific Appendix 4 is also especially dedicated to explain how to practically implement the CESAM framework within a SysML system modeling tool.

---

5 Telling to someone to do something, then sometimes after, to do something else, then again after, to do something again different, will probably never work …

6 The mix between technique and socio-dynamics is of course the core difficulty of systems architecting in practice.

However, we can easily see by reading this book that the SysML syntax is not perfectly adapted to the needs of systems architecting, due to the differences and/or discrepancies that exist between the different views within the SysML framework. The SysML diagrams used to statically specify missions, functions and components together with their interactions are for instance not homogeneous, which is clearly absurd[7], thus leading to lots of easily avoidable – with a good modeling language – technical difficulties while modeling systems. We would thus like to launch a final call to the systems engineering community for creating an architecture-oriented system modeling language with a sound mathematical-based semantics such as the one provided by the CESAM framework.

---

7 Other typical issues are also coming from the fact that, in most modeling languages, environment's objects do not have the same type that system's objects. This is just a terribly bad choice since it prevents us to make use of the natural recursion brought by a system hierarchy.

Appendices

Appendix 1

System Temporal Logic

Formal requirements are expressed in *system temporal logic*[1], a mathematical formalism that we did not present below and that we will discuss in full details in this appendix.

System temporal logic is a formal logic that extends the same classical notion for computer programs (see for instance Pnueli 1977; Manna and Pnueli 1992; Baier and Katoen 2008; Kröger and Merz 2008; Katoen 2009; Murray 2012; Artale 2010-2011). Such a logic intends to specify the sequences of input/output and internal variable observations that can be made on a formal system whose input, output and internal variable sets X, Y, Q and timescale T are fixed. In other terms, system temporal logic specifies the sequences O of values of inputs, outputs and internal variables that can be observed among all moments of time t within the timescale T, as stated below:

$$O = (O(t)) \text{ for all } t \in T, \text{ where we set } O(t) = (x(t), y(t), q(t))[2].$$

It is based on the atomic formulae that may be either "TRUE" or equal to $O(x, y, q)$[3], where x (resp. y or q) is either an element of the input set X (resp. output set Y

---

1 The system temporal logic that we present here is a system-adaptation of the simplest temporal logic used in theoretical computer science, which is called LTL (Linear Temporal Logic; see Pnueli 1977; Baier and Katoen 2008; Kröger and Merz 2008; Katoen 2009; Murray 2012; Artale). However, there exists plenty of other more expressive temporal logics (see Baier and Katoen (2008) or Kröger and Merz (2008)) that can be adapted to a systems engineering context, if necessary, depending on the level of expressivity that may be requested.

2 Using here the formalism of Definition 1.1.

3 As we will see below, $O(x, y, z)$ stands for a predicate that fix the initial value $x(t_0)$, $y(t_0)$ and $q(t_0)$ of the inputs, outputs and internal variables to x, y and q at the initial moment t_0 of the considered timescale.

or internal variable set Q) or equal to the special symbol $\varnothing$ (that models an arbitrary value), except that x, y and q cannot be all equal to $\varnothing$. Atomic formulae within system temporal logic are the following:

> TRUE, O(x, y, q) for all $x \in X \cup \{\varnothing\}$, $y \in Y \cup \{\varnothing\}$ and $q \in Q \cup \{\varnothing\}$ with $(x, y, z) \neq (\varnothing, \varnothing, \varnothing)$. [A1.1]

System temporal logic will then manipulate logical formulae – that is, well-formed predicates – that are expressing the expected properties of the sequences of inputs, outputs and internal variables of a formal system among all moments of time t within a considered timescale. Such a logic involves the following two kinds of logical operators (see Aiguier *et al.* (2012, 2013) for more details):

– two classical truth-function operators: AND (conjunction) and NOT (negation);

– two specific temporal operators X (neXt) and U (Until) whose syntax is provided below:

- X f, meaning that formula f is fulfilled at the next state,

- f U g, meaning that formula f is fulfilled until g becomes fulfilled.

We will provide soon the system semantics of all these different operators. However, we now are in position to syntactically define a *temporal formula* as any well-formed logical formula that may be obtained by recursively applying these different logical operators, starting with an atomic formula.

For the sake of simplicity, we may introduce, on one hand, two other truth-function operators, OR (disjunction) and $\rightarrow$ (implies), and, on the other hand, two other temporal operators, $\lozenge$ (eventually) and $\square$ (always), which can be expressed using the previous operators as provided by the here below four definitions (hence they do not extend the power of expressivity of the underlying logic), since they allow us to state more easily a number of temporal properties:

– additional truth-function logical operators:

- f OR g = NOT (NOT f AND NOT g) (f or g is true),

- f $\rightarrow$ g = NOT f OR g (f implies g is true),

– additional temporal operators:

- $\lozenge$ f = TRUE U f (f will be eventually true at some future moment of time),

- $\square$ f = NOT ($\lozenge$ NOT f) (f is true at any moment of time).

To end our presentation of system temporal logic, we must of course define the *semantics* of the different previous logical operators. In other terms, we need to explain when a formal system S, whose input, output and internal variable sets are X, Y and Q and whose timescale is T, will satisfy to a temporal formula constructed with these operators, which is expressed by writing S $\models$ f, which reads that the system S satisfies the formula f or equivalently that f is satisfied by S.

This satisfaction relationship $\models$, which provides the semantics of all system temporal formulae, can then be inductively defined according to the following properties (where we systematically set below S[t] for the system that has the same behavior as S, but whose initial moment is t instead of t_0):

– S $\models$ TRUE for any system S;

– S $\models$ O(x,y,q) if and only if $x(t_0) = x$, $y(t_0) = y$ and $q(t_0) = q$ (when x, y, q $\neq$ $\varnothing$)[4];

– S $\models$ f AND g if and only if S $\models$ f and S $\models$ g;

– S $\models$ NOT f if and only if we do not have S $\models$ f;

– S $\models$ X f if and only if $S[t_0+]$ $\models$ f;

– S $\models$ f U g if and only if $\exists$ t $\in$ T such that S[t] $\models$ g and S[u] $\models$ f, for all u $\in$ T with u < t.

It is also interesting to explicitly provide the semantics of the two additional temporal operators that we introduced above, as it can be deduced from the previous definitions:

– S $\models$ $\square$ f if and only if we have S[t] $\models$ f, for all t $\in$ T;

– S $\models$ $\lozenge$ f if and only if there exists t $\in$ T such that S[t] $\models$ f.

Our formalism allows us to express all usual temporal properties of the systems. To be more specific, let us now see how to express a system performance property in this system temporal logic framework. To this purpose, we first need to introduce the following two logical predicates that are here modeling intervals, respectively, of input and output values:

X(x0,x1) = AND O(x,$\varnothing$, $\varnothing$) for all x $\in$ [x0,x1],

Y(y0,y1) = AND O(x,$\varnothing$, $\varnothing$) for all y $\in$ [y0,y1].

---

4 Where t_0 stands for the initial moment of the considered timescale T.

A typical performance property stating for instance that a system must always have its inputs lying between two values, a and b, and its outputs lying between two other values, c and d, as soon as its internal variable is equal to q, will then be expressed as follows:

Performance = $\square$ (O(∅, ∅, q) → X(a,b) AND Y(c,d)).

We can also provide the example of a maintainability property that is generically stated as follows, expressing simply here that a system that satisfy such a property must always go back to a normal state, expressed by a suitable "normal" value of the internal variables of the system, when it enters in a non-normal state at a certain moment of time:

Maintainability = $\square$ (NOT O(∅, ∅, "normal") → $\lozenge$ O(∅, ∅, "normal")).

In the same way, a safety property would finally be generically defined by expressing that a system shall never be in a non-safe state, again expressed by a suitable value "non-safe" of its internal variables, which can be stated as a system temporal logic invariant:

Safety = $\square$ (NOT O(∅, ∅, "non-safe")).

Appendix 2

Classical Engineering Issues

We shall now present several classical engineering issues on illustrative examples. These issues are indeed representative of the typical problems addressed by systems architecting. We classified them into two categories: on one hand, *product problems*, referring to purely architectural flaws leading to a bad design of the product, and, on the other hand, *project problems*, that is, organizational issues leading to a bad functioning of the project. An overview of these different problems is presented in Table A2.1 below. The details of our examples and analyses will be found in the sequel of this appendix.

Product system problems
Product problem 1 – The product system model does not capture reality
Typical issue: the system design is based on a model which does not match with reality
Example: the failure of Calcutta subway
Product problem 2 – The product system has undesirable emergent properties
Typical issue: a complex integrated system has unexpected and/or undesired emerging properties, coming from a local problem that has global consequences
Example: the explosion of Ariane 5 satellite launcher during its first flight
Project system problems
Project problem 1 – The project system has integration issues
Typical issue: the engineering of a system is not done in a collaborative way
Example: the huge delays of the Airbus A380 project
Project problem 2 – The project system diverts the product mission
Typical issue: the project forgets the mission of the product
Example: the failure of the luggage management system of Denver airport

Table A2.1. *Examples of typical product and project issues addressed by systems architecting*

A2.1. Product problem 1 – the product system model does not capture reality

To illustrate that first product architecture issue, we will consider the Calcutta subway case[1] which occurred when a very strong heat wave (45°C in the shadow) struck India during summertime. The cockpit touch screens of the subway trains became then completely blank, and the subway drivers were therefore not able to anymore pilot anything. As a consequence, the subway company stopped working during a few days, which lead moreover to a huge chaos in the city and to important financial penalties for the subway constructing company, until the temperature came back to normal, when it was again possible to operate the subways as usually.

To understand what happened, the subway designers immediately tested the cockpit touch screens, but these components worked fine under high-temperature conditions. It took then several months to understand the complete chain of events that lead to the observed dysfunction, which was – quite surprisingly for the engineers who made the analysis – of systemic nature, as we will now see.

The analysis indeed revealed that the starting point of the problem was the bogies, that is, the mechanical structure which is carrying the subway wheels. Each subway wagon is supported by two bogies, each of them with four wheels. The important point is that all these bogies were basically only made with metal. This metal expanded under the action of high temperature and heat, leading to an unexpected behavior of the bogies that we are now in a position to explain.

We must indeed also know that to each bogie is attached a braking system. These braking systems are in particular regulated by the central subway computer where a control law was embedded. The control law obliges each local braking system on each bogie to exert a braking force which shall be between two safety lower and upper borders[2], when braking is initiated. The role of the central computer is thus to ensure that the two safety borders are always maintained during braking, which is achieved by relaxing or increasing the braking force on a given braking system.

The key point was that the underlying control law was not valid at high temperature. This control law was indeed designed – and quite robust in that

1 This case is not public. We were thus obliged to hide its real location and to simplify its presentation, without, however, altering its nature and its systems architecting fundamentals.

2 Braking forces can indeed not be, neither too strong (in order to avoid wheels destroying rails), nor too weak (in order to avoid wheel slip which would result in no braking at all).

case – in an environment, where strong heat never occurs. Hence, nobody knew that the control law was no longer correct in such a situation.

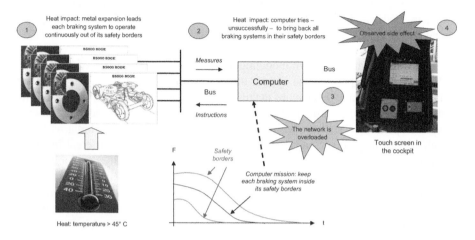

Figure A2.1. *The Calcutta subway case. For a color version of this figure, see www.iste.co.uk/krob/systems.zip*

What happened can now be easily explained. The high temperature indeed provoked the same metal expansion among the different subway bogies. Hence, all bogies were continuously working out of their safety borders during braking. But the computer was not aware of that situation and continued to try to bring back all braking systems inside their safety borders, applying its fixed control law that was unfortunately false in this new context. As a consequence, there was a permanent exchange of messages between the central computer and the numerous braking systems along the subway. It resulted in an overload of the network which was not dimensioned to support such a heavy traffic. The observed effect on the cockpit touch screens was thus just a side effect of this network overload, due to the fact that these cockpit touch screens are also connected to the central computer by the same network, which explains why nothing wrong was found at the cockpit touch screen level.

We can thus see that this case study highlights a typical modeling problem, here the fact that the braking control law was false in the Indian high-temperature context, as well as an integration issue[3], that ultimately led to an operational failure through a

---

3 In that case, all components are indeed working well individually. The problem is a subway system level problem that cannot be found in one single component, but rather in the bad integration of all involved components.

"domino" effect[4], where an initial local problem progressively propagated along the subway and resulted in a global breakdown of the system. We shall thus remember that it is a key good practice to permanently check and ensure the consistency between a system model and the reality that it models, since reality will indeed always be stronger than any model, as illustrated by the Calcutta subway case.

Note finally that this kind of modeling problem is typically addressed by systems architecting, which proposes an answer through "operational architecting" (we refer to both Chapters 4 and 5 for more details). Such an analysis indeed focuses on the understanding of the environment of the concerned system. In the Calcutta subway, a typical operational analysis would have consisted in considering India as a key stakeholder of the subway and then trying to understand what is different in India, compared to the Western countries where the subway was initially developed. It is then easy to find that very strong heat waves statistically occur in India each decade, which creates an Indian specific "high-temperature" context that shall be specifically analyzed. A good operational systems architecting analysis shall then be able to derive the right braking system lifecycle, as presented in Figure A2.2, with two states that are, respectively, modeling normal and high-temperature contexts and two transitions that do model the events[5] that create a change of state and of braking control law.

---

4 Another classical example of a domino effect is provided by de Weck (2006) who described the collapse of the redesign of the US F/A-18 aircraft fighter for the Swiss army, as already presented in Case study 7.1 of Chapter 7. This plane was indeed initially designed in 1978 for the US Navy as a carrier-based fighter and attacker, with 3,000 flight hour's expectation, missions with an average duration of 90 minutes and a maximal acceleration of 7.5 g and 15 years of useful life. Due to the neutral policy, inland, small size and mountainous nature of Switzerland, this country wanted a land-based interceptor aircraft, with 5,000 flight hour's expectation, missions with an average duration of 40 minutes and a maximal acceleration of 9.0 g and 30 years of useful life. Engineers analyzed that it was enough to change some non-robust fatigue components near the engine, made in aluminum, to meet Swiss requirements. These components were then redesigned in titanium. Unfortunately, a shift of the center of gravity of the aircraft was created and we needed to reinforce the fuselage to solve that issue. This other change led to transversal vibrations that required other reinforcements of weights and modifications in the flight control system. Many changes continued to propagate in the aircraft, up to impacting the industrial processes and the organization of the construction factory. Five hundred gram changes lead thus finally to 10 million dollar modifications that were never expected.

5 Here, the fact that the temperature is higher (resp. lower) than some threshold T0 (resp. T1) when the braking system is in "normal temperature" context (resp. "high-temperature" context).

Such a diagram is typically a (operational) system model. It looks apparently very simple[6], but we must understand that introducing the "high-temperature" context and the transition that leads to that state will allow avoiding a stupid operational issue and saving millions of euros …

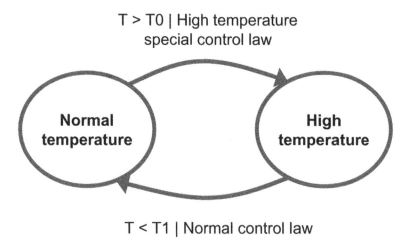

T > T0 | High temperature
special control law

Normal temperature

High temperature

T < T1 | Normal control law

Figure A2.2. *The missing operational analysis in the Calcutta subway case. For a color version of this figure, see www.iste.co.uk/krob/systems.zip*

A2.2. Product problem 2 – the product system has undesirable emergent properties

The second product-oriented case study that we will discuss is the explosion of the very first satellite launcher Ariane 5 which is well known due to the remarkable work of the Lions commission, who published a public detailed and fully transparent report on this accident (see Lions (1996)). This case was largely discussed in the engineering literature, but its main conclusions were mainly focused on how to better master critical real-time software design. We will now present here a systems architecting interpretation – focusing on the underlying integration issues – of that case, which, to the best of our knowledge, was never made up to now.

---

6 This simplicity is unfortunately an issue for systems architecting. Most of the people will indeed agree to the fact that we cannot manipulate partial differential equations without having studied applied mathematics. But the same people will surely think that no specific competency is required to write down simple operational models such as the one provided in Figure A2.2, which is unfortunately not the case. We indeed believe that only good systems architects can achieve such an apparently simple result, which will always be the consequence of a good combination of training and personal skills.

Let us now remember what happened on June 4, 1996 for the first flight of Ariane 5. First of all, the flight of this satellite launcher was perfect from second 0 up to second 36 after take-off. At second 36.7, there was, however, a simultaneous failure of the two inertial systems of the launcher that lead at second 37 to the activation of the automatic pilot which misunderstood the error data transmitted by the inertial systems. The automatic pilot then brutally corrected the trajectory of Ariane 5, leading to a mechanical brake of the boosters and thus to the initiation of the self-destruction procedure of the launcher that finally exploded at second 39 (see Figure A2.3).

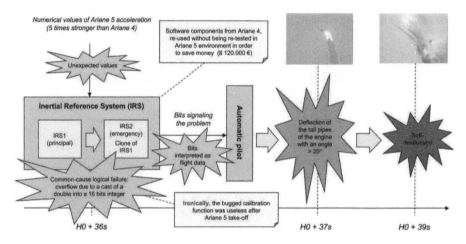

Figure A2.3. *The Ariane 5 case. For a color version of this figure, see www.iste.co.uk/krob/systems.zip*

As we can easily guess, the global cost of this accident was tremendously high and probably reached around 1 billion euros. We know that the direct cost due to the satellite load loss was around 370 million euros. But there was also an induced cost for recovering the most dangerous fragments of the launcher (such as the fuel stock) that crashed in the (quite difficult to access) Guyana swamps, which took one month of work. Moreover, there were huge indirect costs due to the Ariane 5 program delaying: a second test flight was only performed one year later and it took three more years to perform the first commercial flight of the launcher, by December 10, 1999.

As already stated, the reason for that tragic accident is fortunately completely analyzed through the Lions commission report (cf. Lions (1996)). The origin of the accident could indeed be traced back to the reuse of the inertial reference system

(IRS)[7] of Ariane 4. This critical complex software component perfectly worked on Ariane 4, and it was thus identically reused on Ariane 5 without being retested[8] in the new environment. Unfortunately, Ariane 5 was a much more powerful launcher than Ariane 4 and the numerical values of Ariane 5 acceleration – which are the inputs of the inertial reference system – were five times bigger than for Ariane 4. These real values were thus coded in double precision in the context of Ariane 5, when a certain function of the inertial reference system was designed to only accept single precision real numbers as inputs. As a consequence, due to the fact that this software function was coded in C[9], an overflow occurred during its execution. The error codes resulting from that software error were then unfortunately interpreted as flight data by the automatic pilot of Ariane 5, which corrected – one second after receiving these error codes – the trajectory of the launcher from an angle of more than 20°, resulting quite immediately in the mechanical breaking of the launcher boosters and one second after, in the initiation of the self-destruction procedure.

The Ariane 5 explosion is hence a typical integration issue[10]. All its components worked individually perfectly, but without correctly working altogether when integrated. Hence, we shall remember that a component of an integrated system is never correct by itself. It is only relatively correct to the set of its interfaced components. When this set evolves, we must thus check that the target component is

7 An inertial reference system is a software-based system that continuously calculates the position, orientation and velocity of a moving object. In the context of Ariane 5, it is thus a highly critical system since most of the other systems are depending on its calculations.

8 The engineer in charge of the IRS proposed to retest it in the new Ariane 5 environment, but it was decided not to follow that proposal in order to save around 120,000 euros of testing costs.

9 The C programming language is very permissive and does not provide any automatic type control. On the contrary, a C program will always convert any input value into the data type that it is intended to manipulate. In the Ariane 5 context, the inertial reference software system thus automatically converted all double precision float inputs into single precision float values, according to the standard C language rules. This purely syntactic-type conversion destroyed the physical meaning of the involved data, leading thus to the observed overflow.

10 Moreover, they were also a number of software engineering mistakes – which are presented below – that also illustrate the fact that the hardware–software integrated nature of the launcher was not really taken into account by the designers. *Issue 1 – software specificity misunderstanding*: only physical (which are statistical) component failures were considered, but logical (which are systematic) component failures are of totally different nature. Note that this kind of software failure can only be addressed by formal model checking or dissimilar redundancy strategy (which consists of developing two different versions of the software component by two different teams on the basis of the same specification in order to ensure a different distribution of bugs within the two versions); *issue 2 – poor software documentation*: the conditions for a correct behavior of the IRS module were not explicitly documented in the source code; *issue 3 – poor software architecture:* the raise of a local exception in a software component shall normally never imply its global failure.

still properly integrated with its environment, since the fact that the IRS module fulfilled Ariane 4 requirements cannot ensure that it fulfils Ariane 5 requirements.

This example also shows that an – usually not researched – emergent property of integration can be death. The Ariane 5 system was indeed *incorrect by design* since the launcher could only explode as it was integrated. In other words, Ariane 5 destruction was embedded in its architecture and it can be seen as a purely logical consequence[11] of its integration mode. This extremal – and fortunately rare – case illustrates thus well the real difficulty of mastering the integration of complex systems!

Note finally that systems architecting can provide a number of methodological tools to avoid such integration issues. Among them, we can typically cite interface or impact analyses. In the Ariane 5 context, a simple interface-type consistency check would for instance allowed seeing that the input types of the inertial reference system were simply not compatible with the expected ones, which would probably permit avoiding a huge disaster!

A2.3. Project problem 1 – the project system has integration issues

Our first "project architecture" issue is the initial Airbus 380 delivery delay, since it is mainly public (see Wikipedia (2021a) for an extensive presentation of that case study). Let us recall that this aircraft is the world's largest passenger airliner. Its origin goes back to the mid-1988 when Airbus engineers began to work in secret on an ultra-high-capacity airplane in order to break the dominance that Boeing had on that market segment since the early 1970s with its 747 aircraft. It took, however, a number of years of studies to arrive at the official decision of announcing, in June 1994, the creation of the A3XX program which was the first name of the A380 within Airbus. Due to the evolution of the aeronautic market that darkened in that moment of time, it is interesting to observe that Airbus decided then to refine its design, targeting a 15–20% reduction in operating costs over the existing Boeing 747 family. The A3XX design finally converged on a double-decker layout

---

11 The IRS component of Ariane 5 consisted of two exactly similar software modules (which, as explained in the previous footnote, was of no use, due to the logical nature of the failure that similarly repeated in each of these modules). The 36 seconds delay that separated take-off from the crash of the IRS can thus be broken down in two times 18 seconds that are necessary for each module to logically crash. As a consequence, we can typically state the following architectural "theorem" which illustrates the "incorrection" by design of Ariane 5. *Theorem*: let us suppose that the IRS component of Ariane 5 has N similar software modules. The launcher shall then be destroyed at second 18*N+3.

that provided more passenger volume than a traditional single-deck design, perfectly in line with the traditional hub-and-spoke theory as opposed to the point-to-point theory that was the Boeing paradigm for large airliners, after conducting an extensive market analysis with over 200 focus groups.

In the beginning of 2000, the commercial history of the A380 – the new name that was then given to the A3XX – began and the first orders arrived at Airbus by 2001. The industrial organization was then put in place between 2002 and 2005: the A380 components are indeed provided by suppliers from all around the world, when the main structural sections of the airliner are built in France, Germany, Spain and United Kingdom, for a final assembly in Toulouse in a dedicated integration location. The first fully assembled A380 was thus unveiled in Toulouse by January 18, 2005 before its first flight on April 27, 2005. By January 10, 2006, it flew to Colombia, accomplishing both the transatlantic test, and the testing of the engine operation in high-altitude airports. It also arrived in North America on February 6, 2006, landing in Iqaluit in Nunavut, Canada, for cold-weather testing. On September 4, 2006, the first full passenger-carrying flight test took place. Finally, Airbus obtained the first A380 flight certificates from the EASA and FAA on December 12, 2006.

During that entire period, orders continued to arrive from the airline companies, up to reaching a bit less than 200 cumulated orders, obtained in 2007. The first deliveries were initially – in 2003 – planned for end 2006, with an objective of producing around 120 aircrafts for 2009. Unfortunately, many industrial difficulties – that we will discuss below – occurred and it was thus necessary to sharply re-estimate downward these figures each year[12] (cf. Figure A2.4). The very first commercial A380 was finally produced by end 2007 and instead of 120, only 23 airliners were delivered in 2009.

---

12 Airbus announced the first delay in June 2005 and notified airlines that deliveries would be delayed by six months. This reduced the total number of planned deliveries by the end of 2009 from about 120 to 90–100. On June 13, 2006, Airbus announced a second delay, with the delivery schedule slipping an additional six to seven months. Although the first delivery was still planned before the end of 2006, deliveries in 2007 would drop to only nine aircrafts, and deliveries by the end of 2009 would be cut to 70–80 aircraft. The announcement caused a 26% drop in the share price of Airbus' parent company, EADS, and led to the departures of EADS CEO, Airbus CEO, and A380 program manager. On October 3, 2006, upon completion of a review of the A380 program, Airbus new CEO announced a third delay, pushing the first delivery to October 2007, to be followed by 13 deliveries in 2008, 25 in 2009 and the full production rate of 45 aircraft per year in 2010.

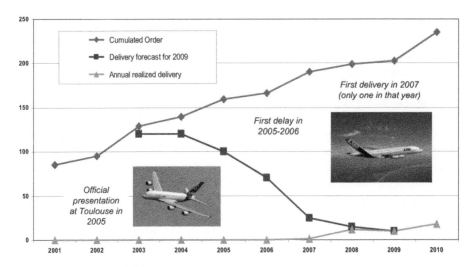

Figure A2.4. *The Airbus 380 case. For a color version*
of this figure, see www.iste.co.uk/krob/systems.zip

These delays had strong financial consequences, since they increased the earnings shortfall projected by Airbus through 2010 to € 4.8 billion. It is thus clearly interesting to try to better understand the root causes of such an important failure.

The source of these delays seems to be connected to the incoherence of the 530 km (330 miles) long electrical wiring, produced both in France and Germany. Airbus cited in particular as underlying root causes the complexity of the cabin wiring (98,000 wires and 40,000 connectors), its concurrent design and production process, the high degree of cabin customization which is requested for each airline company, and failures in configuration management and change control. These electrical wiring incoherencies were indeed only discovered at the final integration stage in Toulouse[13], which was of course much too late …

The origin of this problem could be traced back to the fact that German and Spanish Airbus facilities continued to use CATIA® version 4, while British and French sites migrated to version 5. This caused overall configuration management problems, at least in part because wire harnesses, manufactured using aluminum, rather than copper, conductors, necessitated special design rules including non-standard dimensions and bend radii. This specific information was not easily

---

13 There exists a video where we can see a poor technician in Toulouse that is unable to connect two electrical wires coming from two different sections of the aircraft, due to a lack of 20 cm of wire.

transferred between versions of the CAD[14] software, which lead to incoherent manufacturing activities and, at the very end, created the integration issue that was observed in Toulouse. On a totally different dimension, the strong customization of the aircraft internal equipment also induced a long learning curve for the teams and led thus to other delays.

Independently of these "official" causes, there are other plausible deep causes coming from cultural conflicts among the dual-headed French and German direction of Airbus and lack – or break – of communication between the multi-localized teams of the European aircraft manufacturer.

As systems architects, we may summarize such problems as typical "project architecture" issues. The issues finally observed at the product level are indeed only consequences of lack of integration within the project, that is, project interfaces – to use a system vocabulary – that were not coherent, which simply refer, in more familiar terms, to project teams or project tools that were not coherently working altogether. It is thus key to have a robust project architecture in the context of complex systems development since the project system is always at least as complex as the product system that it is developing. Unfortunately, it is a matter of fact that the energy spent with technical issues is usually much more important than the energy spent on solving organizational issues, which often ultimately leads to obviously bad project architectures in complex systems contexts, resulting, at the very end, in bad technical architectures in such contexts.

A2.4 Project problem 2 – the project system diverts the product mission

As a last example of different types of project issues, we will now consider the case of the Denver airport luggage management system failure, which is fortunately well known due to the fact that it is completely public (see for instance de Neufville (1994) or Schloh (1996)).

Denver airport is currently the largest airport in the United States in terms of the total land area. It was the 6th airport in the United States (the 10th in the world) in terms of passenger traffic. As a matter of fact, it was initially designed in order to be one of the main hubs for United Airlines and the main hub for two local airlines.

The airport construction officially started in September 1989 and it was initially scheduled to open on October 29, 1993. Due to the very large distance between the three terminals of the airport and the need for fast aircraft rotations for answering to

---

14 CAD stands for computer-aided design.

its hub mission, the idea of automating the luggage management emerged in order to provide very quick aircraft inter-connections to travelers. United Airlines was the promoter of such a system which was already implemented in Atlanta airport, one of their other hubs. Since Denver airport was intended to be much wider, the idea transformed into using the opportunity of Denver's new airport construction to improve Atlanta's system in order to create the most efficient and innovative luggage management system in the world[15]. It was indeed expected to have 27 km of transportation tracks, with 9 km of interchange zones, on which were circulating 4,000 remotely controlled wagons at a constant transportation speed of 38 km/h for an average transportation delay of 10 minutes, which was completely unique.

The luggage management system project started in January 1992, a bit less than two years before the expected opening of the airport. For one year, the difficulties of this specific project were hidden since there were many other problems with more classical systems. However, at the beginning of 1993, it became clear that the luggage management system could not be delivered on schedule and Denver's city major was obliged to push back the opening date, first to December 1993, then to March 1994 and finally again to May 15, 1994.

Unfortunately, the new automated luggage management system continued to have strong problems. In April 1994, the city invited reporters to observe the first operational test of the new automated luggage system: they saw instead disastrous scenes where the new system was destroying luggage, opening and crashing their contents before them. The major was then obliged to cancel sine die the opening date of the airport. As we can imagine, no airline – excepted United – wanted to use the new "fantastic" system, which obliged to abandon the idea of a global luggage management system for the whole airport. When the airport finally opened in February 28, 1995, only the United Airlines terminal was thus equipped with the new luggage management system, when the other terminal[16] that also opened was simply equipped with totally classical systems (i.e. tugs and carts).

In 1995, the direct additional costs due to this failure were approximately 600 M$, leading to more than 1 billion dollars over cost at the very end. Moreover, the new baggage system continued to be a maintenance hassle[17]. It was finally terminated by United Airlines in September 2005 and replaced by traditional handlers, manually handling cargo and passenger luggage. A TV reporter who

---

15 The idea was to have a fully automated luggage transportation system, with new hardware and software technologies, that was able to manage very large volumes of luggage.

16 It was initially not possible to open the last airport terminal due to the time which was required for changing the already constructed automatic luggage management system to a standard manual one.

17 Its nickname quickly became the "luggage system of hell"!

covered the full story concluded quite interestingly[18] that "it took ten years, and tons of money, to figure out that big muscles, not computers, can best move luggage".

When we look back at that case, it is quite easy to understand why this new automatic luggage system collapsed. The system had first too many innovations[19]. It was indeed both the first global automated system, the first automatic system that was managing oversized luggage (skis!), the first system where carriages did not stop during their service[20], the first system supported by a computer network and the first system with a fleet of radio-localized carriages. There was also an underlying huge increase in complexity: compared to the similar existing Atlanta system, the new luggage management system was 10 times faster, had 14 times the maximal known capacity and managed 10 times more destinations. Moreover, the project schedule was totally unrealistic with respect to the state-of-the-art: due to the strong delay pressure, no physical model and no preliminary mechanical tests were done, when the balancing – that is, testing and fixing – of the luggage management system lines required up to two years in Atlanta.

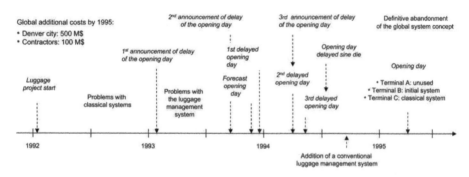

Figure A2.5. *The Denver luggage management system case. For a color version of this figure, see www.iste.co.uk/krob/systems.zip*

18 One must always remember that a system can be formed of people only doing manual operations. In most of the cases, good systems architectures are hybrid with both automatic and manual parts. In Denver's case, the best solution was, however, purely manual, which took 10 years for United Airlines to understand.

19 As a matter of fact, it is interesting to know that Marcel Dassault, the famous French aircraft engineer, was refusing all projects with more than one innovation! A strategy that worked quite well for him.

20 Suitcases were automatically thrown with a catapult ... which easily explains the high ratio of crashes.

It is thus quite easy to understand that the new luggage management system could only collapse. In some sense, it collapsed because the project team totally lost sight of the mission of that system, which was just to quickly transport luggage within the airport and at the lowest possible cost, with a strong implementation constraint due to the fact that there were only less than two years to implement the system. A simple systems architecture analysis would probably have concluded that the best solution was not to innovate, but to simply use people, tugs and carts, as usual. This case study illustrates thus quite well a very classical project issue where the project system forgets the mission of the product system and replaces it by a purely project-oriented mission[21] that diverts the project from achieving the product system mission. Any systems architect must thus always have in mind this example in order to avoid the same issue to occur on its working perimeter.

---

21 In Denver's luggage management system case, "creating the world most innovative luggage management system" indeed became the only objective of the project (which is not any more a product, but a project system mission).

Appendix 3

Example of System Model Managed with CESAM

We shall now dedicate this appendix to the presentation of a quite complete system model managed with the CESAM framework. After introducing the system of interest that we shall use to this aim, we shall present the main – environment, operational, functional and constructional – system views, as proposed by the CESAM approach, on the case study analyzed in this appendix.

A3.1. The system of interest

Figure A3.1. *Our system of interest: a smartphone system. For a color version of this figure, see www.iste.co.uk/krob/systems.zip*

In this appendix, the system of interest that we will study through a system analysis is a *smartphone*. It is a technological system that we easily use all day long and thus seems quite simple, but it is in fact a very complex system, which makes it particularly interesting to study (see Figure A3.1)!

At this point, we shall, however, just stress, for the reader who is not aware of this, that a smart phone is not at all a phone, in its traditional technological meaning, but a computer which was miniaturized and that emulates the main functionality of a phone.

A3.2. Environment architecture

The environment architecture of a smartphone system consists of a stakeholder hierarchy diagram where all stakeholders of the smartphone are hierarchically organized and an environment diagram which elicits the main external interfaces of a smartphone.

A3.2.1. *Stakeholder hierarchy diagram*

The stakeholder hierarchy diagram, which is associated with a smartphone system, organizes the various stakeholders of a smartphone according to the following clusters:

– *end-users* refer to the people – adults or teenagers – who may use a smartphone;

– *services providers* are companies that propose value-added smartphone services, such as applications development services, smartphone user services or banking services;

– *communication system* groups all communication networks and associated operators to which a smartphone may be interfaced during its lifecycle;

– *electrical and electronical devices* are the various electrical and electronical devices which can exchange electricity and/or data with a smartphone;

– *surrounding environment* means the physical environment and the customized devices, such as USB connectors or smartphone cases, with which a smartphone may be in touch;

– *product services* offer services that help the user avoid negative impacts directed to or coming from a smartphone (e.g. anti-virus software, repairers or recycling systems);

– *malicious agents* are all external entities which try to disturb – with malicious motivations – the normal behavior of a smartphone, such as hackers, thieves or malware for instance;

– *technology* refers to the technological platforms and providers used by a smartphone;

– *development teams* correspond to all teams involved in the development of a smartphone (marketing, designers, testing teams, suppliers, etc.);

– *norms and regulations* are the smartphone-relevant communication and health regulations.

The resulting stakeholder hierarchy diagram is provided in Figure A3.2.

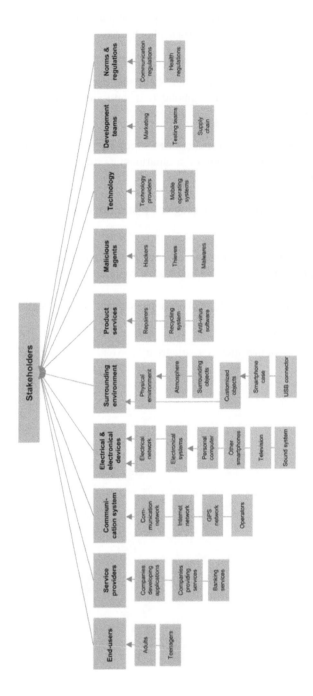

Figure A3.2. *Stakeholder hierarchy diagram of a smartphone system.*
For a color version of this figure, see www.iste.co.uk/krob/systems.zip

A3.2.2. *Environment diagram*

The environment diagram of a smartphone system can then be obtained (see Figure A3.3) by eliciting the various external interfaces that exist between a smartphone and all its high-level stakeholders, as provided by the previous stakeholder hierarchy diagram.

Note that these external interfaces are of very different natures: we find of course data interfaces, such as between the end-users, service providers and communication system and the smartphone, as well as mechanical interfaces, for instance between the end-users, surrounding environment and some product services and the smartphone, electrical and electromagnetic interfaces, for example, between the communication system, electrical and electronical devices and the smartphone, and finally influencing interfaces, for example, between the development teams, technology, norms and regulations and the smartphone. For malicious agents, they are interfaced with the smartphone through data or mechanical interfaces depending on the type of threat they are exerting.

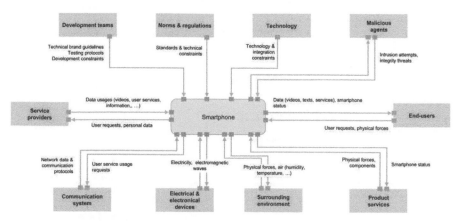

Figure A3.3. *Environment diagram of a smartphone system. For a color version of this figure, see www.iste.co.uk/krob/systems.zip*

A3.3. Operational architecture

The operational architecture of a given system is normally formed by a need architecture diagram, a lifecycle diagram, use case and associated operational scenario diagrams together with an operational flow diagram. For the smartphone system, we will, however, only present – for the sake of simplicity – the two first diagrams, then elicit just the list of its use cases, focus only on one representative operational scenario diagram and finally skip the operational flow diagram.

A3.3.1. *Need architecture diagram*

The need architecture diagram of a smartphone system consists of the following diagrams, grouped within Figure A3.4, where the main needs with respect to a smartphone are listed and hierarchically organized, each of them being stated according to the standard need pattern (see section 3.4.2).

Figure A3.4. *Need architecture diagram of a smartphone system. For a color version of this figure, see www.iste.co.uk/krob/systems.zip*

As we can see, these needs are classified according to six main categories, that is, operability, availability, performance, safety and security, evolutivity and transparency, which are themselves sub-divided into two to three sub-categories in most of the cases.

It is also interesting to see that this hierarchical representation allows us to quickly see the good/bad balance between the different need categories, as shown in Figure A3.5 which gives the distribution of the number of needs per need category: if we expect for instance to have six to seven key needs per category on average, we can clearly see that the performance and availability categories may contain a few too many or not enough needs, when the evolutivity and transparency categories certainly contain too few needs. It is therefore necessary to revisit these last categories to either reduce/increase the needs that they contain, or group existing need categories in order to have a more balanced distribution of needs among them.

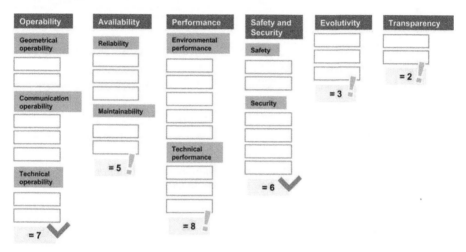

Figure A3.5. *Analysis of the need distribution of a smartphone system. For a color version of this figure, see www.iste.co.uk/krob/systems.zip*

A3.3.2. *Lifecycle diagram*

The lifecycle diagram of a smartphone system synthesizes all its lifecycle phases with their temporal relationships. These lifecycle phases of a smartphone can be organized into three main groups:

– All initial "development", "manufacturing", "delivery", "exposition/storage" and "shipment" lifecycle phases that happen before the end-users arrive.

– The various lifecycle phases that may occur during the normal use of a smartphone by an end-user, that is, included in the global "usage" lifecycle phase, which are conjunctions of situations of life depending on the online/offline, electrical network connection and user identification status and on the temperature and humidity environmental conditions.

– The special "maintenance" and "recycling" lifecycle phases that cover the way the degraded situations – up to its end of life – of the smartphone are managed.

The resulting lifecycle phase diagram can be seen in Figure A3.6.

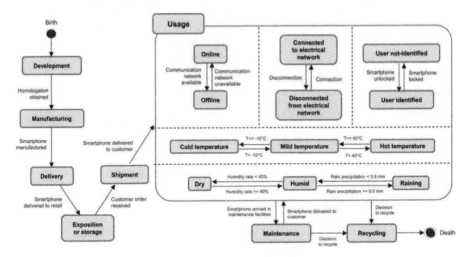

Figure A3.6. *Lifecycle diagram of a smartphone system. For a color version of this figure, see www.iste.co.uk/krob/systems.zip*

A3.3.3. *List of use cases*

Concerning the use cases of a smartphone system, we shall only focus here on providing the list of the use cases of such a system, without beginning to specify each use case through a dedicated use case diagram. This last strategy is indeed quite classical in practice, since it is always better, when of course possible, to directly dig into an operational scenario diagram to specify a given use case, since operational scenario diagrams are much more specific than use case diagrams.

The list of the use cases of a smart phone is therefore provided in Figure A3.7. The different use cases listed in the two tables that we can find in this figure are classified per lifecycle phase, as identified in the previous lifecycle phase diagram. Note that we did not write down any use case, neither for the "disconnected from electrical network" lifecycle phase, nor for the lifecycle phases associated with the three temperature conditions that we considered, since they can easily be obtained with the generic pattern "use smartphone when X", where X is just the considered lifecycle phase.

A3.3.4. *Operational scenario diagrams*

In terms of operational scenarios, which form the last key operational analysis, we shall only develop a single operational scenario diagram for a smartphone system, as a representative example. In this matter, we chose the "use applications and services" use case which is associated with the "online" lifecycle phase of the smartphone, as we can see from the list of use cases of a smartphone that we provided in the previous section. This use case is indeed probably the central use case of a smartphone in the perspective of any end-user, which explains its quite natural choice.

The corresponding operational scenario diagram specifies the "use applications and services" use case by expressing that the three following activities are occurring in parallel during the period of time corresponding to the considered use case:

– The end-user continuously asks for services – up to the end of use – which results, on the one hand, in the normal case when the temperature of the smartphone is OK, in the delivery of the requested service data, done through the communication system by the relevant service provider, and, in the abnormal case when the temperature of the smartphone is not OK, on the other hand, to the deny of the requested service, with explanation sent to the end-user and inhibition of any interfaced electrical and electronical device.

– Temperature from the surrounding environment diffuses on the smartphone and electricity is provided to the smartphone by some electric and electronical device.

– Malicious agents are trying to attack the smartphone by means of intrusion attempts made through the communication system.

The resulting operational scenario diagram is provided in Figure A3.5. The "par" box there represents the parallelism of the different activities separated by dash lines, when the "loop" box expresses a "while" sequence and the "alt" box models an "if then else" sequence, both of them being controlled by the logical condition which is put under brackets at the top of the corresponding box.

Lifecycle phase	Use case	
Usage		
Connectivity	**Offline**	Customise smartphone
		Know smartphone status
		Back up smartphone
		Reset smartphone
		Get smartphone usage advice
		Extend smartphone life
		Use applications and services offline
		Offer applications and services
		Connect customised objects
		Damage smartphone
		Connect E&E devices
	Online	Troubleshoot smartphone
		Diagnose smartphone
		Attack smartphone
		Ensure confidentiality
	Online	Use applications and services
		Add new applications and services
		Update applications and services
		Send network data
		Get network data
Electrical network	**Disconnected from electrical network**	
	Connected to electrical network	Charge smartphone
		Extend smartphone life
End-user	**Absence of end-user**	Unlock smartphone
	End-user usage	Lock smartphone
		Secure smartphone
Temperature	**Hot temperature**	
	Mild temperature	
	Cold temperature	

Lifecycle phase	Use case
Development	Scope smartphone
	Design smartphone
	Verify smartphone
	Validate smartphone
	Test applications and services
	Approve smartphone
Manufacturing	Produce smartphone parts
	Source smartphone parts
	Assemble smartphone
	Check smartphone
Delivery	Pack smartphone
	Transport smartpone
	Trace smartphone
Exposition or storage	Store smartphone
	Identify smartphone
	Make a demo of smartphone
	Experience smartphone features
Shipment	Ship smartphone to customer
	Receive smartphone

Figure A3.7. *List of use cases classified per lifecycle phase of a smartphone system. For a color version of this figure, see www.iste.co.uk/krob/systems.zip*

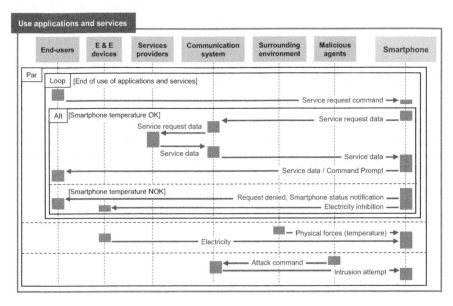

Figure A3.8. *Example of an operational scenario diagram of a smartphone system. For a color version of this figure, see www.iste.co.uk/krob/systems.zip*

A3.4. Functional architecture

The functional architecture of a system is normally formed by a functional requirement architecture diagram, a functional breakdown diagram, a functional interaction diagram and a series of functional scenario diagrams, when relevant, which altogether elicit the functions of the system with their interactions, completed by a functional mode diagram and a functional flow diagram. For the smartphone system, we will, however, only present – for the sake of simplicity – the first diagrams, without showing the functional mode diagram and the functional flow diagram.

A3.4.1. *Functional requirement architecture diagram*

The functional requirement architecture diagram of a smartphone system is the diagram, which is provided in Figure A3.9, where the main functional requirements associated with a smartphone are listed and hierarchically organized, each of them being stated according to the standard functional requirement pattern (see section 3.4.2 for more details).

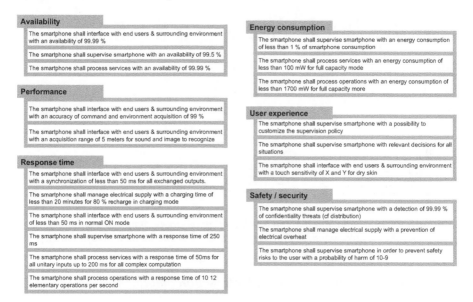

Figure A3.9. *Functional requirement architecture diagram of a smartphone system*

These functional requirements are here distributed among the following six categories of functional requirements: availability, performance, response time, energy consumption, user experience and safety/security. We may, however, observe that the response time category probably has too many functional requirements since it is disbalanced with respect to the other categories of functional requirements in terms of the number of functional requirements that it contains.

We shall of course recall that functional requirements always originate from needs and it is therefore important to maintain traceability between a given functional requirement and the source needs to which it brings an answer. This can be achieved through a need to functional requirement matrix which captures the corresponding traceability relationships. A partial example of such a traceability matrix is sketched in Figure A3.10, where we begin to trace how three needs can be covered by four functional requirements with respect to a smartphone. For the sake of place, note, however, that we only indicated here the functions that were impacted by the considered needs.

	Process services				Operate smartphone		Supervise smartphone		Interface with environment		Protect from environment	Manage electrical supply			Communicate			
	Dispatch contents	Centralize input data	Run services	Convert service and device data	Compute operations	Manage memories	Manage operation priorities & modes	Analyse smartphone health	Deliver environment outputs	Acquire environment inputs	Protect from environment	Distribute electricity	Store electricity	Receive electricity	Send data to services	Acquire service data	Send data to devices	Acquire device data
N1									X	X								
N2							X	X	X									
N3																		

N1	N2	N3
Electronic systems shall be able to exchange data with wired, Wi-Fi, NFC and Bluetooth protocols for all electronic systems built after 2019 in connected usage phase.	End-users shall be able to know the smartphone status about energy level, health, data storage and memory use in real time in usage phase	The recycling system shall be able to recycle 95% of the smartphone components at a cost lower than 2 dollars per smartphone.

Figure A3.10. *Partial need to the functional requirement matrix of a smartphone system. For a color version of this figure, see www.iste.co.uk/krob/systems.zip*

A3.4.2. *Functional breakdown and interaction diagrams*

The functional breakdown diagram – also called the functional breakdown structure – of a smartphone system hierarchically organizes all smartphone functions around the following high-level functions that we classified in four clusters for a better understanding:

– Supervision function:

- supervise smartphone that monitors, decides and chooses the smartphone priorities and modes, depending on the smartphone health.

– Environment interfacing functions:

- interface with environment that realizes the usual input/output mechanisms of the smartphone, when in normal mode;

- protect from environment that protects the smartphone from dysfunctional inputs or outputs, resulting from an abnormal lifecycle phase or functional mode.

– Process functions:

- process services that run all user-oriented/visible smartphone services;

- process operations that run all low-level technical smartphone operations.

– Electrical and electromagnetic support functions:

- manage electrical supply that manages electricity;

- communicate that manages network communications.

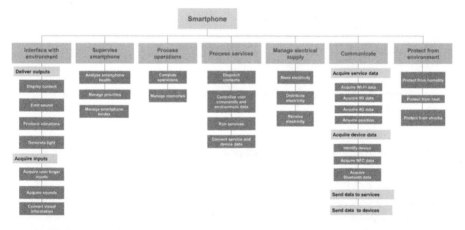

Figure A3.11. *Functional breakdown structure diagram of a smartphone system*

The resulting functional breakdown diagram is provided in Figure A3.11. Note that some sub-functions of the high-level functions that we just introduced were also sub-clustered when relevant.

The only knowledge of the smartphone functions is, however, not enough to master its functional architecture; we also need to understand the functional interfaces of each of these functions which may be either internal interfaces, that is, between two smartphone functions, or external interfaces, that is, between a function and a stakeholder of the smartphone. This is the core objective of the functional interaction diagram which is provided in Figure A3.12. Note that the four functional clusters that we proposed here above, when introducing the functional breakdown diagram, can be easily observed on the functional interaction diagram through the proximity of the functions that we clustered, which reflects the internal or external couplings of these functions.

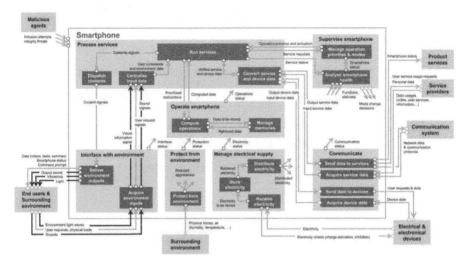

Figure A3.12. *Functional interaction diagram of a smartphone system. For a color version of this figure, see www.iste.co.uk/krob/systems.zip*

A3.4.3. *Functional scenario diagrams*

In terms of functional scenarios, which form the last key functional analysis, we shall only develop here a single functional scenario diagram for a smartphone system, as a representative example. Let us thus again consider the "use applications and services" use case of a smartphone, which we already studied from an operational scenario point of view, in order to analyze the associated functional scenario. As already stated, this use case is indeed probably the central use case of a smartphone for any end-user, which explains its natural choice. Moreover, this example illustrates how a given operational scenario analysis can be naturally refined into a functional scenario analysis.

Note, however, that we here only refined the central part of the considered operational scenario into a functional scenario. This central part corresponds to the situation where the end-user asks for a service which has to be managed, either in the nominal case with a normal smartphone temperature, or in a non-nominal case with an abnormal smartphone temperature.

As an example, let us elicit how the initial "service request command" event issued from an end-user, which is the only external interaction that we can observe from an operational perspective, refines from a functional perspective. First of all, the "interface with environment" function has to acquire the user requests, which are then sent to the "process services" function. This new function sends then the service status and user requests to the "supervise smartphone" function which shall make the decision of delivering or not the requested services, depending on the smartphone temperature. To this aim, the "supervise smartphone" function also receives, on one hand, the electrical supply status – since it may have an impact on the smartphone temperature – from the "manage electrical supply" function and, on the other hand, the internal temperature status from the "protect from environment" function. With all these information, the "supervise smartphone" can now make the right decision of allowing or not the execution of the requested service. Two alternative functional sequences are then managed depending on whether the smartphone temperature is OK or not. We refer to the below Figure A3.13 for the details of these remaining sequences.

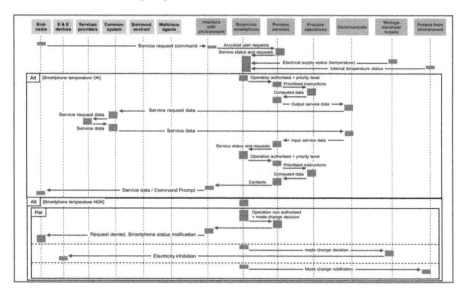

Figure A3.13. *Example of a functional scenario diagram of a smartphone system. For a color version of this figure, see www.iste.co.uk/krob/systems.zip*

A3.5. Constructional architecture

The constructional architecture of a system is formed by a constructional requirement architecture diagram, a constructional breakdown diagram, a constructional interaction diagram and a series of constructional scenario diagrams, when relevant, which altogether elicit the components of the system with their interactions, completed by a configuration diagram and a constructional flow diagram. For the smartphone system, we will, however, only present – for the sake of simplicity – the very first diagrams, without showing the constructional scenario diagrams, the configuration diagram and the constructional flow diagram.

A3.5.1. *Constructional requirement architecture diagram*

The constructional requirement architecture diagram of a smartphone system is the diagram, which is provided in Figure A3.14, where the main constructional requirements associated with a smartphone are listed and hierarchically organized, each of them being stated according to the standard constructional requirement pattern (see section 3.4.2 for more details).

These smartphone constructional requirements are distributed among the following six categories of constructional requirements: material properties, geometry, protection, economic performance, evolutivity, compatibility, connections. We may observe the difference between these categories, which all refer to some implementation-oriented/dependent physical or technological properties of a smartphone system, and the categories we used to organize the functional requirements which were only referring to implementation-independent input/output properties of the smartphone.

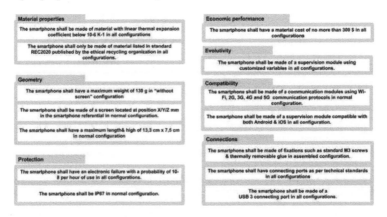

Figure A3.14. *Constructional requirement architecture diagram of a smartphone system. For a color version of this figure, see www.iste.co.uk/krob/systems.zip*

We shall recall that constructional requirements always originate from needs and/or from functional requirements and it is thus key to maintain traceability between a given constructional requirement and the source needs and/or functional requirements to which it proposes an implementation choice. This can be typically achieved through a need and functional requirement to constructional requirement matrix which just maintain the corresponding traceability relationships.

A partial example of such a traceability matrix is sketched in Figure A3.15, where we begin to trace how two needs and one functional requirement associated with a smartphone can be covered by a quite large number of constructional requirements on a smartphone. For the sake of place, note, however, that we just indicated in this partial matrix the smartphone components whose implementation was impacted by the considered needs and functional requirements: we shall therefore make use of the previous constructional requirement architecture diagram – refined at a smartphone component level (which was not done here) – in order to get the statements of the relevant constructional requirements on the impacted components.

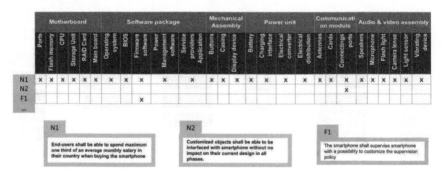

Figure A3.15. *Partial need and functional requirement to the constructional requirement matrix of a smartphone system. For a color version of this figure, see www.iste.co.uk/krob/systems.zip*

A3.5.2. *Constructional breakdown and interaction diagrams*

The constructional breakdown diagram – also called product breakdown structure – of a smartphone system hierarchically organizes all smartphone components around six high-level components that can be clustered into three main categories:

– The *technical core* of the smartphone that consists of a *motherboard* which orchestrates the computations made by the smartphone.

– The *technical supporting modules* which form the *software package* that contains all the key software modules of the smartphone.

– The external interfacing modules:

- the *mechanical assembly* with the purely mechanical parts of the smartphone;

- the *power unit* with all electrical management smartphone modules;

- the *communication modules* with communication-oriented smartphone parts;

- the *audio and video assembly* with all user-oriented audio and video modules.

The resulting constructional breakdown structure is provided in Figure A3.16.

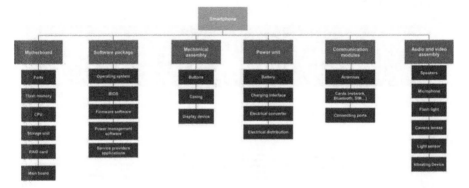

Figure A3.16. *Product breakdown structure of a smartphone system. For a color version of this figure, see www.iste.co.uk/krob/systems.zip*

Note that we presented the smartphone components according to a classical generic encapsulation pattern (see Figure A3.17). The components of most systems can indeed be usually organized into three layers, respectively, formed, first by the external interfacing modules that manage the interactions of the system with its stakeholders, secondly by the technical support modules that implement the supervision/monitoring functions of the system and finally by the technical core that achieves the elementary technical functions of the system.

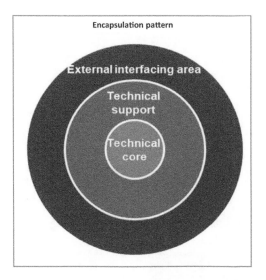

Figure A3.17. *Encapsulation pattern. For a color version*
of this figure, see www.iste.co.uk/krob/systems.zip

The knowledge of the smartphone components is, however, not enough to master its constructional architecture; we also need to know the constructional interfaces of each of these components which may be, either internal interfaces, that is, between two smartphone components, or external interfaces, that is, between a component and a stakeholder of the smartphone. This is the core objective of the constructional interaction diagram which is provided in Figure A3.18. Note that this interaction diagram involves three types of interaction flows: the data flows, depicted in black, the electrical flows, depicted in red, and the mechanical flows, depicted in yellow.

It is important to point out that these constructional breakdown and interaction diagrams shall be understood as generic systems architecture views of a smartphone and shall thus not be confused with concrete smartphone implementation representations. The main idea of these views is indeed to capture in a single diagram all possible implementations of a smartphone – which therefore means that they cannot precisely describe a given implementation – in order to be able to quickly derive from them the systems architecture representations of any real implementation.

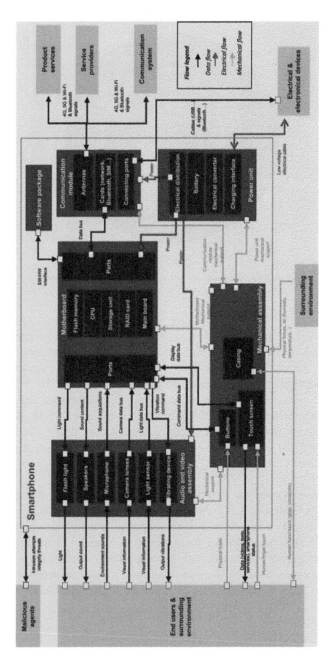

Figure A3.18. *Constructional interaction diagram of a smartphone system. For a color version of this figure, see www.iste.co.uk/krob/systems.zip*

In order to better understand that key idea, let us show an example of how to manage a smartphone implementation. In this context, the designer has to first choose both a concrete implementation and an adequate make or buy policy for all components listed in the constructional breakdown structure (see Figure A3.19). In this matter, he/she must both take into account the supply chain constraints and the company make or buy strategy and guarantee the coherence of the resulting architecture. In this last matter, a key tool may be the implementation architecture of the smartphone under design that can be easily obtained by instantiating the generic constructional interaction diagram, based on the specific implementation choices made by the designer. Figure A3.20 illustrates such an implementation architecture, as obtained from the component implementation choices provided in Figure A3.19.

Component	Building block	Make or buy policy
Main board & Ports	Equipped main board MBS1	Make
Flash memory	Flash BX 440	Buy
CPU	CPU11 1.7 GHz 6 Cores	Make
Storage unit	WD 64GB-SAS 2Gb/s-5000rpm	Buy
RAID Card	Adaptec SmartRAID 3151-4i 12 Gb/s	Buy
Operating system	OS S1	Develop
BIOS	BIOS S1	Develop
Firmware software	Firmware software S1	Develop
Power mgt software	Power mgt software modules PMSS1	Develop
Service providers application	software modules M1, M2, M3, M4	Develop
Buttons	Equipped outer bodies O1, O2, U1, U2, X12	Make
Casing		
Display device	Touch screen Sony TSX1	Buy

Component	Building block	Make or buy policy
Battery	Lithium-ion charging block 3,7 V 800 mAh GML900078	Buy
Charging interface		
Electrical converter		
Electrical distribution		
Antennas	Standard antenna set PHY22.5	Buy
Cards	Communicating card set SCD1	Buy
Connecting ports		
Speakers	Yin electronics Speakers S12	Buy
Microphone	ADK Microphone MK8	Buy
Flash light	PETZL m6	Buy
Camera lenses	Sony mobile lenses L34, L82	Buy
Light sensor	Amzel Light sensor S28	Buy
Vibrating Device	LRA Coin Vibration Motor 1.8V	Buy

Figure A3.19. *Implementing a constructional architecture of a smartphone system. For a color version of this figure, see www.iste.co.uk/krob/systems.zip*

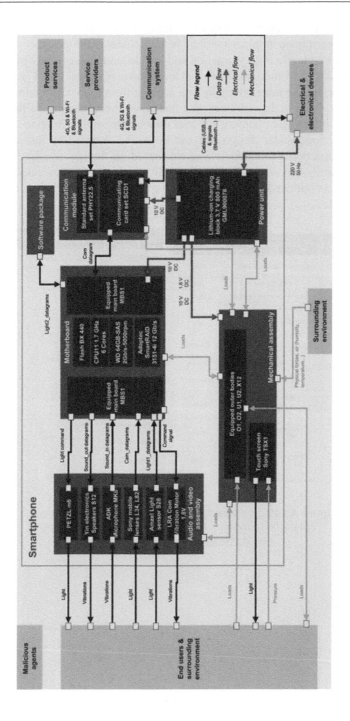

Figure A3.20. *Implementation architecture of a smartphone system. For a color version of this figure, see www.iste.co.uk/krob/systems.zip*

Appendix 4

Implementing CESAM through a SysML Modeling Tool

This appendix is dedicated to the presentation of a *generic organization of a concrete system model* based on the CESAM systems architecting framework, using the classical SysML modeling language[1] (see for instance Friedenthal *et al.* (2012)). Note, however, that organizing a concrete system model is always dependent on the chosen SysML modeling tool, since the different modeling tools that are existing on the market are not at all implementing in the same way the SysML standard that we may use to develop a system model. This appendix tried to be as implementation-independent as possible, but beware that its contents shall be adapted, depending on the modeling tool that you are using.

A4.1. Generic structure of a SysML system model based on the CESAM framework

We shall recall first that, from the perspective of a modeling tool, a system model consists of a set of technical data, associated with the considered system, that can be expressed in textual and graphic formats. These technical data are stored in a structured database that can be accessed by systems engineers through the modeling tool, with which they can manage the system model by adding, deleting and/or modifying its key elements that are of the following two different types:

---

1 We will not discuss here how to implement the CESAM framework within the proprietary modeling framework proposed by Capella, which is still possible, though a little bit more difficult due to the misalignment of Capella with usual systems engineering practices, as promoted for instance by INCOSE or NASA (cf. INCOSE (2011) and NASA (2016)).

1) *Elementary objects*, that is, the system and its stakeholders, lifecycle phases, use cases, functions, functional modes, components, configurations, needs, requirements and flows.

2) *Systems architecture diagrams* – such as environment, lifecycle, functional or constructional interaction diagrams – that synthetize architectural views made with elementary elements.

All system modeling tool interfaces are indeed always organized according to this core distinction, as we can see on the generic example provided in Figure A4.1.

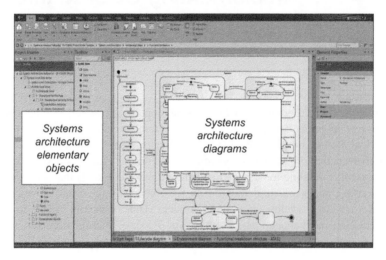

Figure A4.1. *Example of a system modeling tool interface. For a color version of this figure, see www.iste.co.uk/krob/systems.zip*

The main principle for organizing a given system model, based on the CESAM framework and managed using the SysML standard, consists then of breaking down the system model into three main parts that are corresponding, respectively, on one hand, to all systems architecture diagrams and, on the other hand, to all elementary objects, split between architectural objects (use cases, lifecycle phases, functions, functional modes, components, configurations, flows, etc.), on one side, and needs and requirements, on the other side. A system model shall thus be organized through adequate packages (in the SysML meaning Friedenthal *et al.* (2012)) – see Figure A4.2 – dedicated to the following contents:

– 0 – Views

This initial part of a system model shall be dedicated to the storage of all the diagrams that are modeling the operational, functional and constructional architectural views, as provided by the CESAM framework, of the system of interest which is modeled by the system model.

– 1 – Objects

This other part of a system model shall now be dedicated to the storage of the different operational, functional and constructional modeling objects that are used to construct the views of the system of interest that are stored in the previous part of the system model.

– 2 – Needs & requirements

This last part of the system model shall be specifically dedicated to the storage of the needs and of the functional and constructional requirements associated with the system of interest which is modeled in the considered system model.

The key idea for organizing a system model in such a way is that all modeling objects – such as for instance stakeholders, use cases, functions or components – are always used in many different architectural views. It is therefore not efficient at all to store them in the packages that contain the architectural views where they were initially created. For similar reasons, we also recommend to separate needs and requirements from both architectural views and objects.

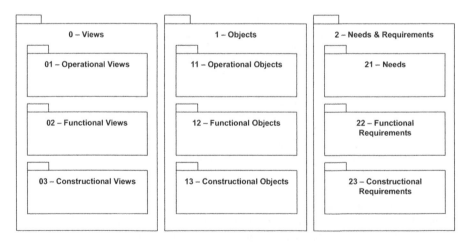

Figure A4.2. *Generic structure of a system model based on the CESAM framework*

These different packages can thus be naturally broken down according to the three – operational, functional and constructional – systems architecture visions, leading to the proposed SysML package organization which is provided in Figure A4.2.

A4.1.1. *Organization of views in a SysML CESAM system model*

Let us first focus on the *views* within such a system model organization. It happens that the CESAM systems architecting framework immediately reflects in the generic organization of the views, that are, respectively, broken down into operational, functional and constructional views, of a system model – through suitable SysML packages (cf. Friedenthal *et al.* (2012)) – as presented in the below Figure A4.3.

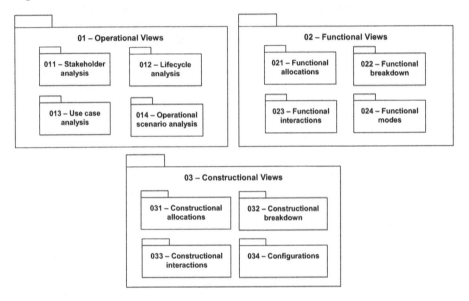

Figure A4.3. *Refined organization of views in a system model based on the CESAM framework*

The CESAM architectural views of a system model, organized as presented in Figure A4.3, can then be modeled using different SysML diagrams (see Friedenthal *et al.* (2012) for more details) which are presented in the below Table A4.1. Note that we also need to express the use case to function and the function to component allocations in such a system model, which led us to introduce specific views to this aim.

Architectural vision	Architectural analysis	Architectural deliverables	SysML representation
1 – Operational architecture	011 – Stakeholder analysis	Stakeholder diagram	Use case diagram
		Environment diagram	Block definition diagram
	012 – Lifecycle analysis	Lifecycle diagram	State machine
	013 – Use case analysis	Use case diagrams	Use case diagram
	014 – Operational scenario analysis	Operational scenario diagrams	Sequence diagram
2 – Functional architecture	021 – Functional allocations	Use case to function matrix	Activity diagram
	022 – Functional breakdown	Functional breakdown diagram	Activity diagram
	023 – Functional interactions	Functional interaction diagram	Activity diagram
	024 – Functional modes	Functional mode diagram	State machine
3 – Constructional architecture	031 – Constructional allocations	Function to component matrix	Block definition diagram
	032 – Constructional breakdown	Constructional breakdown diagram	Block definition diagram
	033 – Constructional interactions	Constructional interaction diagram	Internal block diagram
	034 – Configurations	Configuration diagram	State machine

Table A4.1. *SysML representations of the CESAM architectural views*

A4.1.2. *Organization of objects in a SysML CESAM system model*

Let us now focus on the *modeling objects* within the system model organization that we introduced. Note first that their organization is always highly modeling tool-dependent since the way these objects are connected to the views where they are produced depends on the chosen modeling tool. The proposed generic organization of these objects is, however, naturally the following:

– 11 – Operational objects

Operational objects can be decomposed into three types of objects, that is, stakeholders, lifecycle phases (possibly completed by transitions) and use cases. We may also consider operational flows as other operational objects, especially for external interface definition.

– 12 – Functional objects

The main functional objects are functions and functional modes. It may also be interesting to specifically consider functional flows as other functional objects, as far as we are interested in functional interface definition.

– 13 – Constructional objects

The main constructional objects are components and configurations. It may also be useful to consider constructional flows as other constructional objects, in particular when we need to specify constructional interfaces.

The resulting organization of objects, according to a classical SysML package breakdown (cf. Friedenthal *et al.* (2012)), is presented in the below Figure A4.4.

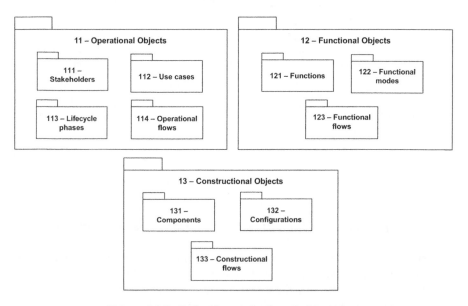

Figure A4.4. *Refined organization of objects in a system model based on the CESAM framework*

A4.1.3. Organization of needs and requirements in a SysML CESAM system model

Concerning finally *needs and requirements*, their organization is quite generic since any need and any functional or constructional requirement shall always be first stated, if necessary derived and allocated to a suitable object of a system model, then organized in a hierarchical way.

Following this pattern, the proposed organization for needs and requirements is the following:

– 21 – Needs

Stakeholder needs can be structured around two main views that are dedicated, first, to their derivation from the various stakeholders and to their allocation to the different use cases of the system of interest and, secondly, to a hierarchical organization of all needs. We may also maintain elsewhere the hierarchy of all need statements.

– 22 – Functional requirements

Functional requirements can be structured around two main views dedicated, first, to their derivation from the needs and to their allocation to the functions of the system of interest and, secondly, to a hierarchical organization of all functional requirements. We may also maintain in another place the hierarchy of all functional requirement statements.

– 23 – Constructional requirements

Constructional requirements can be structured around two main views dedicated, first, to their derivation from the needs and the functional requirements and to their allocation to the components of the system of interest and, secondly, to a hierarchical organization of all constructional requirements. We may also maintain in another place the hierarchy of all constructional requirement statements.

This mode of organizing the needs and requirements of a system model is presented – through the introduction of adequate SysML packages (see Friedenthal *et al.* (2012)) – in the below Figure A4.5.

Note that each view used to represent needs or requirements within a SysML system modeling tool shall always be based on a SysML requirement diagram (see again Friedenthal *et al.* (2012) for more details). Such diagrams can indeed be used both for specifying derivation and allocation relationships, for expressing hierarchical relationships and for stating requirements, if necessary.

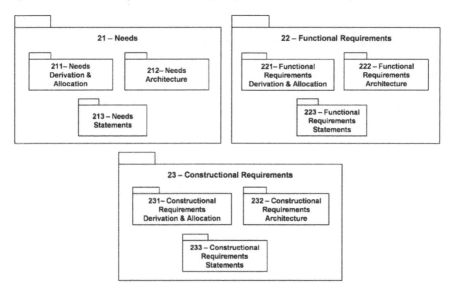

Figure A4.5. *Refined organization of needs and requirements in a system model based on the CESAM framework*

A4.2. Example of organization of a SysML system model based on the CESAM framework

As a synthesis, we just quickly show here how the SysML system model organization, based on the CESAM framework, that we introduced in the last section, practically reflects into a SysML modeling tool. In this matter, the following Figure A4.6 illustrates such a generic practical organization of a system model, here using the SysML Enterprise Architect™ modeling tool. We can see that such an organization is just an obvious instantiation within the modeling tool of all the generic material that we developed and presented in the previous section.

The remaining part of a modeling activity consists then of course of concretely developing a given system model, by filling the above different packages with suitable system views and corresponding technical data, associated with a given system of interest.

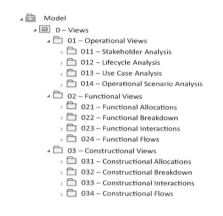

- ▲ 🗄 Model
  - ▲ 🖽 0 – Views
    - ▲ 🗀 01 – Operational Views
      - ▷ 🗀 011 – Stakeholder Analysis
      - ▷ 🗀 012 – Lifecycle Analysis
      - ▷ 🗀 013 – Use Case Analysis
      - ▷ 🗀 014 – Operational Scenario Analysis
    - ▲ 🗀 02 – Functional Views
      - ▷ 🗀 021 – Functional Allocations
      - ▷ 🗀 022 – Functional Breakdown
      - ▷ 🗀 023 – Functional Interactions
      - ▷ 🗀 024 – Functional Flows
    - ▲ 🗀 03 – Constructional Views
      - ▷ 🗀 031 – Constructional Allocations
      - ▷ 🗀 032 – Constructional Breakdown
      - ▷ 🗀 033 – Constructional Interactions
      - ▷ 🗀 034 – Constructional Flows

c

- ▲ 🖽 1 – Objects
  - ▲ 🗀 11 – Operational Objects
    - ▷ 🗀 111 – Stakeholders
    - ▷ 🗀 112 – Use Cases
    - ▷ 🗀 113 – Lifecycle Phases
    - ▷ 🗀 114 – Operational Flows
  - ▲ 🗀 12 – Functional Objects
    - ▷ 🗀 121 – Functions
    - ▷ 🗀 122 – Functional Modes
    - ▷ 🗀 123 – Functional Flows
  - ▲ 🗀 13 – Constructional Objects
    - ▷ 🗀 131 – Components
    - ▷ 🗀 132 – Configurations
    - ▷ 🗀 133 – Constructional Flows

- ▲ 🖽 2 – Needs & Requirements
  - ▲ 🗀 21 – Needs
    - ▷ 🗀 211 – Needs Derivation & Allocation
    - ▷ 🗀 212 – Needs Architecture
    - ▷ 🗀 213 – Needs Statements
  - ▲ 🗀 22 – Functional Requirements
    - ▷ 🗀 221 – Functional Requirements Derivation & Allocation
    - ▷ 🗀 222 – Functional Requirements Architecture
    - ▷ 🗀 223 – Functional Requirements Statements
  - ▲ 🗀 23 – Constructional Requirements
    - ▷ 🗀 231 – Constructional Requirements Derivation & Allocation
    - ▷ 🗀 232 – Constructional Requirements Architecture
    - ▷ 🗀 233 – Constructional Requirements Statements

Figure A4.6. *Organization of a system model based on the CESAM framework within a SysML modeling tool*

Appendix 5

Some Good Practices in Systems Modeling

Good practice 1: a system architectural model shall be done **to solve a specific problem**
Good practice 2: system modeling activities shall be fully **part** of any system development project and this from the very beginning of the project
Good practice 3: be clear about advantages provided by system modeling and adopt a **simplicity principle** coupled with a permanent **methodological doubt** (why do we need that? what is it for?)
Good practice 4: the natural evolution of a system makes it **very difficult to define its "true" operational reality**: never hesitate therefore to use all methods and tools which seem adapted to settle all operational uncertainties
Good practice 5: it is necessary to integrate all **technical and human dimensions** of the system to be built, and this from the very beginning of the system development project
Good practice 6: the more a system modeling is done in an **iterative way** – based on a permanent questioning between the stakeholders and the systems architect – the more it will be effective
Good practice 7: **"black-box" system modeling, without any feedback from the customer, must be banished**: stakeholders must be involved in the systems architecting process
Good practice 8: the **validation** of a system architectural model is a **permanent process** which must create trust in the system model, from the points of view of both the systems architect and the domain engineers and customers who will verify and validate it
Good practice 9: the achievement, as soon as possible, of a **"simple, but not simplistic", preliminary system model** which "works" is fundamental to make the systems architecting approach credible by the stakeholders: details can typically be added later if necessary (a coarse-grained system model can turn out to be sufficient)

Good practice 10: a **complete and coarse-grained coherent system model** is more important than an accumulation of details, which are often not relevant to the system project objectives
Good practice 11: systems architect expertise is primary: one must avoid beginners who know only how to use modeling tools (which is very different from architecting)
Good practice 12: the developed systems architectural models shall be considered as **assets of the organization** and managed coherently, in configuration and traceability and in space and time, by the organization in charge of the system design

Table A5.1. *Some good practices in systems modeling[1]*

---

1 Adapted from a personal communication of Professor J. Printz.

References

Abts, C., Boehm, B., Brown, W.A., Chulani, S., Clark, B.K., Horowitz, E., Madachy, R., Reifer, D.J., Steece, B. (2000). *Software Cost Estimation with COCOMO II (with CD-ROM)*. Prentice-Hall.

Aiguier, M., Golden, B., Krob, D. (2010). Complex systems architecture and modeling. In *First International Conference on Complex Systems Design & Management (CSD&M 2010)*, Aiguier, M., Bretaudeau, F., Krob, D. (eds).

Aiguier, M., Golden, B., Krob, D. (2012). Modeling of complex systems II: A minimalist and unified semantics for heterogeneous integrated systems. *Applied Mathematics and Computation*, 218(16), 8039–8055. doi:10.1016/j.amc.2012.01.048.

Aiguier, M., Golden, B., Krob, D. (2013). An adequate logic for heterogeneous systems. In *Proceedings of the 18th International Conference on Engineering of Complex Computer Systems (ICECCS' 2013)*, Liu, Y. and Martin, A. (eds). IEEE. doi:10.1109/ICECCS.2013.19.

Alur, R. and Dill, D.L. (1994). A theory of timed automata. *Theoretical Computer Science*, 126(2), 183–235.

ANSI/GEIA (2003). *ANSI/GEIA EIA-632 – Processes for Engineering a System*.

ANSI/IEEE (2000). *ANSI/IEEE 1471-2000 – Recommended Practice for Architecture Description of Software-Intensive Systems*.

Antonopoulos, J. (1992). The great Minoan eruption of Thera volcano and the ensuing tsunami in the Greek archipelago. *Natural Hazards*, 5(2), 153–168.

Artale, A. (2010–2011). Formal methods – lecture III: Linear temporal logic. Free University of Bolzano [Online]. Available at: https://web.iitd.ac.in/~sumeet/slide3.pdf.

Aslaksen, E.W. (1996). *The Changing Nature of Engineering*. McGraw-Hill.

Aslaksen, E.W. and Belcher, R. (1992). *Systems Engineering*. Prentice Hall.

Baier, C. and Katoen, J.P. (2008). *Principles of Model Checking*. MIT Press.

Barwise, J. (1972). *Handbook of Mathematical Logics*. North-Holland.

Bellman, R.E. (1957). *Dynamic Programming*. Princeton University Press.

Berrebi, J. and Krob, D. (2012). How to use systems architecture to specify the operational perimeter of an innovative product line? In *Proceedings of INCOSE International Symposium of 2012 (IS 2012)*, Celentano, M. (ed.). INCOSE.

von Bertalanffy, K.L. (1976). *General System Theory: Foundations, Development, Applications*. George Braziller.

Blanchard, B.S. and Fabricky, W.J. (1998). *Systems Engineering and Analysis*. Prentice Hall.

Bliudze, S. and Krob, D. (2005). Towards a functional formalism for modelling complex industrial systems. In *Proceedings of the European Conference on Complex Systems (ECCS'05)*, Bourgine, P., Képès, F., Schoenauer, M. (eds). article 193.

Bliudze, S. and Krob, D. (2006). Towards a functional formalism for modelling complex industrial systems. *ComPlexUs, Special Issue: Complex Systems – European Conference*, November 2005, Selected Papers, Part 1, 2, (3–4), 163–176

Bliudze, S. and Krob, D. (2009). Modeling of complex systems – Systems as data-flow machines. *Fundamenta Informaticae, Special Issue: Machines, Computations and Universality*, 91, 1–24.

Boehm, B. (1981). *Software Engineering Economics*. Prentice-Hall.

Booch, G., Jacobson, I., Rumbaugh, J. (2004). *The Unified Modeling Language Reference Manual*, 2nd edition. Addison-Wesley.

Börger, E. and Stärk, R. (2003). *Abstract State Machines*. Springer.

Caseau, Y., Krob, D., Peyronnet, S. (2007). Complexité des systèmes d'information : une famille de mesures de la complexité scalaire d'un schéma d'architecture. *Génie Logiciel*, 82, 23–30.

Cha, P.D., Rosenberg, J., Dym, C.L. (2000). *Fundamentals of Modeling and Analyzing Engineering Systems*. Cambridge University Press.

Chalé Gongora, H.G., Doufene, A., Krob, D. (2012). Complex systems architecture framework. Extension to multi-objective optimization. In *Proceedings of the 3rd International Conference on Complex Systems Design & Management (CSDM 2012)*, Caseau, Y., Krob, D., Rauzy, A. (eds). Springer Verlag.

Cousot, P. and Cousot, R. (1996). Abstract interpretation. *Symposium on Models of Programming Languages and Computation, ACM Computing Surveys*, June, 28(2), 324–328.

Dauron, A., Doufène, A., Krob, D. (2011). Complex systems operational analysis – A case study for electric vehicles. In *2nd International Conference on Complex Systems Design & Management (CSDM 2011)*, Hammami, O., Krob, D., Voirin, J.L. (eds).

Doufène, A. and Krob, D. (2013). Sharing the total cost of ownership of electric vehicles: A study on the application of game theory. *Proceedings of INCOSE International Symposium of 2013 (IS2013)*.

Doufène, A. and Krob, D. (2014). Model-based operational analysis for complex systems – A case study for electric vehicles. *Proceedings of INCOSE International Symposium of 2014 (IS2014)*.

Doufène, A. and Krob, D. (2015). Pareto optimality and Nash equilibrium for building stable systems. *IEEE International Systems Conference*.

Forrester, J.W. (1971). *World Dynamics*. Productivity Press.

Friedenthal, S., Moore, A.C., Steiner, R. (2012). *A Practical Guide to SysML: The Systems Modeling Language*. Morgan Kaufmann OMG Press.

Giakoumakis, V., Krob, D., Liberti, L., Roda, F. (2010). Optimal technological architecture evolutions of information systems. In *Proceedings of the First International Conference on Complex Systems Design & Management (CSDM 2010)*, Aiguier, M., Bretaudeau, F., Krob, D. (eds). Springer Verlag.

Giakoumakis, V., Krob, D., Liberti, L., Roda, F. (2012). Technological architecture evolutions of Information Systems: Trade-off and optimization. *Concurrent Engineering: Research and Applications*, 20(2), 127–147.

Godfrey, M.D. and Hendry, D.F. (1993). The computer as von Neuman planned it. *IEEE Annals of the History of Computing*, 15(1), 11–21.

Grady, J.O. (2006). *System Requirements Analysis*. Elsevier.

Grady, J.O. (2007). *System Verification – Proving the Design Solution Satisfies the Requirements*. Elsevier.

Gruhl, W. (1992). *Lessons learned, cost/schedule assessment guide*. Internal presentation, NASA Comptroller's Office.

Hofstadter, D.R. (1979). *Gödel, Escher, Bach: An Eternal Golden Braid*. Basic Books.

Honour, E.C. (2014). Understanding the value of systems engineering. *Proceedings of INCOSE 2014 International Symposium, 14, 1207–1222*, Toulouse, 20–24 June 2014, France [Online]. Available at: http://www.seintelligence.fr/content/images/2015/12/ValueSE-INCOSE04.pdf.

IEEE (2005). *IEEE 1220-2005 – Standard for Application and Management of the Systems Engineering Process*. Institute of Electrical and Electronics Engineers.

INCOSE (2011). *Systems Engineering Handbook, A Guide for System Life Cycle Processes and Activities*. INCOSE.

ISO (2018). *ISO 20077 – Road Vehicles — Extended Vehicle (ExVe) Methodology*. ISO.

ISO/IEC/IEEE (May 2015). *ISO/IEC/IEEE 15288:2015 – Systems and Software Engineering – System Life Cycle Processes*. ISO.

Katoen, J.P. (2009). *LTL Model Checking*. University of Twente.

Korzybski, A. (1950). *Science and Sanity: An Introduction to Non-Aristotelian Systems and General Semantics*. International Nonaristotelian.

Kossiakoff, A. and Sweet, W.N. (2003). *Systems Engineering – Principles and Practice*. Wiley.

Krob, D. (2006). Modelling of complex software systems: A reasoned overview. In *26th IFIP WG 6.1 International Conference on Formal Methods for Networked and Distributed Systems (FORTE'2006)*, Najm, E., Pradat-Peyre, J.-F., Viguié Donzeau-Gouge, V. (eds). Lecture Notes in Computer Science, 4229, Springer Verlag.

Krob, D. (2007). Architecture of complex systems: Why, what and how? In *Proceedings of Cognitive Systems with Interactive Sensors (COGIS'07)*, Aghajan, H., Lecadre, J.P., Reynaud, R. (eds). Stanford University.

Krob, D. (2008). Comment sécuriser la conception et le déploiement des logiciels métiers par une démarche d'architecture collaborative ? In *Proceedings of journée française des tests logiciels*, Homès, B. (ed.). CFTL.

Krob, D. (2009). Eléments d'architecture des systèmes complexes. In *Gestion de la complexité et de l'information dans les grands systèmes critiques*, Appriou, A. (ed.). CNRS Editions.

Krob, D. (2012). Eléments de systémique – architecture de systèmes. In *Complexité-Simplexité*, Berthoz, A. and Petit, J.L. (eds). Editions Odile Jacob.

Krob, D. (2013). Eléments de modélisation systémique. In *L'Energie à découvert*, Mossery, R. and Jeandel, C. (eds). CNRS Editions.

Kröger, F. and Merz, S. (2008). *Temporal Logic and State Systems*. Springer.

Lamport, L. (2003). *Specifying Systems – The TLA+ Language and Tools for Hardware and Software Engineers*. Addison-Wesley.

Leveson, N. (2012). *Engineering a Safer World: Systems Thinking Applied to Safety (Engineering Systems)*. The MIT Press.

Leveson, N. (2020). *System Safety Engineering: Back to the Future*. Aeronautics and Astronautics Massachussetts Institute of Technology.

Lions, J.L. (1996). Ariane 5 – Flight 501 Failure. Report by the Inquiry Board, ESA.

Luzeaux, D. and Ruault, J.R. (2010). *Systems of Systems*. ISTE Ltd and John Wiley & Sons.

Maier, M.W. and Rechtin, E. (2002). *The Art of Systems Architecting*. CRC Press.

Manna, Z. and Pnueli, A. (1992). *The Temporal Logic of Reactive and Concurrent Systems*. Springer.

Marwedel, P. (2003). *Embedded System Design*. Kluwer.

Meadows, D.H., Meadows, D.L., Randers, J., Berhens III, W.W. (1972). *The Limits to Growth*. Universe Books.

Meinadier, J.P. (1998). *Ingénierie et intégration de systèmes*. Hermes.

Meinadier, J.P. (2002). *Le métier d'intégration de systèmes*. Hermes Lavoisier.

Miles, L.D. (1972). *Techniques of Value Analysis and Engineering*. McGraw-Hill.

Murray, R.M. (2012). *Linear Temporal Logic*. California Institute of Technology.

Murschel, A. (1995). The structure and function of Ptolemy's physical hypotheses of planetary motion. *Journal for the History of Astronomy*, xxvii, 33–36.

NASA (2016). *Systems Engineering Handbook*. NASA SP-2016-6105 Rev2.

de Neufville, R. (1994). The baggage system at Denver: Prospects and lessons. *Journal of Air Transport Management*, December, 1(4), 229–236.

von Neuman, J. (1945). First draft of a report on the EDVAC, June 30. Moore School of Electrical Engineering, University of Pennsylvania.

Novikova, T., Papadopoulos, G.A., McCoy, F.W. (2011). Modelling of tsunami generated by the giant Late Bronze Age eruption of Thera, south Aegean sea, Greece. *Geophysical Journal International*, 186(2), 665–680.

Parnell, G.S., Driscoll, P.J., Henderson, D.L. (2001). *Decision Marking in Systems Engineering and Management*. Wiley.

Pnueli, A. (1977). The temporal logics of programs. *Proceedings of IEEE 54th Annual Symposium on Foundations of Computer Science (FOCS'77)*, 46–57, IEEE.

Printz, J. (2001). *Productivité des programmeurs*. Hermès.

Rauzy, A. (2008). Guarded transition systems: A new states/events formalism for reliability studies. *Journal of Risk and Reliability. Professional Engineering Publishing*, 222(4), 495–505.

Sage, A.P. and Armstrong, J.E. (2000). *Introduction to Systems Engineering*. Wiley.

Schloh, M. (1996). *The Denver International Airport Automated Baggage Handling System*. February 6, Cal Poly.

Severance, F.L. (2001). *System Modeling and Simulation – An Introduction*. Wiley.

Sillitto, H. (2014). *Architecting Systems – Concepts, Principles and Practice*. College Publications.

Simon, H. (1962). The architecture of complexity. *Proceedings of the American Philosophica*, December, 106(6), 467–482.

Simpson, T.W., Siddique, Z., Jiao, J.R. (2006). *Product Platform and Product Family Design, Methods and Applications*. Springer Verlag.

Smith, D.J. (2017). *Reliability, Maintainability and Risk: Practical Methods for Engineers*. Butterworth-Heinemann

Smith, D.J. and Simpson, K.G.L. (2020). *The Safety Critical Systems Handbook: A Straightforward Guide to Functional Safety: IEC 61508 (2010 Edition), IEC 61511 (2016 Edition) also Related Guidance on Cyber Security & Including Machinery and Other Industrial Sectors*. Butterworth-Heinemann.

Strauss-Kahn, D. (2020). L'être, l'avoir et le pouvoir dans la crise. Politique Internationale [Online]. Available at: www.leclubdesjuristes.com/letre-lavoir-et-le-pouvoir-dans-la-crise/.

The Open Group (2011). *TOGAF® Version 9.1 – The Book*. The Open Group.

Turner, W.C., Mize, J.H., Case, K.H., Nazemetz, J.W. (1978). *Introduction to Industrial and Systems Engineering*. Prentice Hall.

Valerdi, R. (2008). *The Constructive Systems Engineering Cost Model (COSYSMO), Quantifying the Costs of Systems Engineering Effort in Complex Systems*. VDM Verlag Dr. Muller.

de Weck, O. (2006). *Strategic Engineering – Designing Systems for an Uncertain Future*. MIT.

de Weck, O., Krob, D., Liberti, L., Marinelli, F. (2009). A general framework for combined module- and scale-based product platform design. In *Proceedings of the Second International Engineering Systems Symposium*, Roos, D. (ed.). MIT.

de Weck, O., Roos, D., Magee, C.L. (2011). *Engineering Systems – Meeting Human Needs in a Complex Technological World*. The MIT Press.

de Weck, O., Krob, D., Lefei, L., Lui, P.C., Rauzy, A., Zhang, X.G. (2020). Handling the COVID-19 crisis: Towards an agile model-based approach. *Systems Engineering*, 23(5), 656–670.

White, S.A. and Miers, D. (2008). *BPMN Modeling and Reference Guide, Understanding and Using BPMN*. Future Strategies.

Wikipedia (2020). COSYSMO [Online]. Available at: https://en.wikipedia.org/wiki/ COSYSMO [Accessed 10 July 2020].

Wikipedia (2021a). Airbus A380 [Online]. Available at: https://en.wikipedia.org/wiki/ Airbus_A380 [Accessed 23 November 2021].

Wikipedia (2021b). COCOMO [Online]. Available at: https://en.wikipedia.org/wiki/ COCOMO [Accessed 29 July 2021].

Wikipedia (2021c). Deferent and epicycle [Online]. Available at: https://en.wikipedia.org/ wiki/Deferent_and_epicycle [Accessed 17 November 2021].

Wikipedia (2021d). Enterprise architecture framework [Online]. Available at: https://en.wiki pedia.org/wiki/Enterprise_architecture_framework [Accessed 20 November 2021].

Wikipedia (2021e). Nash equilibrium [Online]. Available at: https://en.wikipedia.org/wiki/ Nash_equilibrium [Accessed 25 October 2021].

Wikipedia (2021f). Occam's razor [Online]. Available at: https://en.wikipedia.org/wiki/ Occam%27s_razor [Accessed 13 November 2021].

Wikipedia (2021g). Organon [Online]. Available at: https://en.wikipedia.org/wiki/Organon [Accessed 13 August 2021].

Wikipedia (2021h). OSI model [Online]. Available at: https://en.wikipedia.org/wiki/OSI_model [Accessed 19 November 2021].

Wikipedia (2021i). Predicate [Online]. Available at: https://en.wikipedia.org/wiki/Predicate_(mathematical_logic) [Accessed 3 September 2021].

Wikipedia (2021j). Systems architecture [Online]. Available at: https://en.wikipedia.org/wiki/Systems_architecture [Accessed 9 September 2021].

Wikipedia (2021k). Systems biology [Online]. Available at: https://en.wikipedia.org/wiki/Systems_biology [Accessed 10 November 2021].

Wikipedia (2021l). Systems engineering [Online]. Available at: https://en.wikipedia.org/wiki/Systems_engineering [Accessed 9 October 2021].

Wikipedia (2021m). Systems psychology [Online]. Available at: https://en.wikipedia.org/wiki/Systems_psychology [Accessed 5 November 2021].

Wikipedia (2021n). Systems theory [Online]. Available at: https://en.wikipedia.org/wiki/Systems_theory [Accessed 4 November 2021].

Wikipedia (2021o). Trade-off [Online]. Available at: https://en.wikipedia.org/wiki/Trade-off [Accessed 22 September 2021].

Wikipedia (2021p). Von Neuman architecture [Online]. Available at: https://en.wikipedia.org/wiki/Von_Neumann_architecture [Accessed 17 November 2021].

Wikiquote (2021). Systems engineering [Online]. Available at: https://en.wikiquote.org/wiki/Systems_engineering [Accessed 25 August 2021].

Winskel, G. (1993). *The Formal Semantics of Programming Languages – An Introduction.* The MIT Press.

World Health Organization (2021). Coronavirus Disease 2019 (COVID-19) situation reports [Online]. Available at: www.who.int/emergencies/diseases/novel-coronavirus-2019/situation-reports/ [Accessed 17 November 2021].

Zeigler, B.P., Praehofer, H., Kim, T.G. (2000). *Theory of Modeling and Simulation – Integrating Discrete Events and Continuous Dynamic Systems.* Academic Press.

Index

A, B, C

activity, 3, 12, 13, 15, 17, 19–21, 29, 30, 32, 34, 35, 37, 45, 51, 56, 81, 110, 128, 131–133, 149, 151, 203, 206
alignment, 3, 34, 37, 59, 60, 105, 133
behavior, 3–8, 10, 11, 29, 32, 34, 43–49, 51, 57, 60, 62, 63, 65, 66, 69, 73, 75, 77, 78, 80, 97, 98, 100, 103–105, 109, 111, 115, 123, 161, 164, 169, 179
collaborative, 12–15, 21, 24, 25, 27, 28, 49, 143–146, 150, 151, 163
component, 43–45, 49–53, 58, 59, 63–69, 71, 72, 75, 77, 78, 91, 104, 115, 117, 118, 121–123, 125, 135, 138, 139, 164–166, 169–171, 188, 192–195, 197, 200–205, 207
configuration, 30–32, 51, 63, 64, 75, 76, 78, 79, 92, 100, 104, 118, 120, 123, 135, 138, 139, 151, 152, 172, 191, 200, 202–204
convergence, 12–14, 35, 36, 154

D, E, F

decoupling, 43, 92, 104, 117
degraded situation, 130, 131, 184
design structure matrix, 116
diversity, 4, 92

encapsulation pattern, 194, 195
external hazard, 127, 134–138, 151, 152
facilitation activity, 12, 13
flexible architecture, 92
function, 22, 26, 30–33, 43–51, 53–61, 63–81, 91–93, 98, 99, 102–115, 118, 119, 122, 123, 125, 132, 134, 136–138, 160, 169, 177, 178, 187–194, 200–205
dysfunctional, 127–139
transverse, 45, 49, 50, 59, 66

G, H, I

genericity, 5, 8, 16
hazard, 127, 129, 134–139
initial version, 13
initiating event, 129–131, 134–136, 138
instantiation, 206
invariant, 10, 50, 162

L, M

lifecycle, 25, 31, 32, 83, 94–97, 99, 134–136, 151, 152, 166, 178, 181, 183–186, 189, 200, 202–204, 207
logical vision, 26, 43

mission, 21, 37, 46–48, 53, 56, 65–69, 78,
   88, 89, 91, 93, 94, 97–100, 103, 110,
   115, 122, 128, 129, 163, 165, 166, 173,
   174, 176

P, R, S

physical vision, 43
process, 2, 3, 8, 12, 14–16, 24–27, 29, 31,
   33, 34, 36, 37, 48–52, 56, 58, 81, 83,
   84, 91, 92, 102, 105, 113, 115, 117,
   126–128, 132, 133, 141, 143–145, 154,
   166, 172, 187–189, 191, 209
product breakdown structure, 52, 56, 122,
   193, 194
risk, 21, 22, 31, 32, 127–132, 134–136,
   138, 142, 145, 146

shared version, 13
socio-dynamics, 60, 154
software component, 26, 49, 68, 169
structure, 3, 4, 6, 8, 16, 31, 43, 44, 47–49,
   51, 52, 55, 56, 60, 63, 73, 75, 103–105,
   110, 111, 115, 116, 122, 143, 150–152,
   164, 188, 189, 193, 194, 197, 199, 201,
   205

T, U

task, 20, 51
technological implementation, 48
use case, 27, 32, 58, 81, 93, 94, 97–100,
   102, 135, 151, 152, 181, 184–186, 190,
   200–205, 207

Other titles from

in

Systems and Industrial Engineering – Robotics

2020

BRON Jean-Yves
System Requirements Engineering

KRYSINSKI TOMASZ, MALBURET FRANÇOIS
Energy and Motorization in the Automotive and Aeronautics Industries

PRINTZ Jacques
System Architecture and Complexity: Contribution of Systems of Systems to Systems Thinking

2019

ANDRÉ Jean-Claude
Industry 4.0: Paradoxes and Conflicts

BENSALAH Mounir, ELOUADI Abdelmajid, MHARZI Hassan
Railway Information Modeling RIM: The Track to Rail Modernization

BLUA Philippe, YALAOU Farouk, AMODEO Lionel, DE BLOCK Michaël, LAPLANCHE David
Hospital Logistics and e-Management: Digital Transition and Revolution

BRIFFAUT Jean-Pierre
*From Complexity in the Natural Sciences to Complexity in Operations
Management Systems
(Systems of Systems Complexity Set – Volume 1)*

BUDINGER Marc, HAZYUK Ion, COÏC Clément
Multi-Physics Modeling of Technological Systems

FLAUS Jean-Marie
Cybersecurity of Industrial Systems

JAULIN Luc
Mobile Robotics – Second Edition Revised and Updated

KUMAR Kaushik, DAVIM Paulo J.
Optimization for Engineering Problems

TRIGEASSOU Jean-Claude, MAAMRI Nezha
*Analysis, Modeling and Stability of Fractional Order Differential Systems 1:
The Infinite State Approach
Analysis, Modeling and Stability of Fractional Order Differential Systems 2:
The Infinite State Approach*

VANDERHAEGEN Frédéric, MAAOUI Choubeila, SALLAK Mohamed,
BERDJAG Denis
Automation Challenges of Socio-technical Systems

2018

BERRAH Lamia, CLIVILLÉ Vincent, FOULLOY Laurent
*Industrial Objectives and Industrial Performance: Concepts and Fuzzy
Handling*

GONZALEZ-FELIU Jesus
Sustainable Urban Logistics: Planning and Evaluation

GROUS Ammar
Applied Mechanical Design

LEROY Alain
Production Availability and Reliability: Use in the Oil and Gas Industry

MARÉ Jean-Charles
Aerospace Actuators 3: European Commercial Aircraft and Tiltrotor Aircraft

MAXA Jean-Aimé, BEN MAHMOUD Mohamed Slim, LARRIEU Nicolas
Model-driven Development for Embedded Software: Application to Communications for Drone Swarm

MBIHI Jean
Analog Automation and Digital Feedback Control Techniques Advanced Techniques and Technology of Computer-Aided Feedback Control

MORANA Joëlle
Logistics

SIMON Christophe, WEBER Philippe, SALLAK Mohamed
Data Uncertainty and Important Measures (Systems Dependability Assessment Set – Volume 3)

TANIGUCHI Eiichi, THOMPSON Russell G.
City Logistics 1: New Opportunities and Challenges City Logistics 2: Modeling and Planning Initiatives City Logistics 3: Towards Sustainable and Liveable Cities

ZELM Martin, JAEKEL Frank-Walter, DOUMEINGTS Guy, WOLLSCHLAEGER Martin
Enterprise Interoperability: Smart Services and Business Impact of Enterprise Interoperability

2017

ANDRÉ Jean-Claude
From Additive Manufacturing to 3D/4D Printing 1: From Concepts to Achievements From Additive Manufacturing to 3D/4D Printing 2: Current Techniques, Improvements and their Limitations From Additive Manufacturing to 3D/4D Printing 3: Breakthrough Innovations: Programmable Material, 4D Printing and Bio-printing

ARCHIMÈDE Bernard, VALLESPIR Bruno
Enterprise Interoperability: INTEROP-PGSO Vision

CAMMAN Christelle, FIORE Claude, LIVOLSI Laurent, QUERRO Pascal
Supply Chain Management and Business Performance: The VASC Model

FEYEL Philippe
Robust Control, Optimization with Metaheuristics

MARÉ Jean-Charles
Aerospace Actuators 2: Signal-by-Wire and Power-by-Wire

POPESCU Dumitru, AMIRA Gharbi, STEFANOIU Dan, BORNE Pierre
Process Control Design for Industrial Applications

RÉVEILLAC Jean-Michel
Modeling and Simulation of Logistics Flows 1: Theory and Fundamentals
Modeling and Simulation of Logistics Flows 2: Dashboards, Traffic
Planning and Management
Modeling and Simulation of Logistics Flows 3: Discrete and Continuous
Flows in 2D/3D

2016

ANDRÉ Michel, SAMARAS Zissis
Energy and Environment
(Research for Innovative Transports Set - Volume 1)

AUBRY Jean-François, BRINZEI Nicolae, MAZOUNI Mohammed-Habib
Systems Dependability Assessment: Benefits of Petri Net Models (Systems
Dependability Assessment Set - Volume 1)

BLANQUART Corinne, CLAUSEN Uwe, JACOB Bernard
Towards Innovative Freight and Logistics (Research for Innovative
Transports Set - Volume 2)

COHEN Simon, YANNIS George
Traffic Management (Research for Innovative Transports Set - Volume 3)

MARÉ Jean-Charles
Aerospace Actuators 1: Needs, Reliability and Hydraulic Power Solutions

REZG Nidhal, HAJEJ Zied, BOSCHIAN-CAMPANER Valerio
Production and Maintenance Optimization Problems: Logistic Constraints and Leasing Warranty Services

TORRENTI Jean-Michel, LA TORRE Francesca
Materials and Infrastructures 1 (Research for Innovative Transports Set - Volume 5A)
Materials and Infrastructures 2 (Research for Innovative Transports Set - Volume 5B)

WEBER Philippe, SIMON Christophe
Benefits of Bayesian Network Models
(Systems Dependability Assessment Set – Volume 2)

YANNIS George, COHEN Simon
Traffic Safety (Research for Innovative Transports Set - Volume 4)

2015

AUBRY Jean-François, BRINZEI Nicolae
Systems Dependability Assessment: Modeling with Graphs and Finite State Automata

BOULANGER Jean-Louis
CENELEC 50128 and IEC 62279 Standards

BRIFFAUT Jean-Pierre
E-Enabled Operations Management

MISSIKOFF Michele, CANDUCCI Massimo, MAIDEN Neil
Enterprise Innovation

2014

CHETTO Maryline
Real-time Systems Scheduling
Volume 1 – Fundamentals
Volume 2 – Focuses

DAVIM J. Paulo
Machinability of Advanced Materials

ESTAMPE Dominique
Supply Chain Performance and Evaluation Models

FAVRE Bernard
Introduction to Sustainable Transports

GAUTHIER Michaël, ANDREFF Nicolas, DOMBRE Etienne
Intracorporeal Robotics: From Milliscale to Nanoscale

MICOUIN Patrice
Model Based Systems Engineering: Fundamentals and Methods

MILLOT Patrick
Designing Human–Machine Cooperation Systems

NI Zhenjiang, PACORET Céline, BENOSMAN Ryad, RÉGNIER Stéphane
Haptic Feedback Teleoperation of Optical Tweezers

OUSTALOUP Alain
Diversity and Non-integer Differentiation for System Dynamics

REZG Nidhal, DELLAGI Sofien, KHATAD Abdelhakim
Joint Optimization of Maintenance and Production Policies

STEFANOIU Dan, BORNE Pierre, POPESCU Dumitru, FILIP Florin Gh.,
EL KAMEL Abdelkader
*Optimization in Engineering Sciences: Metaheuristics, Stochastic Methods
and Decision Support*

2013

ALAZARD Daniel
Reverse Engineering in Control Design

ARIOUI Hichem, NEHAOUA Lamri
Driving Simulation

CHADLI Mohammed, COPPIER Hervé
Command-control for Real-time Systems

DAAFOUZ Jamal, TARBOURIECH Sophie, SIGALOTTI Mario
Hybrid Systems with Constraints

FEYEL Philippe
Loop-shaping Robust Control

FLAUS Jean-Marie
Risk Analysis: Socio-technical and Industrial Systems

FRIBOURG Laurent, SOULAT Romain
Control of Switching Systems by Invariance Analysis: Application to Power Electronics

GROSSARD Mathieu, REGNIER Stéphane, CHAILLET Nicolas
Flexible Robotics: Applications to Multiscale Manipulations

GRUNN Emmanuel, PHAM Anh Tuan
Modeling of Complex Systems: Application to Aeronautical Dynamics

HABIB Maki K., DAVIM J. Paulo
Interdisciplinary Mechatronics: Engineering Science and Research Development

HAMMADI Slim, KSOURI Mekki
Multimodal Transport Systems

JARBOUI Bassem, SIARRY Patrick, TEGHEM Jacques
Metaheuristics for Production Scheduling

KIRILLOV Oleg N., PELINOVSKY Dmitry E.
Nonlinear Physical Systems

LE Vu Tuan Hieu, STOICA Cristina, ALAMO Teodoro, CAMACHO Eduardo F., DUMUR Didier
Zonotopes: From Guaranteed State-estimation to Control

MACHADO Carolina, DAVIM J. Paulo
Management and Engineering Innovation

MORANA Joëlle
Sustainable Supply Chain Management

SANDOU Guillaume
Metaheuristic Optimization for the Design of Automatic Control Laws

STOICAN Florin, OLARU Sorin
Set-theoretic Fault Detection in Multisensor Systems

2012

AÏT-KADI Daoud, CHOUINARD Marc, MARCOTTE Suzanne, RIOPEL Diane
Sustainable Reverse Logistics Network: Engineering and Management

BORNE Pierre, POPESCU Dumitru, FILIP Florin G., STEFANOIU Dan
Optimization in Engineering Sciences: Exact Methods

CHADLI Mohammed, BORNE Pierre
Multiple Models Approach in Automation: Takagi-Sugeno Fuzzy Systems

DAVIM J. Paulo
Lasers in Manufacturing

DECLERCK Philippe
Discrete Event Systems in Dioid Algebra and Conventional Algebra

DOUMIATI Moustapha, CHARARA Ali, VICTORINO Alessandro,
LECHNER Daniel
*Vehicle Dynamics Estimation using Kalman Filtering: Experimental
Validation*

GUERRERO José A, LOZANO Rogelio
Flight Formation Control

HAMMADI Slim, KSOURI Mekki
Advanced Mobility and Transport Engineering

MAILLARD Pierre
Competitive Quality Strategies

MATTA Nada, VANDENBOOMGAERDE Yves, ARLAT Jean
Supervision and Safety of Complex Systems

POLER Raul *et al.*
Intelligent Non-hierarchical Manufacturing Networks

TROCCAZ Jocelyne
Medical Robotics

YALAOUI Alice, CHEHADE Hicham, YALAOUI Farouk, AMODEO Lionel
Optimization of Logistics

ZELM Martin *et al.*
Enterprise Interoperability –I-EASA12 Proceedings

2011

CANTOT Pascal, LUZEAUX Dominique
Simulation and Modeling of Systems of Systems

DAVIM J. Paulo
Mechatronics

DAVIM J. Paulo
Wood Machining

GROUS Ammar
Applied Metrology for Manufacturing Engineering

KOLSKI Christophe
Human–Computer Interactions in Transport

LUZEAUX Dominique, RUAULT Jean-René, WIPPLER Jean-Luc
Complex Systems and Systems of Systems Engineering

ZELM Martin, *et al.*
Enterprise Interoperability: IWEI2011 Proceedings

2010

BOTTA-GENOULAZ Valérie, CAMPAGNE Jean-Pierre, LLERENA Daniel, PELLEGRIN Claude
Supply Chain Performance / Collaboration, Alignement and Coordination

BOURLÈS Henri, GODFREY K.C. Kwan
Linear Systems

BOURRIÈRES Jean-Paul
Proceedings of CEISIE '09

CHAILLET Nicolas, REGNIER Stéphane
Microrobotics for Micromanipulation

DAVIM J. Paulo
Sustainable Manufacturing

GIORDANO Max, MATHIEU Luc, VILLENEUVE François
Product Life-Cycle Management / Geometric Variations

LOZANO Rogelio
Unmanned Aerial Vehicles / Embedded Control

LUZEAUX Dominique, RUAULT Jean-René
Systems of Systems

VILLENEUVE François, MATHIEU Luc
Geometric Tolerancing of Products

2009

DIAZ Michel
Petri Nets / Fundamental Models, Verification and Applications

OZEL Tugrul, DAVIM J. Paulo
Intelligent Machining

PITRAT Jacques
Artificial Beings

2008

ARTIGUES Christian, DEMASSEY Sophie, NÉRON Emmanuel
Resources–Constrained Project Scheduling

BILLAUT Jean-Charles, MOUKRIM Aziz, SANLAVILLE Eric
Flexibility and Robustness in Scheduling

DOCHAIN Denis
Bioprocess Control

LOPEZ Pierre, ROUBELLAT François
Production Scheduling

THIERRY Caroline, THOMAS André, BEL Gérard
Supply Chain Simulation and Management

2007

DE LARMINAT Philippe
Analysis and Control of Linear Systems

DOMBRE Etienne, KHALIL Wisama
Robot Manipulators

LAMNABHI Françoise *et al.*
Taming Heterogeneity and Complexity of Embedded Control

LIMNIOS Nikolaos
Fault Trees

2006

FRENCH COLLEGE OF METROLOGY
Metrology in Industry

NAJIM Kaddour
Control of Continuous Linear Systems

Printed and bound by CPI Group (UK) Ltd, Croydon, CR0 4YY

08/03/2023

03200026-0005